SENTENCING POLICY AND SOCIAL JUSTICE

CLARENDON STUDIES IN CRIMINOLOGY

Published under the auspices of the Institute of Criminology, University of Cambridge; the Mannheim Centre, London School of Economics; and the Centre for Criminology, University of Oxford.

RECENT TITLES IN THIS SERIES:

Cold Case Reviews: DNA, Detective Work, and Unsolved Major Crimes
Allsop

Justice, Mercy, and Caprice: Clemency and the Death Penalty in Ireland
O'Donnell

Young Criminal Lives: Life Courses and Life Chances from 1850
Godfrey, Cox, Shore, and Alker

The Chinese Mafia: Organized Crime, Corruption, and Extra-Legal Protection
Wang

Dirty Money: On Financial Delinquency
Ruggiero

Reinventing Punishment: A Comparative History of Criminology and Penology in the Nineteenth and Twentieth Centuries
Pifferi

Sentencing Policy and Social Justice

RALPH HENHAM

OXFORD
UNIVERSITY PRESS

OXFORD
UNIVERSITY PRESS

Great Clarendon Street, Oxford, OX2 6DP,
United Kingdom

Oxford University Press is a department of the University of Oxford.
It furthers the University's objective of excellence in research, scholarship,
and education by publishing worldwide. Oxford is a registered trade mark of
Oxford University Press in the UK and in certain other countries

First Edition published in 2018

Published in the United States of America by Oxford University Press
198 Madison Avenue, New York, NY 10016, United States of America

British Library Cataloguing in Publication Data
Data available

Library of Congress Control Number: 2017958607

ISBN 978–0–19–871889–5

General Editors' Introduction

The *Clarendon Studies in Criminology series* aims to provide a forum for outstanding empirical and theoretical work in all aspects of criminology, criminal justice, penology and the wider field of deviant behaviour. The Editors welcome excellent PhD work, as well as submissions from established scholars. The Series was inaugurated in 1994, with Roger Hood as its first General Editor, following discussions between Oxford University Press and three criminology centres. It is edited under the auspices of these three centres: the Institute of Criminology at the University of Cambridge, the Mannheim Centre for Criminology at the London School of Economics, and the Centre for Criminology at the University of Oxford. Each supplies members of the Editorial Board and, in turn, the Series Editor or Editors.

In *Sentencing Policy and Social Justice* Ralph Henham poses some challenging questions about the state's responsibility towards its citizens and how best to realise this through sentencing and criminal justice policy. By introducing the concept of 'social justice' Ralph Henham skillfully draws out the suggestion that shared values provide more authority and validate the ideology of punishment. The notion of 'social justice' of course implies that both individual citizens and communities should perceive the punishment of criminalized behaviour as not only fair and non-discriminatory, but as reflecting shared social values and the reality of those values on the ground. In this sense, the book provides a strong critique of the limitations of retributive sentencing—which is the hallmark of sentencing in England and Wales, notwithstanding scope to modify desert principles by reference to other penal theories.

Carefully building up the arguments in the eight chapters which comprise the book, the author presses the argument that the legitimacy of sentencing ultimately depends upon the strength of the relationship between social morality and penal ideology and elucidates ways in which shared moral values can influence sentencing policy. The author draws on problematic areas of sentencing such as women offenders, irregular migrants, serious public disorder and financial crime to illustrate how the ideology underpinning sentencing policy in England and Wales often fails to reflect moral values about the appropriateness or utility of punishment. A seeming failure to engage with the social realities of citizens' lives leads to an absence of moral authority on the part of the state which then undermines the legitimacy of its penal interventions in different social contexts, and arguably weakens the overall credibility and legitimacy of criminal justice.

This is a challenging, thoughtful, and thought-provoking book which reflects modern concerns about sentencing and its distance from the realities of people's lives. The author does not shy away from thorny issues in sentencing but rather embraces them to promote the idea that social justice should be a part of sentencing policy. The recommendations for policy change within are premised on the idea that promoting social justice is both a necessary and practically achievable purpose for sentencing. This means retaining and developing discretionary justice, but without falling into the traps of discriminatory justice. There are heartening lessons for policy-makers, sentencers and citizens alike within the book.

As General Editors, we commend Ralph Henham's book for making significant contribution to the field of criminal justice through scholarly consideration of sentencing and potential links between criminal justice and social justice. We warmly welcome *Sentencing Policy and Social Justice* to the Clarendon Series.

Loraine Gelsthorpe and Kyle Treiber
Institute of Criminology, University of Cambridge
January, 2018

Acknowledgements

In particular, I wish to thank Professor Loraine Gelsthorpe of Cambridge University and Professor Roger Cotterrell of Queen Mary, University of London for their encouragement and support. I also wish to thank Dr Rowan Williams, Professor Mona Siddiqui, and the Editorial Board of the Clarendon Series for their comments and constructive suggestions. The continued support of Professor Janine Griffiths-Baker, Dean of Nottingham Law School, is also gratefully acknowledged.

The invaluable support and encouragement of my wife Annemarie is also acknowledged.

The views expressed herein and any remaining errors are mine.

Ralph Henham
September 2017

Contents

Introduction

Rationale and Scope

This book argues that the promotion of social justice should become a key objective of sentencing policy. It does so by advancing the proposition that the legitimacy of sentencing ultimately depends upon the strength of the relationship between social morality and penal ideology (see Henham 2012, 2014). The book develops reasons for adopting this position and addresses the practical consequences that flow from them.

The degree to which the values that underpin sentencing policy are shared has important implications for social cohesion and the role of penal policy in sustaining the legitimacy of the state. Shared values provide moral authority and validate the ideology of punishment. This ideology then informs the ethics and practical consequences of sentencing. The notion of 'social justice' implies that citizens and communities should perceive the punishment of criminalized behaviour by the state as even-handed and non-discriminatory. This suggests that there should be greater congruence between the values that underpin policy and the reality of those values on the ground. Thus, sentencing is more likely to have moral credibility and influence future behaviour where such perceptions are shared.

Common agreement about which social values should validate sentencing is therefore seen as essential for effective penal governance. Accordingly, the nature of the value system and the extent to which its constituent values are shared must be identified. I argue that such a value system should promote social integration and cohesion, in marked contrast to the values of neo-liberal retributive justice, which tend to reinforce social divisions through the disproportionate use of incarceration. Not only are such policies excessively punitive, they effectively ignore the impact of poverty and inequality on criminality. Aiming for greater social justice in sentencing is designed to reverse this trend. Thus, deciding

Sentencing Policy and Social Justice. First Edition. Ralph Henham. © Ralph Henham 2018. Published 2018 by Oxford University Press.

which values should take priority must precede the formulation of policy.

The book's other main objective is normative. Having identified the value system that should underpin sentencing, this ideological commitment must be carried through into practice so that outcomes have moral credibility and promote the values in question. In this way practice should facilitate rather than damage social relations. Social justice in sentencing is therefore concerned with ensuring that desired values are realized as far as possible. Hence, the degree to which sentencing practice actually contributes to social cohesion is seen as a fundamental measure of social justice.

The book supports the proposition that the state has an overriding moral obligation to promote the welfare of *all* citizens. This carries with it an implication that the state has a moral duty to promote social justice through its sentencing policies and practices. In this, I argue against maintaining a rigid dichotomy between penal and social policy in sentencing matters. Rather, moral values that tend to further social justice should be recognized and promoted more generally within a particular society. In this way sentencing outcomes are more likely to be perceived as socially relevant, and so morally acceptable by the majority of citizens. Consequently, such outcomes are much more likely to prove constructive in promoting social harmony.

However, social morality may conflict about the nature of justice, especially as to which behaviours should be criminalized, or particular offenders punished. The penal apparatus of the state is tasked with reflecting an acceptable balance between these competing social values through its ideological foundations and sentencing practices. Judgments have to be made regarding the 'appropriate' balance between the rights and obligations of citizens and how to ensure that this is respected consistently and fairly through sentencing policy and practice.

Any proposed value system or changes to the existing justificatory framework should therefore be validated empirically. There must be a credible connection between state values and the extent to which such values are shared and understood by individuals, communities, and social networks. This notion is at the core of this study. It is concerned with establishing credible links between ideology and practice, between philosophical justifications and empirical 'truth', and between values and norms.

Hence, policy judgments must be based upon reliable empirical accounts of social values and the extent to which such sentiments are shared.

The degree to which shared values about the appropriateness and utility of punishment should inform sentencing policy and consequently the ethics and practice of sentencing is problematic. In reality, such values overlap and may be reflected ideologically and normatively in many different ways, depending upon their social context. Hence, although the notion of community I employ is tied to a vision of shared values and a need to protect common interests, the fluidity and transient nature of such a shared morality is also recognized.[1]

The book aims to shed more light on how shared values can influence sentencing policy at a time when relationships of community appear increasingly fragmented. Thus, I suggest that sentencing will be better placed to make a positive contribution to social justice if it becomes more sensitive to commonly accepted definitions of the moral boundaries that underpin adherence to the 'rule of law'. In the past, however, penal law has too often served to validate oppression and symbolized an unwillingness, or inability, on the part of the state to engage with alternative moralities (Hall and others 1978). Regrettably, the demands of short-term political expediency often prevent any meaningful engagement with deeply rooted social problems and their impact on criminality.

The late modern era has been characterized by increased secularization and a general polarization of moral values, aggravated by the absence of any sustained debate about the kinds of values and norms which are (or should be) shared generally by those who have a moral stake in promoting social harmony (Siddiqui 2012). My particular concern is with the tendency of processes such as sentencing to exacerbate social disharmony by promoting notions of responsibility that largely ignore the impact of poverty and discrimination on criminality. An important aspect of this is the policy of decentralization to communities of responsibility for crime problems. Such strategies may be viewed as an abdication by the state of its duty to ensure that the moral values underpinning punishment are recognized and consistently reinforced

[1] Philosophical questions concerning the nature and origins of values and the resolution of competing values are beyond the scope of this book.

for the common good of society, rather than secular or competing interests. A reciprocal concern is the role of sentencing policy in promoting mutual awareness and a sense of social responsibility in citizens and communities where the state's social and penal policies consistently reinforce their sense of alienation and social exclusion. Thus, I argue that the ideology informing sentencing policy should reinforce commonly held values of social responsibility.

The need to reflect public opinion in sentencing has recently received significant attention (Roberts 2011a, Ryberg and Roberts 2014), with renewed interest being shown in broadening the scope of lay participation through jury sentencing (Dzur 2012) and 'stakeholder sentencing' (Brooks 2014a), or by ensuring that community views are taken into account by policy-makers in calibrating empirical desert so that rules are more likely to retain moral credibility (Robinson 2013). This volume advocates a different approach, combining a new theoretical focus with practical suggestions for reform. It argues that the contribution sentencing can make towards promoting social justice necessitates a fundamental change in the way shared values are reflected in penal ideology and sentencing policy. Thus, whilst regarding empirical evidence as essential for maintaining the moral credibility of penal law, it goes further in suggesting that modified deserts systems, however well informed by public opinion, will ultimately prove inadequate for delivering social justice. Hence, the book is partly conceptual in arguing for a changed approach, and partly normative in spelling-out how such conceptual changes might impact the ethics and practice of sentencing. The book develops previous theoretical ideas (Henham 2012, 2014) and suggests in as much detail as possible how these changes could be given practical shape within the context of sentencing in England and Wales.

Wherever possible the book uses examples from international, comparative, and domestic contexts to advance the moral and ethical case for challenging the existing ideological paradigm of sentencing. However, my primary focus is the sentencing policy of England and Wales and its recent development, especially the relationship between sentencing policy and sentencing decisions. The book assesses the consequences for penal governance of any increased state regulation of discretionary sentencing power and examines the prospects for achieving the kind of moral transformation regarded as necessary to reverse such a move.

The following problematic areas of contemporary sentencing policy are examined to illustrate the issues raised: namely, the sentencing of irregular migrants,[2] sentencing for offences of serious public disorder, sentencing for financial crime, and the sentencing of women. These areas are chosen in the belief that they demonstrate most effectively how the ideology underpinning sentencing policy in England and Wales often fails to reflect shared values about the appropriateness or efficacy of punishment. This lack of moral authority on the part of the state undermines the legitimacy of its penal interventions in different social contexts and so weakens the overall credibility of criminal justice. The analysis reveals significant points of tension between contemporary sentencing policy and the aim of social justice, suggesting a common thread between them. In particular, it explains how neo-liberal values continue to dominate the ideology, structures and decision-making processes of sentencing, and conditions the responses of successive governments to phenomena that either do not readily conform to the existing paradigm, or present it with new and previously untested challenges. I conclude that the ideology, norms, and structures which currently shape the practice of sentencing in these areas are flawed, and explain the reasons for asserting that the approach proposed in this volume would significantly strengthen sentencing's moral legitimacy and enhance its contribution to social justice.

Summary of the Argument

Ideology

As things stand, the dominant retributive ideology that underpins sentencing posits a narrow interpretation of individualization as a concept, certainly not one that engages constructively with the wider social environment.[3] In other words, the focus

[2] The Institute for Public Policy Research (IPPR) defines 'irregular migrants' as 'people who are liable to be deported for issues related to immigration status', suggesting that the expression 'best captures the complexity of the issue and has fewer connotations with criminality' than the terminology 'illegal migrants' (IPPR 2006).

[3] Individualization in sentencing is the notion that judges and magistrates should have discretion to determine how sentencing norms are to be applied in any particular case (see Thomas 1979). By implication, this approach rejects the imposition of prescriptive sentencing guidelines.

remains very much on punishing the individual offender rather than engaging with the context in which the crime took place. Yet Garland (1990: 253) suggests that punishment should be reflective of generally understood cultural meanings of crime and punishment and, consequently, the boundaries of morally acceptable behaviour. In other words, his perspective invites us to engage with different contexts in order to understand what 'justice' actually signifies in the real world.

Since trial justice has the capacity to alter or distort our ideas about those values that conventionally underpin punishment, it is important to reflect upon the limitations of relying on retributive justice as a primary justification; more especially, how it allocates responsibility for criminality irrespective of the different historical, social, and cultural settings where punishment norms are applied through sentencing. This leads to the conclusion that the only way for sentencing to reach beyond the symbolism of the courtroom is for it to engage more directly with 'real' contexts. I suggest that, for this to happen, criminal justice theory needs to adopt a more normative perspective for conceptualizing trial justice; namely, one that looks at the actual impact of decisions in particular contexts.

Braithwaite (2002: 207) suggests that institutional renewal is a precondition for engaging restorative justice and enforcing human rights. Viewed in this light, the role of criminal justice in exposing 'truth' and defining the capacity of those structures that regulate the behaviour of individual citizens in civil society is crucial for effective state governance. I argue that this potential lies within sentencing policy—to substitute the politics of alienation, exclusivity, and social control with a response that is more sensitive to how the values underlying punishment are perceived by citizens within different communities.

However, to achieve this I believe that sentencing should be evaluated against broader social objectives and measures of satisfaction that go far beyond those which might impact directly on victims and communities. For example, perceptions are influenced by such factors as emotional experiences, feelings about procedural justice, or whether aspirations for trial justice are satisfied. So, retribution and deterrence should be regarded as *part* of the mechanism for penal intervention, not the primary motivator. I suggest that such a fundamental change can be achieved without destabilizing the system's coherence.

The book suggests that the ideology which underpins sentencing needs to be changed in order to provide rationality for a less punitive and more parsimonious approach to sentence decision-making; one that decreases reliance on the use of custody whilst, at the same time, promoting more rehabilitative and restorative alternatives. In this, I agree with the recent British Academy Report (BA Report 2014) (discussed in Chapter 1) that these objectives might be achieved more readily if certain 'core' social values were to form the cornerstone for a more compassionate and reflective kind of sentencing policy. However, I believe that it is necessary to go much further than the report suggests in seeking to reorientate sentencing in this new direction.

As suggested, the state has a moral obligation to ensure that sentencing policy promotes decisions and outcomes that engage directly with questions of social value, not in an abstract sense, but through actual practice. Although one may argue that the ability of sentencing to promote social values in this way is limited, I regard it as fundamental that sentencing should fulfil its potential in penal governance; after all, decisions as to guilt, punishment, and the deprivation of liberty are at the core of what passes as criminal justice. Thus, a socially relevant sentencing policy should always be sensitive to the changing power relationship between citizen and state, a crucial aspect of which concerns the latter's ability (or willingness) to keep pace with social morality in all its diverse forms.

Punishment within democratic states[4] becomes increasingly difficult to justify unless it is tied in a convincing way to contemporary social morality. I believe that the punitive excesses of neoliberal retributive justice have taken us in the wrong direction, so that the morality of sentencing has become distorted and harder to justify in social terms. If, as I argue, this morality is grounded in shared social values, then it follows that sentencing policy should play a significant role in helping to promote such values in practice. Hence, it is for the state to ensure that citizens share the core values chosen to underpin penal policy in a 'real' sense. This means that citizens who live within 'victim' communities must see state values as producing tangible benefits, so that such values are perceived as socially desirable. Factors fostering social

[4] See Cheliotis and Sozzo (2016) for a discussion of the relationship between democratization and punishment.

solidarity rather than exclusion, mutual awareness, and social responsibility might fall within this category. This task becomes more difficult where, as now, increasing social and moral diversity pertains.

The idea that sentencing policy should promote shared social values is therefore regarded as central to effective penal governance. However, the concept of reflecting shared values and promoting social justice in sentencing, especially the relationship between the two, requires further clarification. The state's primary responsibility when formulating sentencing policy lies in identifying and prioritizing what are *presumed* to be desirable and shared social values. But this alone is insufficient. This sharing of moral values may be illusory, so it must be related in some concrete way to social context. As suggested, to be socially desired, citizens must share the view that the values underpinning policy are beneficial for them, their communities and society as a whole—for example, because adherence to such values is likely to promote their own autonomy, liberty, and security, or that of their fellow citizens. However, social justice can only be achieved where citizens also believe that such policies are being applied in a consistent and non-partisan manner.

Accordingly, I believe that sentencing policy and practice must seek to achieve a closer connection with the moralities of crime and punishment within different cultures and communities. Most importantly, research should aim to identify values that are generally accepted as being for the common good of 'civil' society, and, of equal importance, explaining why and how they have been shaped by particular social contexts, so that this knowledge can inform future policy. Sentencing praxis should then be better equipped to engage more meaningfully with the social consequences of penal intervention, for example, in giving offenders, victims, and communities effective rights of access and participation (see Chapter 6). Perceptions of social justice will therefore depend upon the contribution such a reconceived process can make to social cohesion through consistent and impartial practice. Thus, I suggest that a system of values which embodies the common good is one where the relationship between the state's core values and the values that are actually present and shared by the citizens of different communities is at its closest. The closeness of that connection should be consistently monitored because it is a measure of the extent to which the values promoted by sentencing policy retain moral credibility in the eyes of the majority of citizens.

If, as I argue, the state has an obligation to ensure that the values it promotes through sentencing are shared by citizens, the criteria governing the selection of those values and their status must be decided. I suggest that an overarching and uniform system of values similar to the core values of liberty, autonomy, solidarity, dignity, inclusion, and security identified by the BA Report (2014) should inform the sentencing process. Moreover, the state's obligation should be to ensure that the values it promotes through sentencing bear as close a relationship as possible to those of its citizens. Decision-makers must therefore be able to draw upon common understandings of what those values signify within and between different communities. Developing our knowledge of how such values are socially constructed, experienced, and shared is therefore central to developing a workable definition of the common good.

Furthermore, the fact that *all* citizens are potential offenders and/or victims suggests a common or 'public' interest in the promotion of sentences that are perceived to be morally 'just'. In this sense, 'society' as a whole is victimized. Thus, it is in the 'public' interest that sentencing policy should not promote values and practices that are socially divisive. Where values are shared, the state's moral obligation to reflect them in sentencing policy should therefore be firmly tied to a greater understanding of their social significance.

Lacey and Pickard (2015b: 693) similarly recognize the need for a deliberative space in effecting a reconceptualization of purpose for the criminal process by extending the scope for achieving reparation and reintegration through dialogue and discussion, but *within* the existing sentencing framework and guidelines. Whilst also seeing the effectiveness of sentencing as essentially tied to the ideology that informs sentencing policy, my argument differs in that I regard this ideology as outmoded and in need of change, so that the purposes of sentencing, whether retributive, deterrent, rehabilitative, or reintegrative, are tied to the wider moral purpose of promoting shared social values. The core objectives of my argument are therefore: (a) to break free of the current paradigm, and, (b) to reconceive the process and reposition sentencing so that outcomes contribute more effectively to social cohesion. In this way ideological change should provide meaning and social relevance to rights of equality and non-discrimination at the point of sentencing.

Given that sentencing is inextricably linked to social values, social theory currently lacks a sufficient appreciation of how values are translated into 'meaningful' outcomes through institutionalized processes such as sentencing. Coherence between ideology and practice is fundamental in achieving this objective. I argue that, as currently conceived, social theory falls short of providing an adequate account of the fundamental links that exist between the ideology that underpins sentencing and how the outcomes of that process act as normative guides to conduct. Understanding how a shared belief in the value of penal intervention actually translates into socially meaningful outcomes in individual cases is therefore vital.

Contextual validation should therefore provide a conceptual and operational link between the universal system of values underpinning state policy and the way such values are perceived and embedded within different communities. So conceived, sentencing would not find its guiding values solely by reference to local contexts, nor would particular social contexts define the nature of the common good. Rather, detailed context-specific information would assist policy-makers in deciding how the balance between state values and the competing values and interests of different cultures and communities should be maintained, so promoting overall coherence and consistency.

However, notions of 'community' are notoriously opaque. 'Communities' may occupy a particular physical space but vary significantly in their composition. Typically, they are culturally, racially, or ethnically diverse, with various kinds of overlapping social networks based on religion, ethnicity, kinship, linguistic heritage, or shared history or traditions. Hence, there may be problems in reconciling the different perceptions of interests and values requiring protection within and between differing communities. Thus, for present purposes 'communities' are defined as geographically distinct entities within identifiable regional divisions, such as metropolitan areas, whilst recognizing the overlapping nature of communal networks, their origins, and social significance.

Norms, ethics, and structures

Changing the ideology that underpins sentencing is vital if its processes and practices are to have the coherence and direction needed to move away from the socially debilitating effects of neo-liberal retributive justice, such as the excessive use of custodial sentencing. I therefore advocate a complete transformation of the sentencing process, explaining in detail how a new moral purpose for sentencing might be reflected in structural reforms to domestic sentencing. Suggested reforms include the adoption of a trial programme, changed evidential rules for admissibility and burden of proof to facilitate a new factual basis for sentencing, increased possibilities for judicial intervention and diversion through enhanced discretionary power, modified rules for victim and community access and representation, changed roles and ethical codes for legal professionals within the process, reconceptualized roles for plea and sentence bargaining, and the merging of the sentencing and enforcement phases of the trial.

The exponential expansion of out-of-court and alternative forms of penal intervention has destabilized conventional understandings of proportionality within the just deserts framework. In rejecting this framework, I argue that measures of proportionality should take account of social values. As Lacey and Pickard (2015a) suggest, the underlying forces that shape concepts such as proportionality are essentially political, social, and contextual. So the state cannot simply 'secure' legitimacy by imposing or co-opting values that do not engage with social context.

To sum up, the political project of convincing citizens of the moral virtue of the values the state espouses through its sentencing policy is, in my view, best achieved by pursuing them, firstly, by adopting such values as core elements of penal ideology. However, as suggested, values such as those identified as desirable by the BA Report (2014) cannot be viewed as shared values in any 'real' sense unless they are socially embedded. For this to occur, values have to relate in some concrete way to citizens' shared experiences of everyday life, with meanings that resonate with the way morality is shaped and lived by people in different social environments. The extent to which perceptions of 'fairness' or 'justice' are shared thus reflects the experiences of offenders, victims, and communities over time. Furthermore, perceptions of procedural fairness and the perceived social benefits of sentencing all contribute to the overall perception of 'justice'.

Changes in the way the trial is conceptualized are therefore advocated to reflect the fact that the goals set for the trial and sentencing would be grounded in a new morality of core social values. In this, I explain how the ideology, institutions, and practice of sentencing are intimately related, so that the core values underpinning policy and practice are positively reinforced in areas where the relationship between state values and their perceived value is at its closest. Policymakers therefore need to devise ways in which the institutional structures of sentencing can accommodate value-related information in individual cases, whilst maintaining the overall consistency of the system.

Outcomes and reform

From a theoretical perspective, I highlight the self-perpetuating and recursive nature of sentencing's processes and systems. This suggests that sentencing practice tends to develop in ways that reinforce sentencing's underlying ideology, and so its norms, processes, and outcomes. I argue that neo-liberal retributive ideology has perpetuated a punitive system of criminal justice that has become increasingly resistant to change, both ideologically and institutionally, in terms of adopting more parsimonious or caring approaches to sentencing. This trend has hampered the integration of restorative and more socially constructive forms of penal intervention, and accelerated the state's control of sentencing, particularly in restricting judicial discretion.

Most significant, in practical terms, is the need for decision-makers to take greater account of social factors when sentencing. Not, however, in the conventional sense of mitigation within the adversarial paradigm, but through a much more integrated engagement with the moralities of crime and victimization; particularly in terms of how they are shaped and shared within different communities. Thus, I explain how the court's engagement could reach far beyond conventional accounts of offender/victim impact by developing a principled approach for taking greater account of the social significance of crime. This would demand a far more intimate knowledge of the normative consequences of the sentencing decision, for offenders, victims, and the wider community in which the crime was committed, than currently pertains.

The difficult normative questions regarding which social factors should actually count in sentencing and the weight to be attached to them in individual cases is addressed in Chapter 7. I argue that sentencing should take account of social and cultural factors in terms of their possible influence on criminality, and, more particularly, how that criminality and any proposed punishment might be perceived within the community in question. As mentioned, the social goals set for sentencing should be informed by an overarching set of values, with factors influencing the way such values are generally perceived within the community where the offence was committed taken into account when developing a trial programme. Hence, consideration of both the crime and any proposed punishment would take account of different perceptions of value within victim communities. Within the state's overarching policy remit, regional branches of the Sentencing Council would be charged with developing contextually informed guidelines to assist decision-makers with factoring in value-related information at relevant stages of the trial process. The task of policy would be to ensure that such guidelines retain coherence and that social factors are considered in such a way that they do not contravene core principles of fairness such as proportionality and consistency within the reconceived process.

To be realized effectively in practice, the core values identified by the BA Report (2014) would need to be operationalized within a framework of distributive principles. Specific boundaries would need to be established within which value-related information could be assessed and evaluated. Where, for example, social or cultural factors are shown to have influenced the decision as to plea, this might be reflected in the discount given. Arguably, the present system prioritizes economic rather than social values, resulting in the marginalization of such evidence and diminished rights protection.[5] Calibrating value-related factors within a nationally overseen rights-protected framework should help to reduce this kind of inequality and discrimination in sentencing.

The kind of localized regulatory system proposed should not therefore be regarded as a dangerous devolution of the state's responsibility for formulating sentencing policy and practice—an unprincipled descent into localism and uncontrolled discretion. The opposite is intended. Rather, the objective is to counter a fragmentation of state accountability that threatens the overall legitimacy of sentencing policy as a core component of penal governance.

[5] The Sentencing Council's definitive guideline on guilty plea sentence discounts perpetuates this trend (Sentencing Council 2017). See Treacy (2016) for a contrary view.

My argument is that devolved accountability for sentencing within the context of a coherent national penal strategy is the best way forward if courts are to engage effectively with social value at the community level. It offers a more meaningful engagement with the social priorities and challenges faced by local people and communities, and more constructive ways in which discretion exercised in individual sentencing decisions can foster social cohesion.

However, my fundamental point is that the reforms suggested are predicated on the proposed change in ideology being translated into policy at the state level. Hence, the state's duty is viewed in terms of facilitating the realization of 'core' social values through sentencing practice. Whereas state sentencing policy would supply ideological coherence for the proposed changes, regional branches of the Sentencing Council are advocated to facilitate their local implementation. Policy would therefore be operationalized effectively at the local level through guidance and training aimed at ensuring that judges and magistrates have the necessary discretion and knowledge to enable them to take account of social value when sentencing.

Moreover, the Sentencing Council's role would increasingly become one of providing clarification and guidance regarding the overarching principles of sentencing within the new paradigm, since these are crucial for maintaining overall consistency and proportionality. This approach, together with the constant review and development of definitive guidelines, would determine the national sentencing framework. The local deployment and implementation of this framework would be achieved through modification and adaptation of the national guidelines. Social values would be monitored through ongoing independently conducted social research funded through local taxation. Consequently, utilization, adaptation, and continuous modification of sentencing guidelines would occur at the grass roots level, as would accountability. This process would be overseen centrally by the Sentencing Council and facilitated through the practical implementation of sentencing policy.

To sum up, the main points developed in the book are as follows:

- The primary task for government is the identification of 'core' values to inform sentencing policy. This is seen as a moral obligation that falls to the state.

- To be effective as a new morality for sentencing, such values must be embedded as the foundational values of a changed penal ideology.
- However, state values must also have 'real' moral and social credibility—this is an empirical question.
- Policy-makers must have this knowledge otherwise values cannot be effectively realized in practice—an important aspect of this is the notion that the whole process is recursive, in the sense that outcomes reinforce ideology, which then feeds through into practice and outcomes and so forth, similar to an amplificatory system. However, ideology cannot be positively reinforced unless it engages with social reality.
- Late modern society has become increasingly pluralistic and fragmented, so different and overlapping views exist about the morality of certain behaviours—why they occur and how they should be dealt with by the state, if at all.
- Hence, to be realized, the values that sustain penal ideology must, when put into practice, engage with this moral diversity at the community level—particularly as accountability for crime and criminal justice continues to be devolved.
- Contextual empirical research aimed at discovering why and how social values about crime and punishment are shaped over time is therefore essential if sentencing is to engage effectively with these views at the grass roots level.
- Implicit in recasting penal ideology is the notion that the criminal process and sentencing in particular should change to provide a more flexible and constructive forum for realizing the state's aims—thus, numerous changes to practice and guidance are advocated in Chapters 6 and 7, the most important being that judges and magistrates should be given more discretion, not less, to be able to facilitate the changes proposed.
- The BA Report (2014), discussed in Chapter 1, identifies a system of universal values based on our common humanity, developing Durkheim's notion of moral individualism. Such a system would favour policies that promote social integration and cohesion. However, I argue that this vision requires empirical (contextual) validation if the proposed value system is to connect with social reality in a meaningful way. Chapter 4 compares moral individualism with religious belief to make this point—emphasizing that a sharing of trust and belief in the value system that underpins penal ideology must exist on

the ground to make it viable. Although universal belief in such a value system is unlikely ever to be realized, greater moral credibility is necessary to secure the legitimacy of sentencing. Attempts to embed values through education, civic engagement, or citizenship classes, although valuable, are limited in scope. Ideology and social reality need to be drawn closer together to make the value system work practically. For this reason penal value systems need to have 'real' moral purchase before they can function in a coherent and egalitarian manner.

- Sentencing policies that fail to facilitate what is perceived as fair and just at the community level, and naively persist in refining and expanding neo-liberal retributive solutions to crime problems, particularly through the excessive and disproportionate use of imprisonment, will tend to polarize popular opinion and work against social cohesion. To be respected, values such as autonomy, liberty, solidarity, dignity, inclusion, and security must be secured at the grass roots level. The most obvious way to maximize such values is through reforms that realize meaningful (i.e. effective) rights of participation for offenders, victims, and communities, thereby enabling them to work together in devising restorative and integrated solutions to criminality. Regrettably, the combined effects of the adversarial trial model and neo-liberal retributive justice policies continue to hamper the mainstreaming of this approach, so reforms remain constrained and reactive. There is no sense in which engagement, inclusion, and equality are embedded as fundamental principles of conventional trial justice.
- To conclude, sentencing policy would be far more effective in delivering outcomes that sustain the core values identified by the BA Report if its moral foundations were aligned with such values and translated into practice via a completely transformed system. As suggested, this does not mean abandoning conventional penal purposes, such as retribution and deterrence. Rather, it means reconfiguring and repositioning the forum for resolving crime problems as a system of trial justice that is less punitive, more parsimonious, has more emotional sensitivity, is more caring and compassionate, and able to recognize and take greater account of the negative effects of social environment on behaviour. In short, one that provides a deliberative space where responsible local agencies can fashion the most appropriate solutions to crime for offenders, victims, and communities.

The Structure of the Book

Chapter 1 begins by exploring the meaning of 'social justice' in the context of sentencing policy. Although it focuses on explaining the relationship between social justice and sentencing in terms of its social reality, the arguments developed in the book are based on a particular view of this relationship and the duties and obligations it imposes on the state and individuals and communities. The position taken is that the state has a moral obligation to ensure that sentencing policy promotes social justice. Correspondingly, individuals and communities have a moral obligation to promote the welfare of all citizens (Williams 2012a).

In reality, however, the ideologies, policies, and practices of sentencing are forced to reflect what amounts to an unsatisfactory compromise or accommodation between competing social values. Views regarding the 'appropriate' balance between the rights and obligations of citizens and how to ensure they are respected consistently and fairly by the state are matters of ongoing debate. The chapter considers the implications of this debate for developing a sentencing policy that engages with social justice and illustrates the issues raised through a detailed examination of the relationship between sentencing policy and social justice in England and Wales over the last twenty or so years, focusing on the extent to which social change and value pluralism have affected the relationship between penal ideology and sentencing policy. More specifically, it considers how the fragmentation of communities and social values and the ensuing breakdown in social cohesion has affected public perceptions of punishment. The analysis explains how the penal apparatus of the state has responded to these dilemmas through a narrow interpretation of community interests and an increasing politicization of penal policy that has obfuscated those social values justifying state intervention. By way of illustration, the chapter explores how these tensions between sentencing policy and social values have played out in the sentencing of irregular migrants.

Chapter 2 advances the case for adopting a normative approach in conceptualizing the social reality of sentencing. The ability to reflect upon and engage with social context is seen as fundamental for any paradigm which is intended to influence policy, especially if policy-makers aim to predict interactions between sentencing and social justice. The chapter reflects particularly on the problems of relating social values to legal processes such as sentencing and how this prevents policy-makers from promoting social justice as a significant sentencing objective. It also reflects upon what can be gleaned from international criminal justice about the relationship of sentencing to social justice issues, particularly in terms of its engagement with victims and communities. The chapter concludes by exploring how sentencing policy and practice might help to redress or stabilize social relations where the moral cohesion of 'communities' is threatened or no longer exists; in other words, where the institutional structures of governance and their decisions are more likely to be perceived as partial by particular interests. I argue that the provision of universal rights for citizens or communities of interest does not replace the need for sentencing to reinforce 'bonds of community', and, more especially, commonly held social values (Cotterrell 2012).[6]

Where poverty renders economic ties of community less relevant to socially marginalized groups or communities, their perceptions of punishment are more likely to mirror what they regard as the repressive and punitive nature of state penal policy. The implications of this assertion are explored through an analysis of the sentencing approach taken following the English riots of 2011, focusing particularly on community perceptions regarding the legitimacy of state intervention in such circumstances, and the deployment of state penal power through sentencing as a form of social control.

Chapter 3 considers the global and comparative dimensions of sentencing and explains their significance for developing a positive relationship between sentencing policy and social justice. It begins by assessing the effect of globalization on the formulation of sentencing policy in England and Wales. The discussion then reflects on the problems of comparison and policy transfer in the sentencing field and speculates whether greater judicial involvement in the enforcement of sentences or early release might enhance social justice. The chapter concludes with some reflections about sentencing as a transitional concept, drawing

[6] The expansion of victims' rights may be used by a political system to justify greater identification with it. The idea of the victim can generate public empathy and give false legitimacy to other measures that may turn out to be politically repressive (Dubber 2006).

on the justifications, concepts, and practices of various transitional justice settings and examining their relevance in the domestic context. I argue that notions of transitional justice offer some useful insights into how one might think about sentencing policy's potential contribution to social justice, particularly in situations where the state lacks a coherent moral mandate for criminalizing and punishing offenders. By way of illustration the chapter considers whether, in the aftermath of global recession, the juxtaposition of social values with those of global capitalism has influenced the approach taken to the sentencing of financial crime in the domestic arena.

Chapter 4 evaluates the implications for sentencing policy of the prevalent view that sentencing should engage more directly and effectively with the emotions and sensibilities of its relevant audiences, especially those of victims and the wider community. It reflects on the work of Doak (2009) and Loader (2011) in seeking to explain how sentencing impacts on emotions, perceptions, and motivations in both the public and the private sphere, and considers how such knowledge might better inform penal ideology and so influence sentencing policy and practice, referring to work by Roberts and Hough (2005) and Tyler (2008). The chapter then explores how sentencing might better serve the 'public interest' by developing its potential for promoting social justice and thereby contributing to the 'common good'. Reasons for recasting the moral underpinnings of sentencing policy are examined in the light of increasing secularization and value pluralism, weakening political legitimacy, and diminishing economic resources. One argument is that consideration of the 'public interest' in sentencing policy should move away from its present narrow focus on the individual towards a greater recognition of collective forms of accountability. Thus, penal ideology should acknowledge that states and citizens share responsibility for reflecting the 'public interest' in criminal justice interventions.

Chapter 5 explores the gap between political and penal legitimacy. It argues that in order to achieve some kind of clarity about the contextual reality of 'social justice', it is necessary to consider the dynamics of the relationship between penal policy and the political economy. The chapter explores the implications for sentencing policy of work by Cavadino and Dignan (2006) and Lacey (2008a) on enhancing relationships between political and penal legitimacy. In particular, it considers Lacey's suggestion that communitarian justice requires the adoption of a conception of 'consistent pluralism' through which the values each society places on the goods in question are given equal prominence in criminal justice practice. In this way fundamental community values and interests are consistently reinforced. Clearly, the practical realization of this imperative through sentencing will depend upon its capacity to reflect pluralistic conceptions of the good in a non-partisan fashion. An important aspect of this is the nature and quality of the 'truth' concerning the social reality of crime that sentencing relies on, and its public perception. I argue that the ability of sentencing policy to reflect the social meaning of 'justice' necessitates a recasting of penal ideology. The greatest difficulty lies in establishing clear links between ideology and practice so that sentencing policy becomes sensitive to changes in social values. To illustrate these problems in a domestic context, the chapter explains how the ongoing tensions between neo-liberal retributive ideology and utilitarian values continue to define the approach taken by the courts to the sentencing of women. This tendency works against developing a socially relevant policy commitment to 'consistent pluralism'; rather, it encourages sentencing outcomes that exacerbate social exclusion and reinforce existing divisions in social morality.

Chapter 6 considers the case for recasting the moral values that inform sentencing and the policy implications of such a fundamental change of approach. It draws on work by Findlay and Henham (2005, 2010) arguing for new foundational principles, and explores how such a moral transition might be reflected through structural reforms to domestic sentencing. Emphasis is placed on the difficulties of recasting values and structures to reflect the changing governance role of sentencing as a tool for engaging with issues of social justice. The chapter examines specific areas of policy change within England and Wales and the problem of moving from theory to practice through the analysis of recent government reforms, highlighting how changes in social values and moral diversity might be better accommodated in sentencing policy and practice. In particular, it explores the implications of the diminishing role of judicial discretion in sentencing, the prioritizing of procedural justice over substantive justice, as exemplified by the disproportionate sentence discounts given to guilty pleas, and the renewed policy focus on 'swift and sure' justice with its thinly disguised cost-cutting agenda.

Chapter 7 makes some practical suggestions for reforming sentencing in England and Wales based on the arguments developed in the earlier chapters. These include greater coordination between the national regulation of sentencing discretion through the Sentencing Council[7] and regional or community-based sentencing practices; the creation of regional branches of the Sentencing Council; new principles and practice directions to ensure that sentencing discretion is exercised within a nationally coordinated, but locally relevant, policy framework; guidance from the Sentencing Council to integrate the rules governing out-of-court disposals with existing principles of proportionality and consistency relevant to sentence; and ensuring that all penal interventions are informed by a publicly justifiable framework of penal objectives.

Further practical suggestions include the merging of the sentencing and enforcement phases of the criminal process within a reconceptualized and broadened normative framework that prioritizes social impact; the monitoring and evaluation of social impact by multi-agency, community-based panels; establishing new objectives and principles to ensure that social impact evidence relevant to sentence is given greater consideration during the trial phase; the creation by the Sentencing Council of an interdisciplinary policy working group to monitor the degree of congruence between sentencing objectives and social impact within and between different regions in order to inform the framing of sentencing guidelines and any preceding impact assessment; a greater role for the Sentencing Council in the ethical surveillance of sentencing, the development of procedural rules, and the training of judges and magistrates; and, finally, working together with the Crown Prosecution Service (CPS), defence lawyers and other agencies to develop guidance clarifying their role within the new sentencing framework.

Chapter 8, the final chapter, draws together the common themes emerging from the book and considers their broader implications for the future development of sentencing policy. It suggests that, where divergence exists between perceptions of social justice and the values that inform sentencing, policy-makers are more likely to be in a position to respond effectively by adopting the ideological

[7] See Ashworth and Roberts (2013) on the history and function of the current sentencing guidelines system in England and Wales.

approach and normative changes proposed. The book's recommendations for policy change are premised on the notion that promoting social justice is a necessary and realistically achievable purpose for sentencing. However, these suggestions depend upon developing judicial discretionary power in sentencing, not restricting it. Ultimately therefore, the success of the book's proposals for a more egalitarian and community-focused sentencing system will depend upon the strategies policy-makers adopt to restore public confidence and trust in discretionary justice and its ability to engage with social justice issues. The book ends by exploring what this might entail.

1

Sentencing Policy and Changing Notions of Social Justice

Introduction

The core of the thesis developed in this book is that the future of sentencing policy as a key element of criminal justice governance depends upon the extent to which the sentencing is able to achieve a measure of 'social justice'. However, notions of 'social justice' tend to be somewhat opaque, so this chapter begins by exploring its meaning and significance in the context of contemporary debates about sentencing and penal justice more generally.

Fundamentally, the relationship between sentencing policy and social justice is described and explained in terms of its social reality. From a sociological standpoint, this means exploring what the values and norms relating to punishment and sentencing signify in their social context. My particular concern is the degree to which shared values about the appropriateness and utility of punishment are reflected in the ideology that informs sentencing policy, and therefore, the practice of sentencing.

Notionally, shared values may exist at the local (community), societal (state), or international (global) levels. However, in reality, such values overlap in degree and extent and are reflected ideologically and normatively in many different ways, depending upon their social context. Since 'communities' at whatever level may vary significantly in their composition, reasons for existence, and types of social network, significant difficulties exist in reconciling conflicting interests and values within and between differing communal networks. Hence, although the notion of community employed throughout the book is one tied to shared values and a need to protect common interests, the fluidity and transient nature of any shared morality and its social context is also recognized.

The book's aim of shedding more light on why and how values about crime and punishment are shared comes at a time when relationships of community appear increasingly fragmented (Cotterrell 2013: 63). Accordingly, a specific concern is the notion that sentencing should become more instrumental in promoting social harmony and social cohesion. The arguments developed in the book are based on a particular view of the relationship between social values and sentencing and the reciprocal obligations and duties this imposes on the state, citizens, and communities. The position taken is that the state has a moral obligation to ensure that sentencing policy promotes social justice. Correspondingly, citizens and communities have a moral obligation to promote the welfare of all citizens (Williams 2012a).

However, the approach taken by the state as to what should be the 'appropriate' relationship between sentencing policy and social policy invariably depends upon the political realities. Such nationally significant strategic decisions are determined by central government. Regrettably, the right-wing neo-liberal justice policies of recent years have largely ignored the adverse social consequences of sentencing, most notably in the United States (Tonry 2011). Such policies tend to exacerbate social divisions, thereby pre-empting further social problems and a fragmentation of policy responses on the part of the state. This tendency has spawned numerous, largely uncoordinated, alternatives to trial justice, many involving a multi-agency approach, offering mediation or various other restorative strategies designed to bridge the 'moral credibility' gap that exists between the sanction and its perceived value. More often than not policy appears to be shaped by political dogma that prioritizes economic values and so lacks the coherence or empirical justification beyond that necessary to satisfy such aspirations.

Recent years have witnessed a proliferation of problem-solving and specialized courts operating at the intersection of criminal justice and social policy (Donoghue 2014). However, I suggest that this dichotomy reflects a dangerous paradox. Not only does it serve to insulate conventional forms of criminal trial and sentencing from social policy debates, it also reinforces the existing retributive foundations of contemporary penal policy, thereby hindering sentencing courts from engaging directly with the social reality of criminalization and victimization within already deprived and marginalized communities. As a consequence, the ethics and norms of sentencing have become increasingly distinct from other more 'socially sensitive' forms of penal resolution. Sentencing remains constrained by deserts principles of proportionality and consistency operating within a predominantly neo-liberal retributive paradigm. This conception dictates the parameters within which social impact evidence is conceptualized, filtered, and synthesized by the courts.

Since I argue that the promotion of social justice should be a primary consideration for sentencing, it follows that its ideologies, policies, and practices ought to reflect a socially 'acceptable balance' between competing moral values and those of the state. In 'democratic' societies, the electoral process is meant to shape the political and social contours of this moral debate, but universal suffrage is no guarantor of rights. Hence, judgments about what should be the 'appropriate' balance between the rights and obligations of citizens and how to ensure that they are respected consistently and fairly by the state remain matters of fervent moral and philosophical debate.[1] Accordingly, I begin by considering the implications of this debate for developing a sentencing policy that engages with social justice before exploring the normative significance of this discourse from a sociological perspective. The analysis emphasizes the importance of reflecting social values in the practice of sentencing and, by so doing, reinforces the need for more appropriately theorized empirical research.

The discussion then moves on to consider the issues raised in the specific context of the sentencing policy of England and Wales during the past twenty-five years, focusing on the extent to which social change and value pluralism has damaged the essential connections between penal ideology and sentencing policy. More specifically, I examine how the fragmentation of communities and the ensuing breakdown in social cohesion has affected public perceptions of punishment. In particular, the analysis considers how the increasing politicization of penal policy has obfuscated the values justifying state intervention. Thus, I argue that neo-liberal values have taken priority at the expense of any broader consideration of which social values should inform a more inclusive and socially constructive approach to sentencing.

[1] For a useful overview see Ashworth (2015).

The argument is illustrated by describing how these tensions have impacted the sentencing of so-called 'irregular' migrants.

Punishment and the Relationship between Citizen and State

The rationales that inform state penal policy are frequently unclear beyond exhortations that particular measures are a necessary response to criminalized behaviour. States often assume the moral right to inflict punishment on perceived wrongdoers, offering this rationale as a general justification for the creation of institutions dedicated to the infliction of retributive punishment. Within this framework, unregulated judicial discretionary power is increasingly discouraged as something subversive and to be avoided. It is typically characterized as dangerously eclectic or pragmatic, with a tendency for constructing and offering alternative rationalizations in individual cases.[2]

The vision of a more liquid ideology (Bauman 2000), where there is no overriding vision of what society is, or what it is for, has changed the penal politics of late modernity (Schwarzmantel 2008). A retreat towards a more reflexive, individualistic society where ideologies have become more polarized and competitive, leaving the field open for neo-liberal hegemony, appears counter intuitive to the notion of shared social values promoting the common good. Thus, rather than polarizing ideologies or facilitating hegemony, one might argue that the political function in late modernity should now be transformed into one that supports a changed vision of society; one reflecting shared values through a reflexive and responsive ideological commitment that carries through into social policy and practical solutions. As perceived, social values of integrity, liberty, security, and autonomy vary according to religion, culture, and community. Hence, the state's moral obligation should be to draw upon, interpret, synthesize, and present an ideology that gives substance to these various meanings.

The incremental polarization of citizen and state has significant ramifications for the rationalization of punishment. Existing trial

[2] Hutton (2013) argues that a more sociologically informed understanding of sentencing could generate consistent guidelines that exist alongside an individualized definition of justice.

structures and normative frameworks reflect a democratic deficit in accountability that not only hinders the prospects for developing shared values and principles for criminal justice, but also undermines settlements negotiated at the community level. This deficit is manifest in the failure of sentencing to engage effectively with the complex relationships that exist between criminality and social disadvantage, as well as social and cultural differences, particularly in terms of shaping moral values and attitudes to punishment. Such structural weaknesses facilitate the state's prioritization of retributive justice over utilitarian and humanitarian objectives.[3]

The key point to draw from this is the difficulty of the state's task in providing ideological foundations for sentencing policy that promote practices which are sensitive to, and capable of, reconciling competing values and interests, whilst at the same time keeping abreast of changing notions of social morality. Whereas philosophical ideas and debates about the nature of punishment and 'justice' have a crucial role to play in informing the penal policy-making process, it is the normative implications of these debates that concern us here. These are essentially matters of sociological import. An implication is how one might conceive of an ideology that is likely to promote social justice through sentencing in a practical sense. A second concern is the extent to which such philosophical debates might influence the theory and methodology of social scientific investigation upon which policy research draws, so impacting decisions about the normative reach of sentencing.

Differing philosophical insights about the justifications and purposes of punishment postulate different normative scenarios whose sociological significance will vary according to context (Henham 2005). This awareness has important implications for those who seek to understand the relationship between social values and sentencing through a sociological lens, particularly where societies are characterized by value pluralism, since it

[3] Lacey (2012) suggests that rebuilding criminal justice is a political and practical problem. Insufficient emphasis is given to institutional reform and delivery and more clarity is needed about the preconditions for realizing reform. A major step forward would be to try to distance and remove criminal justice from political pressure (see also Ashworth 2013a).

necessitates a profound appreciation of why and how values are shaped through social experience and act as guides to conduct. The latter is hugely significant because contested values regarding the role of punishment in society are reflected in sentencing policy and practice.

Justice and Social Context

Many would argue that any failure to reconcile the moral justification for punishment with social reality is surely to be expected. After all, philosophical writing is concerned with answering 'ought' rather than 'is' questions. Nevertheless, as suggested earlier, if one is serious about promoting social justice through changes in penal ideology, policy, and practice, sociological accounts of punishment need to offer more convincing explanations of how morality influences the social world. Understanding the relationship between law and morality is a crucial aspect of this (see Hudson 1993, 2003).

Social justice and the state's moral authority to punish

An important question for those wishing to promote 'social justice' through sentencing is the extent to which the moral message conveyed by censure mirrors the moral values of the powerful elite rather than those shared by the majority of citizens (McBarnet 2013). Such a partisan infliction of punishment by the state is likely to be perceived by those citizens who are targeted as controlling and coercive, rather than representative of a shared morality. Evidently, the existence of such a shared morality remains a matter of empirical fact relative to social context. However, this conjecture raises broader philosophical questions that have important practical implications, since the state's moral authority to punish those who suffer social injustice may well need to be taken into account by policy-makers. Particularly difficult moral choices about the punishment of certain citizens, including those who suffer poverty and social deprivation, may have to be made, decisions that may prove pivotal to the long-term survival of the ruling elite, especially where state policies have contributed to that social injustice (see further Howard 2013).

The Social Reality of Sentencing Policy and Social Justice

Exploring the contextualized meaning and significance of social justice from a sociological perspective is problematic because accounts are likely to vary depending upon the theoretical (and ideological) lens of the observer (see further Boutellier 2005). The need for clarity increases where interdisciplinary and comparative analyses are concerned. This section therefore opens with an explanation of the terminology used throughout this book:

- The term 'social morality' is used to refer to the values that inform norms of action and interaction within a given social context, more specifically, the shared moral values of identifiable social groups and communities within a particular society. Social morality may conflict about the nature of justice, especially the punishment of selected behaviours criminalized by the state, or of particular offenders. This should be distinguished from the notion of 'legitimacy' as referring to the moral attachment of individuals and social groups to the penal ideologies, processes and outcomes of criminal trials. I have argued elsewhere that the penal apparatus of the state is tasked with reflecting an acceptable balance between competing social values through its penal ideology and its punishment practices (Henham 2012).
- The expression 'social values' is used in two senses. Primarily, it refers to those values that the state adopts as the foundational (or 'core') values of penal ideology. However, the way in which such values are *perceived* by citizens and communities is pivotal—in other words, policy-makers need to understand what the foundational values of penal ideology signify in reality. For example, how are values of autonomy, liberty, and security thought of when it comes to punishment and sentencing, and what shapes these perceptions—the important issue here is the extent to which these perceptions *accord* with those of the state.
- The term 'social value' refers to the value that citizens and communities actually *place* on specific penal interventions such as sentencing—the issue here is the degree to which the state's values are translated into something that has 'real' social

worth. In short, the difference between what the state desires and thinks it is achieving, and what is achieved in practice. The most important aspect of this is sentencing's perceived contribution to desistance. Thus, social values guide the ordering of priorities, decision-making and interaction, whereas social value signifies the worth to victims, communities, and society in general, of specific penal measures.

Since 'social value' concerns impact, it has social (i.e. normative) and ideological significance in shaping the objectives of penal policy. Value judgments are made about sentences and the sentencing process, and the extent to which particular sentences are likely to impact on the community or society as a whole. Such judgments are, of course, influenced by individual experiences, either as offenders or victims. The extent to which value judgments are shared within or between communities has immense policy significance:

- Finally, 'social justice' itself concerns the extent to which communities perceive the punishment of criminalized behaviour by the state as even-handed and non-discriminatory—here issues of criminalization, social welfare provision and tackling poverty are relevant—such perceptions are held collectively by citizens within communities. Perceptions of procedural fairness within victim communities may have therapeutic benefits and so contribute to the overall perception of social justice. Again, the extent to which such perceptions are shared depends on the experiences of victims over time. Of significant policy interest is the degree to which norms derived from values promoting social justice actually contribute to the social cohesion of communities. Thus, I argue that identifying and prioritizing shared social values should precede the formulation of policy.

Understanding the link between political ideology and social morality is fundamental to penal governance. Reiner (2012) notes how notions of social democracy encourage reciprocal individualism, with mutual concern for the welfare of all, as distinct from the competitive individualism and punitive penal policies of neo-liberal political ideology. Furthermore, in order to achieve some kind of clarity about the contextual reality of 'social justice' it is necessary to consider the relationship of penal policy to the interplay between economics and politics, in other words, the political economy (Lacey 2008a, 2012).[4]

Garside (2006) asserts that the consistent failure of the criminal justice system to significantly narrow the justice gap illustrates that the state is failing to protect the interests of the weakest members of society: women, children, the elderly, and the poor. Arguably, it also illustrates the moral bankruptcy of state social policy, since the future legitimacy of penal policy depends upon whether it has political authority and is perceived as morally justifiable by the majority of citizens. Realizing criminal justice's potential for enhancing social justice therefore requires a political commitment to developing social policies that actively promote communitarian values and collective notions of responsibility.

Although the institutional legitimacy of criminal justice may be strengthened where citizens have trust and confidence in the operation of the system's processes and procedures (Tyler 2006), effective monitoring and responding to moral change by the state is essential to maintain 'legitimate' authority' (Beetham 1991). This is vital to ensure that there are sufficient moral grounds for citizens to feel obliged to comply and co-operate with the powerful (Gelsthorpe 2013: 13). Accordingly, ongoing dialogue between criminal justice agencies and citizens is crucial in defusing the tensions between law and morality that exist within any institutional normative order (Macormick 2007).

Nevertheless, the moral consensus between citizen and state is often fragmented, or non-existent. Persistent state oppression is likely to exacerbate the so-called 'democratic deficit', with the result that citizens may justifiably feel that they have no moral obligation to co-operate with state authorities and obey the law. Citizens who feel excluded because they are 'disconnected' from mainstream society, and what they perceive to be the values of others, may not be willing to concede that anyone should be allowed to exercise power over them. There is no 'democratic deficit' in this situation; simply an unwillingness to recognize the existence of what power-holders call 'society', acknowledge its common good, and so concede a degree of dominion to others in order to perpetuate its existence. In short, the state is perceived

[4] See ch 5.

as lacking the moral authority to criminalize and punish because the validity of the state itself is not recognized.[5]

Judicial discretionary power is seen as key to deciding how power relations are played out in the sentencing process. Judges create the social reality of 'penal legitimacy' by interpreting and applying rules for punishment that are validated by ideologically inspired penal policies, including neo-liberal forms of retributive justice. In influencing values and behaviour, individualized sentencing decisions can therefore have profound implications for offenders, victims, and communities—by, for example, expressing social values the state seeks to uphold through punishment, and the implications for *all* citizens in terms of enhancing society's 'common' good.

In practical terms, the crucial issue for penal legitimacy is whether or not these shared values *actually* exist and, if so, whether the criminal process and sentencing in particular, recognizes and gives effect to them (Henham 2012). If the criminal process fails to reflect shared values then sentencing decisions may well increase feelings of alienation and exclusion among citizens and communities alike. This will severely limit the contribution that sentencing is able to make towards achieving social justice. Consequently, how the state conceives of the relationship between social values and social justice is fundamental to criminal justice governance.

The British Academy Report (2014)

The British Academy Report *A Presumption against Imprisonment: Social Order and Social Values* (2014) argued that values 'appropriate' to complex modern societies tend to assert themselves because they encourage social conditions that are valued. Accordingly, sentencing policy should promote such core values as shared values if they are likely to have a beneficial impact on social justice—in other words, they could form the basis for developing penal policies that help to secure a more egalitarian and holistic society.

The value of reducing the burgeoning prison population of England and Wales may be a morally defensible objective for

[5] See ch 2 for further discussion in the context of the English riots of 2011.

humanitarian reasons, but the sentencing implications of such a policy still remain morally and politically contentious. Hence, whatever penal goals or normative changes are proposed as solutions to deal with the prisons' overpopulation issue, there are significant ideological repercussions and moral choices to be made. The BA Report (2014) recognizes social values as key to promoting more socially responsive and egalitarian forms of penal intervention, more particularly in England and Wales, and a principled response to tackling the rising prison population. The report recommends the creation of a Penal Policy Committee reporting to Parliament whose primary responsibility would be the formulation of policies on the appropriate use of imprisonment, greater attention by the Sentencing Council to the costs and effectiveness of different kinds of sentences, and a review of IPP sentences.[6]

However, the most significant aspect of the report in the context of the present discussion is the stress it places on social values as the primary focus for the development of future policy on the use of imprisonment. In particular, the report draws attention to the need for penal policy to promote what it singles out as the core social values that the UK should uphold for each citizen, namely: liberty, autonomy, solidarity, dignity, inclusion, and security, values that 'play a central role in the way in which contemporary democracies understand themselves (as evidenced by the ways in which aspects of them figure in international human rights conventions)' (BA Report: 37). Hence, these values should inform attempts to formulate new options for punishment, reserving imprisonment for only the most serious cases.

The report acknowledges the values of autonomy, solidarity, and dignity as central to Durkheim's notion of moral individualism and in binding individuals together because they encourage concern for the welfare of the self and others (BA Report: 41), whereas the unprincipled use of imprisonment fosters social

[6] IPP (imprisonment for public protection) sentences were introduced by s 225 of the Criminal Justice Act (2003). Although abolished in 2012 by s 122 of the Legal Aid, Sentencing and Punishment of Offenders Act, some 6,000 prisoners remained subject to the terms of their original sentence. Many of these sentences were imposed for less serious offences where the minimum term had expired and the prisoners involved were unable to obtain release, such detention having been held unlawful by the European Court of Human Rights (ECtHR) in *James, Wells and Lee v United Kingdom* Application nos 25119/09, 57715/09, and 57877/09 HEJUD [2012] ECHR 1706 (18 September 2012).

fragmentation. The exclusory effects of imprisonment promote social breakdown by destroying the essential fabric of society, the essential 'bonds of community' that bind communities together and give them a sense of belonging to a greater whole. The report makes clear that means can and should be found to strengthen society's fundamental values against those who would threaten them, but, so far as possible, these means should not themselves undermine this value system by rationing autonomy and dignity only to those thought to 'deserve' them and excluding others from their reach (BA Report: 73).

The report regards a liberal political community as one informed by values of mutual respect and autonomy, 'such respect marks a recognition of the dignity of the individual as an autonomous agent' (BA Report: 75), recognizing that imprisonment threatens such values and undermines social solidarity. Similarly, the social value of security should be measured in terms of its capacity to reinforce the values of moral individualism, consistent with broader calls for penal policy to be linked more directly to social conditions (BA Report: 77).

Whilst the report (BA Report: 108) repeatedly calls for penal policy to be more grounded in public opinion, one may argue that it deals inadequately with the fundamental problems of developing policy based upon the core social values it identifies. As I will point out, more needs to be done, not only in terms of the kind of empirical research necessary to monitor change and inform sentencing policy, but, more fundamentally, in ensuring that penal ideology itself is reconfigured, so that shared social values become the fundamental driver of policy. This move is considered necessary to counter the social and political hegemony of penal policy as presently conceived, and to help re-establish credible penal governance. In other words, I do not believe that the report goes far enough in addressing the fundamental conundrum of penal policy, so clearly articulated by Hudson (1993), namely, how to bring about a shift towards a more socially 'just' kind of penal policy.

Articulating the need for the penal system to respect core social values and devising strategies and structures to achieve the goal of reducing the prison population does not address the key question that Durkheim failed to answer, namely, how to develop a shared morality that promotes the common good of moral individualism (Cotterrell 1999). This book argues for ideological change as a necessary precursor to infuse penal ethics and practice with the moral credibility it currently lacks. Thus, a philosophical change informed by a fundamental understanding of social reality, a truly normative approach, is advocated. Recognizing that the state has a moral duty to promote social justice in public policy is seen as a crucial step towards ensuring that core social values are embedded in sentencing policy. In consequence, the political rhetoric of mainstreaming alternative forms of penal intervention (such as restorative justice) is more likely to have 'real' social purchase because structures and outcomes would operate within an ideological and structural space that takes proper account of social values, rather than the current distorted penal lens of deserts and deterrent policy.[7]

Furthermore, 'networks of community', and therefore, values and social norms, are now far more fluid and complex than ever before, social morality tending to coalesce rapidly around issues 'of direct concern'[8] to citizens and the communities in which they live, influencing perceptions of criminality and the 'appropriateness' of any penal response. Hence, the existence of 'shared values' about punishment and sentencing—the morality underpinning the rule of law—cannot be presumed. This trend has accelerated during late modernity with value pluralism, secularization, and increased tensions between different cultures and communities exacerbated by the neo-liberal penal governance focus on risk and security. And, in England and Wales, the rapid devolution of penal governance to communities, central government failing to provide an overall vision or strategic direction for policy linked to identifiable and shared moral concerns, particularly those based on shared values of 'citizenship' of the kind identified by the BA Report (2014).

The BA Report (2014) points directly to the difficulties of incorporating social values into penal policy; providing a commonly acceptable methodology for identifying just deserts has meant that 'even handed justice is easily subverted by political imperatives' (BA Report: para 93). The report suggests further that, whilst the values it identifies are both morally and politically 'attractive' to

[7] See also Dignan's (2003) proposal for a systemic model of restorative justice.

[8] Globalized and instantaneous forms of media communication now play a significant role in shaping and sharing perceptions about the morality of crime and criminality.

liberal democracies, the dynamics of economic restructuring in particular have largely obscured their vital role in fostering solidarity and community cohesion (BA Report: paras 96, 97). Part II of the report concludes with the observation that actualizing social values 'for all member of political society (including those who break the law') will at least provide some kind of moral benchmark against which to evaluate the use of imprisonment, but the methodology for achieving this is vaguely articulated.

In sum, the BA Report (at 83) argues that the values it identifies as appropriate to foster social solidarity are compromised by continued overreliance on imprisonment. Hence, there is an urgent need to counter policies that continue to subvert such values. For example, the report emphasizes the dangers of pursuing punishment policies that increase the extent to which offenders see themselves as excluded. Despite difficulties in quantifying the social costs, such policies create costs to society that simply cannot be ignored (BA Report: 74, 75). The report outlines a number of strategies it believes will achieve a more parsimonious use of custody.[9] However, I suggest that the rationale to underpin parsimony—the need to foster values promoting social solidarity—requires a more fundamental shift in penal ideology that allows those values to be maximized for all forms of penal intervention. Adopting this as the primary rationale for penal intervention would outweigh the negative impact of values that tend to undermine social cohesion.

Finally, the BA Report (2014) does not address effectively how such values might be reflected and operationalized within a socially inclusive penal policy. The report's recommended creation of an independent Penal Policy Committee, similar to the Monetary Policy Committee created by the last Labour administration, is unlikely to fill the gap in moral credibility that currently exists (BA Report: 89). The report glosses over the inherent difficulties of composition,[10] and the proposed Committee's

[9] These include: greater use of diversion from the courts, promoting greater use of alternative forms of sentence, prohibiting or restricting the imposition of short custodial sentences, removing or restricting the sanction of imprisonment for certain offences, reviewing sentence lengths, and, removing mentally disordered and addicted persons from prison (ibid: 91–102).

[10] There are echoes of the ill-fated Penal Affairs Consortium of the 1970s (see Blom-Cooper and McConville 2014 for renewed arguments in support).

relationship with the Sentencing Council. Yet perceived partiality and insufficient detachment from the 'establishment,[11] particularly over-representation of the judiciary and lawyers, are factors likely to undermine the Committee's moral credibility, and so its utility as a vital arm of penal governance. Without a sea change in penal ideology and sentencing policy the report's laudable objectives (BA Report: para 59: 107) are likely to flounder in the wake of significant budgetary restrictions and the further outsourcing and marketization of penal services.

As argued in the chapters that follow, ideological change is seen as the fundamental precursor to reforming the norms, ethics, and practices of sentencing. This would provide judges and magistrates with the moral authority and the capacity needed to realize social values such as those identified by the BA Report (2014) in a real sense. Thus, the positive benefits of promoting social cohesion would in time enhance the moral credibility and legitimacy of criminal justice overall.

The Relationship between Rights, Norms, and Ethics

For present purposes I use the term 'norms' in the conventional sense of referring to rules or practices having an impact upon conduct. This raises two distinct issues in the context of my argument, the first of which concerns the notion of sentencing practice as being informed by a 'normative' framework. Sentencing ethics are moral rules or principles for conduct that reflect the values underpinning penal ideology and policy. Hence, the normative framework of sentencing provides ethically informed guidance for sentencing practice (Ashworth and Redmayne 2010: ch 2). The second issue arising from the 'normative' context of sentencing concerns the impact of sentencing decisions on offenders, victims, and the wider community—the individual and social consequences of an ethically informed sentencing practice (Doak, Henham, and Mitchell 2009). Hence, whilst ethics infuse the normative framework with state values, the social value placed upon decisions reached within that framework by citizens and

[11] A problem exemplified by the public inquiry into historical allegations of child sex abuse.

communities—the value attributed to sentencing—determines the degree to which the state's ethical prescriptions are effectively translated into practice.

A crucial factor influencing how the norms and outcomes of sentencing are perceived is the social reality of rights accorded to participants in the sentencing process—in other words, how rights are allocated, understood, acted upon, and impact attitudes and behaviour. Thus, the social significance of rights mirrors broader socio-political contingencies, such as the predominant political ideology of the time and the extent to which citizens are able to exert influence over the ruling elite. Poverty and social exclusion tend to exacerbate the state's marginalization of citizens and the amplification of deviancy (Cohen 1972). This is evidenced particularly through increasing confrontation and violence between citizen and state, greater victimization, and a reciprocal failure by the state to secure fundamental rights of liberty and protection for citizens.

The right of citizens to liberty and security has both individual and collective dimensions. Rights are individual in the sense that citizens have the right to expect the state will protect their intellectual and physical integrity, and collective in that the social groups and communities to which individuals belong have corresponding rights of protection by the state. The ambit of rights and the 'public interest' raises difficult questions in the penal context (Ashworth 2002; Starmer 2014). These include defining the nature of the public interest, whether public interest arguments are contrary to the intrinsic nature of fundamental rights, and how conflicts between fundamental rights and the public interest (or conflicting public interests) should be resolved. Although several 'interests' might be identified as relevant, arguments for balancing basic rights and interests depend, ultimately, on our perception of how the goals of punishment come to be defined and resolved. If the aims and solutions are perceived as partial or repressive, then it may be seen as appropriate to challenge the basis upon which particular rights are secured and upheld in criminal trials. However, rights norms per se cannot change the underlying penal ideology of the state; within that paradigm rights merely regulate the norms and practices of sentencing and those of its legal actors. I argue that to be effective—to retain moral credibility—the social values validating rights norms should be embedded in penal ideology. However, the legitimacy attached to rights will depend ultimately upon the extent to which the state's values are shared and capable of being translated into practice.

The State's Duty to Promote Social Justice through Sentencing

In applying sentencing laws and principles, judges employ norms that implicitly represent some kind of morality. Conventionally, this has been thought of as a social morality, one that can be characterized in holistic terms, since trial and punishment by the state is meant to be carried out on behalf of *all* citizens, reflecting a moral consensus. However, value consensus in the sense supposed by Durkheim no longer exists. Sentencing law embodies many untested assumptions about the nature of social morality. Thus, the sanction's moral message may be not be socially relevant or, at worst, impose a partisan and socially divisive moral agenda upon citizens (Henham 2012). Instead, it has been argued that the moral vacuum left by neo-liberal values should be filled by values around which society, and communities in particular, can coalesce.

Discharging the state's overriding moral obligation to promote the social welfare of *all* citizens necessarily involves promoting particular social values in the process of policy-making. As suggested, in terms of sentencing policy, this is an aspect of the BA Report (2014) that remains underdeveloped. Gelsthorpe (2010) argues that greater attention should be given to promoting the notion of 'citizenship', with its potential for increasing social cohesion. The 'citizenship' concept is closely allied to that of 'social capital' and may include values promoting neighbourliness, trust, community involvement, volunteering, social networking, and political participation. An enhanced awareness of 'citizenship', with its associated rights and obligations, may provide a credible way forward in developing a sense of shared values.

A related and contentious issue is the extent to which it is appropriate for the state to criminalize and punish actions that contravene the cultural mores of the 'majority' population, for example, laws demanding conformity in language, dress, or marriage practices (Cotterrell 2011). Arguably, such laws discriminate unfairly against religious and other minorities, polarize allegiances and may ultimately precipitate greater social evils, including terrorism.

Alternatively, one may argue that they enhance moral coherence, social solidarity, and feelings of belonging and national identity, especially in times of increased poverty and economic depression, by reflecting the moral boundaries that underpin the 'rule of law'.[12] Unfortunately, too often in the past, such laws have merely served to validate oppression and prejudice.[13] Depressingly, they may signal an unwillingness, or inability, on the part of the state to engage with alternative moralities. Instead, social morality coalesces around a set of profoundly negative values expressly designed to exploit fear and prejudice among citizens for political advantage (Hall and others 1978).

A more constructive approach might be for political strategists to develop penal policies that take more account of what Cotterrell (2012: 10) refers to as 'bonds of community'. Cotterrell argues that 'bonds of community' of varying degrees of stability or fluidity, transience, or permanence, arise from: common or convergent interests, shared beliefs, or ultimate values, coexistence in particular cultural or physical environments,[14] or emotional allegiances. He points out that different types of communal bonds typically feature in varying forms of social network with overlapping and fluid memberships. However, since the coherence of social networks is largely a function of religion, ethnicity, kinship, common linguistic heritage, or shared history or traditions, understanding how moralities of crime and punishment are shaped by these contexts, and their interrelationship, is a vital precursor to predicting the effects of penal change when developing policy.

[12] Williams (2012a: 2) draws an important distinction between the notion of 'procedural secularism', where the state declines to prioritize one religious body over another, as in India, and that of 'programmatic secularism', wherein the state demands conformity and loyalty to the state, confining public manifestations of religion to the private sphere, as in France.

[13] To demand allegiance where the state lacks political legitimacy is characteristic of repressive totalitarian regimes.

[14] This includes racially distinct or ethnic minority communities, multicultural environments, areas of social deprivation and poverty, and areas of social transition.

The Politics of Sentencing and the Relevance of Social Values

The consequences of neglecting the broader social impact of sentencing policy are readily visible in retrospect. In what follows I argue that the rapid social change and increased value pluralism of the last twenty-five years has had an adverse impact on the relationship between sentencing policy and social justice in England and Wales. Increased politicization has also diminished the moral credibility of state penal policy, resulting in a narrow conceptualization of penal purposes and victims' rights, and hindering the development and integration of restorative practices. In addition, the blurring of penal accountability accompanying the politicization of penal policy has obfuscated the social values that purport to justify state intervention for reasons of preserving liberty or social protection (see Henham 2012). In particular, values that might have promoted social justice have been subjugated to those more concerned with individual culpability and censure.

To illustrate these issues the discussion concludes by exploring how the politicization of penal policy and the continued dominance of the neo-liberal retributive paradigm have effectively marginalized core social values aimed at promoting social justice and social harmony in the sentencing of irregular migrants. More particularly, I explain why an ideology that embodies the core social values identified in the BA Report (2014) is more likely to encourage decision-makers to engage with questions of social value when sentencing such offenders.

Social breakdown and the purpose of punishment

As with other areas of public policy, the continuing 'need' for fiscal prudence often provides a convenient and politically defensible excuse for greater state regulation in the policy and practice of sentencing. In addition, the issue of trust in sentencing has become inextricably linked to a perceived 'need' on the part of the state for greater procedural transparency and a greater emphasis on realizing the cathartic potential of sentencing for 'victims' and the wider community. However, the provision of greater transparency may well result in the triumph of form over substance, since it frequently prompts more regulation to monitor the degree of professed transparency, whilst the practice itself remains largely unaltered. Similarly, cathartic or therapeutic benefits are primarily linked to procedural rather than substantive justice issues. Together with a diffusion of penal accountability by the state to victims and communities through the provision of greater participation and restorative interventions, the political message has been one of promoting the benefits of local democracy through enhanced citizen involvement and satisfaction.

However, the global economic crisis of 2008 and the increased financial constraints placed upon the delivery of public services that followed served to deepen the divisions between social and criminal justice policy. Thus, economic considerations precipitated a decentralization of penal accountability and penal policy, prompting a search for alternative interventions to the criminal trial and conventional forms of sentencing based upon vaguely articulated appeals to communitarian values and the benefits of localism. This was coupled with a return to a revitalized form of rehabilitative policy firmly tied to the predominant 'what works' cost-cutting agenda typical of the new austerity, rather than any shared ideological commitment to promote particular social values.

The White Paper 'Swift and Sure Justice' published in July 2012 exemplified this trend, being clearly motivated by the need for further economic stringency rather than any other principled argument for substantive reform. Notwithstanding its rhetorical focus on victims and community engagement, with its underlying message of 'swift and sure justice' as synonymous, the White Paper's provisions symbolized a further concerted attack on due process rights and liberal notions of fair trial. Moreover, I suggest that its theme of increasing decentralization amounted to a thinly disguised reduction in the state's criminal justice mandate and, more importantly, its moral authority over decisions of responsibility and accountability for crime.

Paradoxically, it may be argued that, by devolving responsibility through decentralization,[15] and providing economic inducements, the state effectively distanced itself from the social moralities of crime and punishment at the local and community level, and, therefore, the social consequences of policy. So, for

[15] Paragraph 69 proposed state funding of up to 40 per cent and emphasized that 'solutions' are 'best determined and delivered locally'.

example, beyond asserting the presumed economic benefits, the UK government failed to consider how social bonds within and between different communities would be affected by its proposed measures. In other words, the source of the state's moral authority for the decentralization of criminal justice responsibility remained unclear. This obfuscation was reflected in terms of penal accountability. Thus, penal policy took no account of the relative inability of many citizens and communities to have their interests and values represented politically, either nationally, or at the local level. Crucially important here is the extent to which local cultural sensitivities were taken into account in developing community responses to harm, particularly understanding its social context and the causes of multiple victimization.

Arguably, the pursuit of criminal justice or other social policies from a purely 'what works' or 'evidence-led' perspective is flawed because it fails to address a major threat to social cohesion,[16] the inability or unwillingness of states to ensure that penal ideology and criminal justice policy engage with different moral values about crime and its punishment. Rather, it encourages social exclusion—a 'criminology of the other' (cf Garland 2001).

Furthermore, the absence of any morally or socially relevant foundations for penal policy may be concealed by what Hall and others (1978) describe as the state's ability to persuade the public to 'misrecognise the enemy'. Economically justified interventions are often defended morally on the basis that they are essentially required for the 'common good'. However, criminal justice policies that fail to recognize the significance of social inequality and the social causes of crime, or whose moral credibility is diminished because they advocate measures which serve to reinforce the status quo, are complicit in working against the 'common good'—they do nothing to enhance social cohesion because they do not promote social justice.

The UK government's proposals thus perpetuated a trend that effectively reduced the role of sentencing and trial justice in favour of diversionary and other alternative mechanisms; for example, extending the out-of-court disposals available to the police. Indeed, as Brownlee (2007) argues, extending the use of

[16] Underdown (2001) draws attention to social factors beyond individual application and reinforcement as crucial to compliance, engagement, and the future success of probation 'what works' initiatives.

conditional cautions by the police is a form of pre-trial sentencing that is not subject to the same constraints as trial sentencing.[17] Such practices are merely another form of 'net-widening' (Cohen 1985),[18] and, although perhaps desirable in principle, do not form part of a coherent and rational penal strategy that includes sentencing. Rather, policy development remains piecemeal and constrained by current penal ideology.

Hence, community-focused alternatives to conventional forms of criminal trial and sentencing may be justified in a variety of ways:

Bifurcation—providing more constructive and cheaper alternatives to short prison sentences, thereby suggesting that they have a rehabilitative and an economic justification.

Social control—allowing politicians to dictate the parameters for criminalization and penal policy by promoting the use of longer and harsher custodial sentences for 'dangerous' offenders while simultaneously increasing the use of community punishment for designated others. Such tendencies raise significant questions about the reasons for including particular social groups and individuals within these categories.

Retributivism—making it difficult for policy-makers to continually justify what are essentially consequentialist measures within the context of what is a predominantly retributive deserts-based system of sentencing.

Communitarianism—implying that community-based interventions tend to fit in well with restorative justice objectives by providing multi-agency, socially supportive and integrative approaches to desistance.

Such a wide variety of possible justifications make it relatively easy for policy-makers to obfuscate the underlying rationale(s) for community interventions. In England and Wales this has resulted in a sustained focus on combining welfare and retributive elements in

[17] The abolition of police cautions and their replacement with a more punitive system of community resolutions and suspended prosecutions would increase the exercise of 'extra-trial' discretion (Bowcott 2014).

[18] New guidance restricting the use of simple cautions was issued by the Ministry of Justice in November 2013 as part of a wider strategy to restrict the use of out of court disposals generally and focus on 'bringing serious crime to justice' (Ministry of Justice 2013a).

community interventions that are not circumscribed by the desert constraints of criminal sentencing. Therefore, although successive UK governments have struggled to convince the public of the 'punitive credentials' of community punishments, increased community control over the shape and form of penal interventions for low risk offenders has effectively narrowed the state's obligations in this respect. Instead, it has tasked local justice with the burden of accountability, so shifting the underlying moral imperative for delivering the diverse forms of community intervention that now pertain.

It may be argued that the UK government's introduction of a mandatory punitive element to community sentences in the Crime and Courts Act 2013 (Schedule 16, Part I) represented a further attempt to bolster the moral credibility of community sentences by assuaging the perceived public desire for punitive justice. However, the legislative changes appeared to be motivated by more pragmatic empirical arguments which suggested that combining the punitive element in community orders with certain requirements could improve their effectiveness without having a detrimental effect on reoffending rates (Ministry of Justice 2012b). Notwithstanding, the essential point is that the state's message was delivered against the emerging backdrop of devolved penal accountability to local areas and communities, yet it failed to encourage the development of appropriate guidelines with the necessary flexibility for local decision-makers to exercise their discretion within a more principled framework (Prison Reform Trust 2011). Arguably, such centralized control when combined with a punitive ideology sits ill with the rhetoric of community justice, citizens' rights, and the benefits of therapeutic jurisprudence.

Sentencing policy and social justice

The growing importance attached to the risk and security agenda has influenced the development of penal policy in neoliberal states over recent years (O'Malley 2009). During this period such states increasingly focused their attention on the control of more 'serious' offenders through various forms of incapacitation. Correspondingly, state penal policy became highly politicized and hypersensitive to perceived populist demands for harsh punishment. As the state's perceived capacity for promoting successful penal interventions diminished, so greater emphasis was placed on the individual offender's moral accountability; whilst state intervention in the penal sphere correspondingly reduced through privatization, outsourcing, and increased community involvement. The identification of social conditions emerged as an important variable for assessing potential risk, particularly in the development of crime prevention strategies, this leading to a blurring of penal and welfare policy (Wacquant 2009). Despite this, discreet welfare and therapeutic programmes were refined and developed within the new penal framework, rather than eclipsed as some commentators had forecast (Feeley and Simon 1992).

In the sentencing context, decision-makers focused increasingly on the principle that the penalty should be proportionate to the 'risk' posed to the community by the offender, rather than the conventional deserts approach advocating proportionality with the 'seriousness' of the offence. As a consequence, judicial discretionary power was often deployed in avoiding or mitigating the impact of risk-based sentencing, stressing instead the desirability of sentence individualization and offence proportionality. Paradoxically, the emphasis on rights protection and due process diminished the influence of consequentialist rationales for sentencing and countered the worst excesses of risk-based sentencing.

For trial-based sentencing the emphasis on individual moral accountability was reinforced by a rigid adherence to the traditional adversarial paradigm. The trial's conventional focus on establishing the offender's guilt or innocence within a rigid and narrowly conceived evidential framework was increasingly perceived as excluding evidence relevant to social accountability, thus further distancing the trial's 'truth' from the social reality of victims' experiences of crime in their daily lives. Arguably, this was exacerbated by the state's accelerated decentralization of penal governance to the regions and communities. Any discussion of the role of social morality was precluded, so offender culpability continued to be judged with limited reference to social factors.

Thus, I would argue that the gradual falling away of any shared moral commitment underlying state penal policy has provided increasingly fertile ground for the popularization of distorted offender stereotypes and their subsequent institutionalization through populist measures. This tendency is clearly illustrated by the approach of the courts to the sentencing of so-called 'irregular migrants'.

Social Justice and the Sentencing of Irregular Migrants

It has been suggested[19] that irregular migrants[20] have distinctive individual needs that are neglected by the criminal justice agencies and the sentencing courts of England and Wales when considering their potential for rehabilitation and desistance (Canton and Hammond 2012). I argue that the ideology underpinning the criminalization and punishment of irregular migrants by the state has disproportionately adverse social consequences when compared to other offenders. Accordingly, current practice hinders reintegrative prospects, so reinforcing social exclusion and damaging social cohesion, and signifying the diminished worth of such offenders to victims, communities, and civil society in general. Thus, for this group of offenders, the core values of liberty, autonomy, solidarity, dignity, inclusion, and security

[19] A person can become an irregular migrant in the UK by:

- Remaining after permission to stay has expired or application to stay has been refused.
- Entering the country illegally.
- Birth—children born to irregular migrants may lack the right to stay in the UK.
- Failing to comply with conditions attached to leave to remain or the purpose for which leave was granted.

The measurement of irregular migration is a complex and politically sensitive issue. See further Gordon and others (2009); The Migration Observatory (2011) http://www.migrationobservatory.ox.ac.uk/resources/briefings/

[20] Canton and Hammond (2012: 6, 7) point out that 'foreign nationals' from within the EU who are in the UK are not 'irregular migrants' in the sense that they are exercising their treaty rights of free movement, unlike those from outside the EU. The latter may be further distinguished on the basis of type of leave to remain and status, asylum applicants and those requiring visas, thus leaving 'undocumented migrants, illegal entrants and over-stayers' as the only 'real' irregular migrants. Canton and Hammond (2012) make the point that 'the groups designated by these terms overlap although they are, conceptually and in terms of associated legal rights, quite distinct'. However, they go on to suggest that 'It is also likely ... that all offenders who come from other countries ... have problems in common, regardless of their legal entitlement to reside. To this extent, the challenges of providing fair and relevant criminal justice services are sometimes the same for irregular migrants as for other foreign nationals'. Note that the above summary represents the pre-Brexit position.

identified by the BA Report (2014) are significantly compromised by current sentencing policy.

Comparative evidence lends support to the conclusion that this form of penal exclusion carries through to the enforcement stage and impacts significantly on the ability of irregular migrants to integrate into society. They have neither legal status nor rights. Certain jurisdictions actively promote the social exclusion of such groups through discriminatory social policies, and further stigmatize and alienate them through criminalization and oppressive criminal justice measures. The discussion that follows explores this issue by examining the extent to which the current sentencing framework provides a socially constructive response to the problems posed by the sentencing of irregular migrants. It concentrates particularly on the capacity of sentencing policy to recognize and respond to the social tensions created by increased irregular migration in certain areas of England and Wales, and considers how a more direct engagement with community perceptions of punishment's social value might achieve a greater measure of social justice for such offenders.

The political construction of social value

The role of penal policy in maintaining the social order is shaped by the partisan nature of politics and the deployment of state power. Paradoxically, penal policy reflects the degree to which socially disadvantaged or subordinate populations are deemed likely by the state to tolerate penal oppression through policies of selective criminalization, thereby forming part of its apparatus of social control (Wacquant 2009).

However, the late modern penal state has become less relevant as a means of regulating the kind of 'socially unacceptable' behaviours that result where social groups or communities with competing ideologies or moralities are forced, or attempt, to coexist. Typically, when social tensions increase, the reaction of the state is to resort to populist policies, with the introduction of 'new' or more draconian penalties for repeat offenders. Such measures are designed to appease as speedily and publicly as possible what the state perceives as an impending threat to its moral authority, especially that of its penal policy, which is always tenuous at best.

Nevertheless, the greatest danger to minority groups from penal oppression lies in the public anxiety and moral panic created by a politically motivated media (Cohen 1972). In Italy, for example, where contemporary penal policy is strongly driven by political aims, the legislature has frequently deployed the criminal law in order to appease perceived public anxieties about migrants inflamed by the media, especially concerning risk and security issues associated with certain crimes or types of offender (Pavarini 2001: 414). More recently, Italian public opinion has demanded harsher penalties and a more effective application of sentences (Mannozzi 2011). However, most public concern was directed, not so much at the excessive severity of punishments, but rather, the perceived excessive leniency of certain sentences. The legislature responded by imposing limits on judicial discretionary power in cases where public opinion appeared more sensitive, such as those involving minor offences committed by migrants or ethnic minorities. This tendency for the state to manipulate penal policy and react oppressively against 'demonized' minority groups in response to media-led campaigns is not new, and is likely to increase in times of economic recession, increasing poverty, and unemployment (Hall and others 1978).

However, more widespread concern has been expressed, within EU countries in particular, about the treatment of irregular migrants by criminal justice agencies (Boone 2012; Bosworth 2014). An important aspect of this is the way in which the concept of rehabilitation has been defined and applied by the courts when sentencing irregular migrants in England and Wales. Canton and Hammond (2012) argue that popular perceptions regarding the criminality of such migrants, fuelled by certain sections of the media, particularly that they are largely responsible for recent increases in crimes of violence, theft, and fraud, is not borne out by the criminal and judicial statistics. This finding may be surprising, given the fact that irregular migrants are excluded from the resources and opportunities available to citizens and others having a legal entitlement to remain.

Despite the social value of rehabilitation, Canton and Hammond (2012) describe how the social exclusion of irregular migrants from mainstream society is mirrored in their discriminatory treatment by sentencing courts, and reinforced through their further exclusion by the enforcement agencies from opportunities associated with desistance from crime. Evidently, the notion that the state is obliged to pursue policies that enable individuals to maximize their potential whilst contributing to civil society, does not appear to apply in the case of irregular migrants, or others having no legal right to remain.

The result of such exclusionary policies is that irregular migrants are effectively denied the support of the community and others who might help to prevent them reoffend. Following the approach taken by McWilliams and Pease (1990), Canton and Hammond (2012) argue that this may be seen as denial of the opportunity offered to an offender of the right to be restored to full citizenship through rehabilitation; in other words, as someone who may seek atonement and be redeemed in the eyes of civil society because they have renounced crime and will henceforth lead a law-abiding life. The key reason for the denial of this right to irregular migrants is, of course, because they are non-citizens and therefore cannot logically be restored to a status they do not, and cannot, hold.

Hence, the existence of such a right, whether or not legally enshrined, will always remain a myth, since irregular migrants cannot have access to public funds or services. As Canton and Hammond (2012: 16) rightly suggest, the social value of criminal justice interventions as being designed to protect the public appears not to extend to the citizens of other nations whose vulnerability is exacerbated by social exclusion and discriminatory practices. As a result, the state's approach is predicated on the untested assumption that greater social value lies in pursuing a partisan policy of exclusion and the removal of irregular migrants than attaches to the right of all individuals, irrespective of status, to be treated equally, and with dignity and respect.

Procedural justice and the right to rehabilitation

Considerable debate persists among legal scholars regarding the question of whether there is, or should be, a right to rehabilitation, and, if so, the extent of its legal enforceability at various stages of the criminal process.[21] However, the social significance of the right to rehabilitation for irregular migrants, where it does exist, is a different matter. Its value may be seriously diminished by exclusionary penal and social policies, especially in countries

[21] The right to 're-socialisation' is a fundamental principle of prison law in the Netherlands, for example (Boone and Kox 2012). However, it is not directly enforceable as such, unlike in Germany (van Zyl Smit and Snacken 2009).

where, as in the Netherlands, considerable numbers of such migrants are never expelled once convicted (Boone and Kox 2012: 65).[22]

Therefore, one would assume that some clarification of the right to rehabilitation is a necessary prerequisite to the formulation of an effective penal policy, whether that right has direct legal enforceability or not. Unfortunately, arriving at such an understanding is a matter of some conjecture, since there is no settled meaning attributable to rehabilitation as a concept, this being dependent upon time and place. In the minds of many, rehabilitation is associated with the idea of reform, or moral change, rather than with the notion that offenders have a *right* to be given an opportunity to re-establish their credentials as full members of civil society.[23] Clearly, the meaning attributed to rehabilitation should depend upon its social value and the context of its attribution, although such clarity has not been evident in English law.[24]

This moral obfuscation is exacerbated in the case of irregular migrants, since they are effectively excluded from civil society in many countries. On the one hand, they are legally excluded, so they are discriminated against and disadvantaged by the criminal process; on the other hand, they are socially excluded from the resources and opportunities routinely available to full citizens. Thus, many states presently interpret the 'public interest' in terms of penal strategies that promote the detention, exclusion, and expulsion of irregular migrants over the social value

[22] Irregular migrants in the Netherlands are subject to the same prosecutorial sentencing guidelines for persistent offenders as ordinary citizens. They receive no treatment for drug addiction or mental health problems (Boone and Kox 2012: 61).

[23] There is a clear distinction between an offender having a legal right to an opportunity and a court having discretion to decide whether or not an offender should be given an opportunity.

[24] See the ECtHR decisions in *Vinter and Others v United Kingdom* (2013) (Grand Chamber application nos.66069/09, 130/10 and 3896/10) and *Hutchinson v United Kingdom* (2015) (Grand Chamber Application no 57592/08). Arguably, *Hutchinson* obfuscated what may be viewed as an attempt by the ECtHR in *Vinter* to force the liberalization of criminal punishment in the UK by endorsing programmes of rehabilitation and promoting reintegration for dangerous criminals. Hence, it may not be too implausible to suggest that *Hutchinson* weakened the effectiveness of human rights review in the UK, and, more significantly, the influence rights can exert over the political and economic decisions that shape the strategic direction of criminal justice policy.

of their possible rehabilitation. In other words, adherence to the core social values of liberty, autonomy, solidarity, dignity, inclusion, and security is seriously diminished in the case of irregular migrants who commit crime.

Such a trend signals a moral failure as well as a failure of policy, suggesting that the state sees no value, social or otherwise, in adhering to principles of equality or non-discrimination when it comes to the punishment of irregular migrants. Even if irregular migrants had a legally enforceable right to rehabilitation, this alone would not deal with the question of whether the citizens of the society in question regarded that as morally acceptable, or the extent to which extending rights to irregular migrant offenders might be viewed as undermining the moral authority of state punishment. My point here is that the moral value of punishment is not set by the law, but by social values. Thus, the moral authority of the state to punish anyone within its jurisdiction, regardless of their legal status, is diminished unless it recognizes the moral value of treating *all* who come into contact with the criminal justice system with equal respect and dignity. Citizens are currently asked to accept that those who fall outside the law because they have no legal status have no rights to rehabilitation or otherwise. But this is tantamount to saying that they have no value as human beings within that society.

The distinctive needs of irregular migrants are currently neglected by the criminal justice agencies and sentencing courts of England and Wales when considering their potential for rehabilitation and desistance (Canton and Hammond 2012). Comparative evidence lends support to the conclusion that this form of penal exclusion carries through to the enforcement stage and impacts significantly on the ability of such offenders to integrate into society. There is also a tendency in some countries for the state to actively promote their social exclusion through discriminatory social policies and to further stigmatize and alienate them through criminalization and oppressive criminal justice measures (Demleitner 2013).

Reconceptualizing the moral justification for penal intervention

I have argued that where neo-liberalism prevails the penal state's response to the problems posed by the sentencing of irregular migrants is likely to be both morally suspect and socially damaging. More particularly, it lacks the capacity to recognize and respond effectively to the social impact of increased irregular migration in certain parts of England and Wales over recent years. Contemporary sentencing policy in this area does not adhere to the principle that the state has a moral obligation to value the humanity of *all* individuals, regardless of their legal status. Accordingly, the state's moral duty should extend beyond risk-based policies of social exclusion by promoting inclusive values of community and the prevention of unjustifiable hardship. I suggest that a penal ideology which embodies such a morality and advocates a more direct engagement with its values when sentencing irregular migrants might achieve a greater measure of social justice.[25]

One might therefore question the social value of imposing harsher sentences and other collateral sanctions upon irregular migrants, as does the UK government's Immigration Act 2016.[26] The political message appears designed to appease those who perceive irregular migrants as threatening citizens' rights to labour, property, and social welfare, yet its social impact is likely to be the further marginalization of vulnerable individuals through exploitation and victimization. Such policies are unlikely to reduce the demand for 'illegal' labour; rather, they reflect a further dangerous politicization of risk control, a trend that conflicts with the notion of promoting social justice in sentencing. In the absence of any empirical justification or impartial risk assessment, the ongoing demonization and harsh punishment of particular social groups only serves to reinforce prejudice and polarize opinion. Accordingly, criminal justice systems that value social justice should accord irregular migrants basic human rights, including legally protected trial rights, *regardless of their citizenship status*.

Williams (2012a) is surely correct in asserting that the state's moral obligations regarding punishment should reflect the collective responsibility we each share for one another's welfare, and extend to *all* human beings regardless of their legal status

[25] Thus, I have argued that the penal state should take a moral lead by reconnecting with the core values suggested in the BA Report (2014) in order to justify sentencing policy and practice in this area. Crucially, as explained below, such values must exist, be shared, and realized in a normative sense through sentencing practice.

[26] Pt 1, ch 2.

or rights as 'citizens'. In principle, such a morality is intrinsically good. Thus, the penal state has a moral obligation to promote social justice in its dealings with citizens—and beyond, to all human beings who fall within the purview of its criminal jurisdiction. Furthermore, as du Bois-Pedain (2017) observes, a political commitment to pursuing policies with 'high associational value' needs to match the perceptions and expectations of citizens. However, in order to attain this goal the social value of particular penal outcomes should be judged against state values *as normatively practised*, not simply ideological positions or policy commitments.

From a political standpoint, the prospects for changing penal ideology or engaging with social value when sentencing irregular migrants may appear illusory, particularly so when the vagaries of political pragmatism rather than social values advocating mutual awareness and social responsibility continue to drive penal policy. Regrettably, penal and social values tend to drift apart where neo-liberalism predominates, thereby weakening the basis for securing the moral and social legitimacy of state sponsored punishment. I suggest that a reconceived sentencing policy is necessary to rectify this moral disjuncture and ameliorate its adverse social consequences. Neo-liberal values and political pragmatism will doubtless continue to define the nature of the 'public interest' in deciding whether or not to pursue harsh and exclusory penal policies in the case of irregular migrant offenders. A more direct ideological and normative engagement with the core social values advocated by the BA Report (2014) would assist in countering the negative impact of such punitive and repressive measures on social cohesion.[27]

Punishment is significant in symbolizing the moral value of penalizing certain crimes and certain types of offender. The current neo-liberal model for sentencing irregular migrants remains exclusory, socially divisive, and individualistic (Hudson 2006: 269). However, the political conditions necessary to bring about the adoption of a fresh ideological and normative paradigm require a mandate for rebalancing 'public interest' values. This is only likely to occur when the morality underpinning present policies is challenged and becomes insufficient to sustain state penal

[27] See Dallo (2015) for recent discussion of these issues in the context of the Italian penal system

power. Thus, policies perpetuating social injustice may ultimately force a re-evaluation of the state's approach to justifying penal intervention on the basis of values of community, social welfare, and mutual responsibility. The shared moral demands of civil society then become the political driver for ideological and normative change. Without change, the present distorted vision may well become a self-fulfilling prophecy; the social exclusion, alienation and criminality of irregular migrants being compounded by the criminal justice system.

2

Sentencing Policy as a Force for Social Cohesion

Introduction

This chapter sets out the case for adopting a normative approach to conceptualizing the social reality of sentencing.[1] I argue that a more profound understanding of the relationship between social values and sentencing practice is urgently required. More particularly, policy-makers need to comprehend how sentencing is implicated in realizing state values and take greater account of the social forces that diminish the moral credibility of state sponsored punishment. Hence, the state's ability to reflect and engage with different social contexts is seen as a fundamental prerequisite for any paradigm that is intended to influence policy. Finally, I reflect on the problems of relating social values to legal processes such as sentencing and how this hinders progress towards promoting social justice as a significant sentencing objective.

If one accepts the proposition that the state has a moral obligation to promote the welfare of all citizens, this obligation should logically extend to all things necessary to ensure their physical and psychological integrity. This implies freedom from cultural and social oppression and, correspondingly, imposes a positive duty on the state to maximize those freedoms for citizens. Thus, in theory, the moral state values social justice and, consequently, its ethics, norms, and actions. Furthermore, the moral virtue of the penal state depends upon a mutual recognition of values, and a conception of justice where notions of responsibility and

[1] By 'normative' I suggest a focus on the extent to which the rules, procedures, processes, and outcomes of sentencing influence offenders, as well as victims, communities, and society at large.

consequential accountability are demonstrably shared between the state and its citizens.

Such a moral vision suggests that sentencing policy has an important role to play in promoting social cohesion, but only if underpinned by an ideology which recognizes that perceptions of value and accountability differ in social significance according to time and place. Consistent with this perspective is the notion that the reinforcement of social values through sentencing is achieved via a recursive process of amplification[2] involving the entire criminal justice process, beginning with the ideology that underpins policy and extending to the eventual sentencing outcome and its social impact (Wilkins 1964). Thus, the substantive content of values is translated into some identifiable aspect of social reality; meanings are interpreted through the processes of sentencing and given practical shape in the form of outcomes. However, the realization of social values that truly mirror those shared by diverse communities, groups, and interests depends in the first instance upon the existence of impartial structures and methods for their identification and for monitoring change.

I therefore argue that crude notions of 'top down' or 'bottom up' approaches to policy-making should be replaced by a process of contextualized policy-making, ensuring that each level of process or structure is infused with socially relevant and meaningful knowledge about the social value of punishment. Such an approach is sensitive to both moral and normative change. It suggests how the adoption of a penal ideology shaped by shared social values could, through their reflection in the normative framework of sentencing, improve the quality of justice, and hence the perceived legitimacy of sentencing policy.[3]

Finally, I stress the need for sentencing policy to reflect those moral attachments that bind citizens together in a relational or communitarian sense. Hence, the focus should be on values that reinforce 'bonds of community' (Cotterrell 2012). As argued,

[2] Amplification is characteristic of the ability of criminal justice systems to reproduce patterns of social (in)equality and (in)justice. Harcourt and others (2005: 318) argue (citing Marx), that the key to understanding what should be done about social inequality is to understand the phenomenon itself in its historical context.

[3] The current impetus for sociology, and criminology in particular, to engage more effectively with policy and its impact owes much to the work of Burawoy (2005) and Loader and Sparks (2011).

where poverty and social disadvantage render economic ties of community less relevant to socially marginalized groups or communities, their perceptions of the morality of punishment are more likely to mirror what they regard as the repressive and punitive values of state penal policy. This assertion is explored in the light of the sentencing approach taken by the courts following the English riots of 2011, focusing particularly on community perceptions regarding the legitimacy of state intervention in such circumstances and the deployment of state penal power as a form of social control.

Conceptualizing Sentencing as a Normative Function

A conventional sociological understanding of sentencing in normative terms would invariably look to its processes, practices, and outcomes rather than its ideology. However, the normative function of sentencing cannot be detached from its ideological foundations. As argued, if the state aspires to fulfil its moral obligation to promote the social welfare of citizens through sentencing policy, the values, ethics, processes, practices, and outcomes of sentencing should be viewed as essentially integrated, and recursively constituted. Hence, as an identifiable and observable aspect of social reality, penal normativity should be conceived as contextually grounded, or otherwise remain largely meaningless in terms of its social value.

Yet, the social significance of sentencing as a key element of penal governance appears to be in decline. Alternative forms of disposal, many of them pre-trial, administered by an array of justice professionals with seemingly disparate ethical codes and institutional objectives, have made considerable inroads into the supremacy of the trial mode (Tata 2014). This trend is likely to continue with the expansion of restorative and community justice initiatives. However, it is by no means clear what these developments signal for normative conceptions of sentencing, particularly its future role in penal governance.

To begin with, one might argue that the rapid introduction of alternative processes has simply diminished the governance role of sentencing, so that its function as an expressive, symbolic, and effective social institution is no longer regarded as central to delivering the state's core penal mission, particularly in terms of its capacity to promote social values. Adversarial trial and retributive justice are increasingly reserved for cases of 'serious criminality'. Sentencing now sits within a plethora of alternative mechanisms, many of which are driven by cost-benefit evaluations of risk rather than desert principles, let alone considerations of social welfare (O'Malley 2010). As O'Malley (2009) paradoxically observes, the diminution of social welfare and therapeutic practices as key elements of criminal justice policy has meant that criminological accounts of offending behaviour stressing social breakdown and demanding social assistance or therapeutic aid are marginalized in favour of risk based concepts for determining individual accountability rather than shared social values. Thus, the social function of penal policy has become increasingly detached from the notion that punishment exists in order to infuse citizens with a greater sense of moral responsibility, so enhancing social capital.

It might also be argued that, given the relative importance of non-judicial or 'quasi' sentencing, inter-professional dynamics now play an increasingly important role in shaping the ethics and practice of sentencing (Tata 2014). In addition, the ways in which the cultures of particular professionals, such as probation, prosecutorial, police, or parole decision-makers, influence the perception and relative importance attached to information and processes relevant to sentencing and the social interactions of professionals is becoming more significant in determining sentence outcomes (Tata 2010, Bibas 2012).

Deconstructing professional dynamics and understandings should therefore become a vital task of policy-making. As Rogers and Erez (1999) suggest, the meanings that different professionals attach to what are assumed to be commonly understood concepts such as 'objective' and 'subjective' are highly influenced by their professional culture. It is also clear that this influence not only extends to what might be thought of as external and unequivocally defined legalistic concepts, such as 'proportionality' or 'mitigating circumstances', but goes to the very essence of what may be described as 'frameworks' of understanding, and the cognitive processes that shape them. The significance of these findings cannot be overstated. They represent a rare attempt to fix the meaning or contextualize an interactive process relevant to sentencing by deconstructing the subjectivity of trial participants' experiences. Hence, the methodology is culturally contextual in that it can suggest ways in which the 'objectivity' of process is constructed subjectively within a particular legal culture.

Accordingly, Rogers and Erez's research is highly significant in changing the way one might conceptualize the 'normativity' of sentencing. It acknowledges that everyone, especially legal professionals, has 'working definitions' that influence how information, particularly emotive personal information of the type contained in pre-sentence recommendations (PSRs) and victim impact statements (VISs), is conceptualized for the purposes of sentencing. Although different frames of meaning or 'working definitions' may well be to a degree generalizable between legal professionals, as with all areas of decision-making there is considerable discretion, each individual's construction of 'objectivity' including shades of meaning which are based purely on their own feelings and experiences and cannot be generalized. Hence, deconstructing different frameworks of cognition and interaction among court professionals may well serve to dispel common misunderstandings about the social significance of what were previously thought of as generally accepted concepts or patterns of behaviour.

However, as things stand, such diversity in normative understanding may prove detrimental to penal governance. Thus, the relative absence in sentencing policy of a core moral mission reflecting shared values may encourage the development of system-based values, rationalizations, and understandings. Conflicting moralities at the centre would be hugely detrimental to the contribution that sentencing, or indeed any penal intervention, might make in promoting social values. Thus, penal policy-makers would struggle to develop structures and processes capable of linking outcomes to identifiable social values. Instead, the likelihood of achieving any socially relevant objective beyond censure would be diminished.

Whereas successive UK governments have addressed the moral credibility gap with measures designed to increase transparency, or other 'therapeutic' procedural adjustments, the state has remained aloof from the morally and socially divisive consequences of sentencing policy. In such circumstances, the 'success' or otherwise of penal policy might be measured by the state's ability to respond adequately to individualistic demands (cf Sen 2001; Nussbaum 2013). Accordingly, what the state perceives as the essence of these demands would ultimately determine the extent of its accountability, so shaping its penal policy objectives. However, one may argue that such a sentencing policy would be driven by individualistic values and a socially impoverished vision of accountability and justice.

Alternatively, a sentencing policy reflecting classical liberal values might place explicit limits on the unfettered use of judicial discretionary power, particularly where its partiality is perceived as posing a direct threat to citizens' rights of equality before the law. Paradoxically, however, social inequality already characterizes the social reality of many citizens' daily lives (Hudson 1993). Instead, one may argue that discretionary power should be reconceived to recognize different levels of individual and collective accountability for crime, and for situating that accountability within a more nuanced understanding of social morality and sentencing's social value. Seen in this light, sentence individualization, far from posing a consummate threat to human liberty because of its potential to destabilize the status quo, might flourish within a penal ideology that values social cohesion. Broadening sentencing's commitment to achieving social objectives may therefore serve to secure its legitimacy more effectively in the eyes of citizens than simply restricting the judicial remit on the narrow grounds of potential abuse of power.

It is also important to recall the normative function of sentencing as a public and symbolic ritual. Sentencing's role, and, I would argue, its moral credibility, is consistently threatened by the introduction of various alternative forms of penal intervention, designed for different kinds of offender or offence, many of which are discreetly administered and notably removed from public scrutiny. The introduction of measures that may be justified on the basis of disparate and possibly competing values increases incoherence and hinders the effectiveness of the penal system. It also devalues the integrity of human beings as members of a society where individuals have equal worth.

This tendency is magnified when the overarching ideology remains unchanged. Such obfuscation may be compounded where relevant structures and processes are community or neighbourhood-based, since state accountability is correspondingly reduced. Thus, it seems reasonable to suggest that the reactive and volatile nature of state penal policy (O'Malley 2004), coupled with cost-driven management strategies of decentralization and localism, fragments penal governance, and incrementally diminishes the normative impact of the ideology that underpins sentencing.[4]

Similarly, McNeill and Robinson (2013: 122) argue that the legitimacy attached to community sanctions by regulatory bodies cannot be taken for granted owing to their fluid and unstable relational contexts. As suggested, the contingent nature of the value appropriated to community sanctions applies to penal interventions more generally. This, together with adverse evaluations of the 'moral performance' of those institutions and structures charged with 'justice' delivery (Liebling and Arnold 2005; Tankebe and Liebling 2013), increases the need for the state to identify a framework of values that draws its authority from relational contexts of community (Lacey 1988).

Social divisions and competing values may obscure the state's vision of what is, or should be, the normative function of punishment. Lack of social cohesion may also conceal a wider moral failure on the part of the state to ameliorate inequality and discrimination. As I will argue in the final section, the current sentencing paradigm in England and Wales is complicit in this failure. It lacks moral credibility because its underlying ideology fails to mobilize social values that are sufficiently connected to social justice.

Problems of Relating Social Values to Sentencing

Most discussions concerning the value of sentencing define its legitimacy and governance role in terms of maintaining the rule of law (Ashworth 2015). In Kantian terms, the normative function of sentencing in maintaining the rule of law within the neo-liberal state is best conceptualized as that of a facilitator (Thorburn 2012: 279). Sentencing exists to serve the citizens of the state and to maximize their claims to freedom. However, the state's duty also extends to ensuring that the institutions and principles of sentencing mark out clear boundaries, explaining the extent to which citizens' claims to freedom may be breached. It is essentially a delimiting or negative duty, rather than a positive interventionist one. This paradoxical stance justifies the state's deployment of proportionality as a mechanism for maximizing the freedom of

[4] The significance of this observation for the future development of sentencing guidelines is discussed in ch 7.

the individual being sentenced, whilst concurrently reaffirming the limits of individual liberty and the state's control over it. The state is also able to retrench its control through rights ostensibly designed to uphold citizens' claims to freedom. However, various systems of participatory democracy determine the balance of power in the neo-liberal penal state, and so the extent to which individual freedoms may be sacrificed and rights protected in the pursuit of competing interests.

Hence, as Hudson (1993) and others have pointed out, a Kantian justification for the state's normative function in sentencing excludes broader utilitarian considerations aimed at promoting social justice, notwithstanding that such consequences may enhance the freedom of citizens. Whilst these arguments have long preoccupied social reformers and legal philosophers, the role of social theory and methodology in linking the normative and social realities of sentencing has not been fully explored. In the present context, a sociological perspective should provide more profound understandings of the relationship between social values and the state's capacity to maintain the rule of law. The conceptual distinction made by Hart (1968) between the aims of punishment and the principles for their distribution is unhelpful in this respect because it reveals nothing about the social reality of penal repression and the social value of punishment (Lacey 1988: 173). Lacey's (1988: 187) normative vision is socially instrumental in that punishment is conceived as serving interests and values of community, its justifying arguments and their application both being integral to the meaning of punishment. Thus, the state is charged with resolving the inherent tensions between individual and social demands in the distribution of punishment by making conscientious efforts to balance its impact consistently and fairly across a plurality of values.

In communitarian terms, the state's criminalization of behaviour should flow only where the repression of that behaviour is necessary to restrict threats and protect fundamental community values (Lacey 1988: 189). Significantly, the state should take seriously those who distance themselves from political participation because they effectively withdraw from any commitment to actively promote social values, including those associated with punishment. Any such withdrawal weakens the state's capacity to balance politically expressed claims for greater individual autonomy against the development of policies favouring social welfare.

Viewed from this perspective, the social value to be derived from the criminalization, prosecution, trial, and sentencing of particular behaviours is a relational question that depends upon the state's ability to identify and respond to legitimately expressed communitarian concerns. However, it is difficult to explain the social value of penal norms in governance terms where the moral line between deviance and crime is impossible to draw, or is morally unconvincing. Where its moral foundations are contested, the governance capability of sentencing policy may be reduced to one of ensuring strict compliance and asserting dominion over minority groups with conflicting values. The moral attachment of individuals and social groups to the ideologies, processes and outcomes of criminal trials may then signify little more than a myth, part of the political rhetoric used to justify social oppression by the secular penal state (Box 1983).

The public and declaratory nature of the trial and sentencing invests the criminal process with a particular communicative function that goes beyond the social value of allowing public rights of scrutiny and participation (Duff and others 2007a: 269). Sentencing, as a public affirmation of wrongdoing, not only reflects the moral norms implicit in sentencing law, it has a broader normative function normally associated with the policies and practices of criminal justice. The idea that sentencing is in some way a public affirmation of shared social values depends upon the degree to which that portrayal accurately reflects social reality (Hudson 1993).

Social morality is often unclear as to whether retributive, deterrent or restorative considerations should prevail. Hence, the state may have difficulty in justifying the morality of sentencing decisions in terms that satisfy the justice demands of victims, communities or civil society. Perceptions of sentencing in death by driving cases usefully illustrate the point. In May 2014, the then UK Justice Secretary, Chris Grayling, announced a comprehensive review of driving offences and penalties (Ministry of Justice 2014)[5] following an announcement in 2013 that the Sentencing Council would review existing sentencing guidelines for the most

[5] An increase from 2 to 10 years' imprisonment was also announced in the maximum penalty for causing death whilst disqualified from driving and a new offence created of causing serious injury whilst disqualified from driving carrying a maximum penalty of 4 years' imprisonment. These changes came into force in April 2015.

serious driving offences. This response followed a long-running campaign by the family victims of those killed or seriously injured by disqualified drivers. Perceived disparity between the seriousness of the harm caused and the appropriateness of the eventual sentence was highlighted in a Sentencing Advisory Panel (SAP) report which formed the basis for the current sentencing guideline (Hough and others 2008).[6]

However, the notion that such concerns can be reflected against clearly identifiable purposes for sentencing in death by driving cases is probably misplaced. Generalizing about sentence proportionality and its relationship to the perception and categorization of harm is unhelpful in explaining the relationship between purposes and outcomes in individual cases. Nevertheless, I would argue that 'harm' assessment in death by driving cases, particularly the weight attached to harm as opposed to individual culpability, should take greater account of social values. However, to objectify social morality in the framing of substantive offences is problematic, since law can at best only provide a static representation of moral values. Offence definitions are also likely to exclude many of the factual situations that shape the perceived morality of driving behaviour in particular situations (see further Duff 1990). Such dilemmas are mirrored in desert-based sentencing regimes more generally, particularly their perceived inability to deliver proportionate penal responses in areas where the morality of certain behaviour is contested. Research evidence indicates a high degree of moral ambivalence regarding many aspects of driving behaviour, with only the more serious and blatant behaviours drawing widespread condemnation (Hough and others 2008). However, it is uncertain how penal law and sentencing should reflect such moral condemnation.

The credibility of sentencing policy rests upon a presumed moral consensus that is objectified in the form of penal norms. In reality, this presumed consensus might have fragile moral foundations. Hence, the perceived 'seriousness' of offending behaviour, both in terms of harm and culpability, will always be contested where the moral purpose underlying the prescribed penalty is

[6] The Sentencing Council's Definitive Guideline on Causing Death by Driving, originally issued by the Sentencing Guidelines Council (SGC) distinguishes between different degrees of risk (see Sentencing Guidelines Council 2008).

unclear. Social values reflect judgments made about sentences and the sentencing process by individuals as offenders, victims, and community members. So the extent to which such values are capable of being realized is a highly significant factor when considering how to enhance the moral credibility of sentencing and its capacity to act as a communicative mechanism.

Control strategies may allow the state to claim the moral 'high ground' by insisting that its actions support ideals or values that are morally just—for example, those expressing democratic principles. Thus, the state may emphasize support for particular values by publicly denouncing those whose actions are motivated by competing values (Mathiesen 1990). Denunciatory sentencing may be regarded as particularly appropriate where persons occupying significant positions of responsibility hold oppositional values. Historically, public denunciation has played a significant and positive role in the establishment of more egalitarian societies. Consequently, it seems reasonable to argue that the public denunciation of wrongdoing as expressed through sentencing *may* have consequences for the common good[7] going far beyond simple deterrence. As a public affirmation of desired values, sentencing undoubtedly has social significance. However, its ability to contribute to social capital will always depend upon the kind of political and ideological constraints that govern its ethics and practices.

The state's moral duty to promote shared social values in sentencing policy derives from its obligation to act on behalf of all citizens for the common good. Moreover, the overriding nature of this obligation stems from the fact that such values are prerequisites for humanity to flourish.[8] Notwithstanding, it is also important to remember that shared values may extend beyond the boundaries of the nation state. Thus, for example, the criminal process and its underlying values may be perceived as key components of an ideological or religious hegemony that validates acts of 'terrorism' or politically motivated crime. Penal interventions

[7] The morality of what is constitutive of the common good is relative to time and place, as is the morality of those penal measures that are deemed necessary to enforce common good values (Foucault 1977).

[8] One may argue further that the human desire for peace and security reflects another intrinsic aspect of the human condition, namely the instinct to act for, and work towards, the welfare of other human beings who are in need.

of whatever character are then perceived as ways of asserting dominion over those with conflicting values.

Ultimately, however, the social value of sentencing is an empirical question. Whilst social theory is key to conceptualizing the role of shared values in penal ideology, contextual analysis is needed to explain the social significance of such values as differentiated concepts of harm, responsibility, and accountability. Such knowledge should then help to define the capacity of those structures that regulate the behaviour of citizens in civil society (Braithwaite 2002). Armed with this knowledge, the penal state should be in a better position to substitute confrontational values of social control with more relational and holistic values that engage constructively with communitarian interests of reconciliation and social harmony.

Sentencing Policy in a Fragmented Society

Promoting communitarian notions of accountability through sentencing is a significant challenge for the state, especially in times of rapid social change. Particular difficulties exist where citizens do not share the values underpinning the exercise of state power. Furthermore, where values sustaining liberty, autonomy, solidarity, dignity, inclusion, and security are diminished, citizens and communities are more likely to regard the state's use of punishment as hegemonic, publicly symbolic of value conflict rather than an expression of shared values promoting social harmony and mutual reconciliation (Box 1983).

This kind of obfuscation is reflected at all levels of penal governance. For sentencing policy, it renders unclear the justifications for punishment and the relationship between them, with adverse implications for rights of access and participation. If sentencing is consistently perceived as a locus for value conflict rather than the reconciliation of competing values this will tend to reinforce social discord and suspicion (Christie 1977). The state's reaction may be to increase regulation or seek to eliminate the discretionary power of judges and magistrates in order to maximize its repressive control over what is perceived as the threat of an increasingly fragmented society. Paradoxically, by tightening its grip on the structures and processes of control, the state reduces the opportunities for engaging with those very groups or communities that feel alienated or excluded from democratic forms of participation (Lea and Young 1984). Thus, social fragmentation may be amplified.

The penal consequences of such an exclusory system are likely to include: a reduction in efforts to promote local accountability and community control over criminal justice delivery; a distancing of sentencing from victims' concerns; increased centralization of risk assessment criteria and dependant decision-making; decontextualized determinations of harm and culpability; and a diminution of multi-agency cooperation and contact within competing groups. More significant, however, is increased reliance on punitive neo-liberal values to justify sentencing policy.

The prolonged coupling of right-wing neo-liberal ideology and retributive values tends to exacerbate social exclusion and poverty, particularly among already socially disadvantaged groups, such as racial minorities (Tonry 2011). In addition to increasing social tensions, retributive norms provide inadequate taxonomies for categorizing contested behaviours, or suggesting the appropriate penal response. This lacuna extends to social factors that might be implicated in crime causation, as well as the categorization of harm in terms of its wider communitarian significance.

There are particular problems in conceiving of 'politically motivated' or other forms of public protest or disorder within conventional retributive conceptions of ordinal and cardinal proportionality (Roberts 2012; Ashworth 2015). Not only is the notion of harm restricted in terms of its wider social significance, but also the concept of culpability is far too narrowly drawn to encompass its broader social dimensions. In other words, the way in which 'harm' and 'culpability' are conceived and calibrated fails to take proper account of the cultural, political, and historical variables implicated in their social construction. Unsurprisingly, therefore, the instantiation of these flawed concepts through the structures and processes of sentencing tends to reflect this failure and exacerbate existing social divisions (Henham 1990).

Historically, social unrest in the form of riots or public disorder has invariably attracted reactive, exemplary, and harsh punishment (Emsley 1996). Invariably, such responses would not have formed part of a wider policy of social reform or reconstruction. Neither would they have resulted from any profound and impartial empirical exercise that sought to explain the influence of contextual variables on social behaviour. Such concerns only came to the fore during the latter half of the nineteenth century with the advent of Gladstone's liberal reforms (Radzinowicz and Hood 1990).

The social history of London, as documented by social reformers such as Booth and Mayhew, provides a detailed and distressing picture of the poverty and sense of lawlessness created by rapid industrialization and social change during the mid-Victorian period in areas such as Deptford (Bullman, Hegarty, and Hill (2012).[9] Significantly, as Emsley (1996: 3) observes, the language and form of the state's penal response more often than not concealed the fact that the protests and riots received collective legitimation, were tacitly condoned by various social groups and communities, and did not conform to commonly perceived definitions of social justice. It is also salient that the greater centralization of penal law and the administration of criminal justice accompanying the massive social changes precipitated by industrialization became more detached from notions of community justice, rather than reflecting the moral consensus and social solidarity envisaged by Durkheim (1984).

Whereas one can never draw firm conclusions from historical interpretations (Burke 1992), more recent sociological accounts offer important insights into the complex relationship between social unrest, crime, and the state's penal response. Cavadino and Dignan (2006), for example, focus on the relationship between the political economy and crime, particularly the social impact of different socio-economic structures and patterns of crime over time, whilst Newburn's (2015) nuanced historical overview and comparative analysis contextualizes competing accounts and rationalizations for the 2011 riots, providing structure, perspective, and a paradigm for the future comparative analysis of disorder. Significantly, Newburn (2015: 60) concludes that 'the nature and extent of the response of the penal state' was perhaps the most distinctive feature of the riots.

Evidently, any policy conclusions drawn from such evaluations must take proper account of the influence of contextual variables on behaviour and social attitudes, relative to time and place (Burke 1992: 140). From the perspective of contemporary penal theory, one of the most significant variables is the extent to which

[9] Poverty and social degradation became linked in the Victorian mind with so-called 'political passions'. Hence, increased lawlessness and immorality were viewed as the inevitable consequence of the rise of socialism and secularization.

citizens and communities, particularly those who might feel disenfranchised, disengaged, or otherwise excluded, view legal and social constraints as unjustifiable restrictions on their autonomy, liberty, and integrity. This suggests that a strong relationship between the social values embodied in penal ideology and citizens' perceptions is fundamental to sustain the moral credibility of sentencing policy.

Functional justifications alone, particularly when adopted by the state in order to justify penal measures, are unlikely to provide satisfactory answers to such empirical questions, and so will do little to assist policy-makers in reconciling competing accounts of social value. Rather, contextualized studies of sentencing as a normative practice are much more likely to suggest appropriate solutions.[10] However, the most difficult challenge for those who seek to interpret such phenomena remains that of countering allegations of partiality or predisposition to a certain theory or methodology (Hammersley 2000).

Notwithstanding, the key questions for social theory remain those of describing how particular social phenomena occur, before attempting to explain them (Burke 1992: 139). Unfortunately, neither of these questions is easy to answer. Nor is it entirely clear what the role of criminology or indeed social theory should be in attempting to do so (Loader and Sparks 2011).[11] Hence, the problem of explaining how and why particular social values predominate at particular moments in time and their relationship to perceptions of crime and punishment persists (Tamanaha 1997). Thus, the task for theory is that of helping us to understand sentencing's role in determining the relationship between value and fact, and the social significance of these decisions over time.

Unfortunately, establishing credible empirical connections between externally observable and quantifiable phenomena such as sentencing decisions and subjectively held feelings about the morality of particular sentences and their influence on future behaviour is hugely problematic. Such difficulties are compounded when approached from a historical or comparative perspective. The following section explores the veracity of these observations in the context of the English riots that took place in

[10] The challenge of deciding which methodology to adopt is addressed in ch 6.

[11] Loader and Sparks (2011) initiated a call for a 'better politics of crime' and a discourse to identify the conditions that are likely to sustain it.

2011, the subsequent response of the sentencing courts and, most importantly, the social significance of that response. I conclude that an ideology, ethics, and practice for sentencing grounded in shared social values would facilitate more socially integrated solutions to any future riot-related offending behaviour than the prevailing neo-liberal paradigm, however modified.

Lessons from the English Riots of 2011

The overt political backing of the exemplary sentences that followed the 2011 riots provoked widespread controversy. For the poorer and socially disadvantaged communities where the rioting took place, it increased their sense of alienation and social injustice. Whilst political rhetoric extolled the virtues of family life, employment, and education, the perception was that the state continued to deny citizens living in socially deprived communities the means for their achievement, consistently using penal policy to punish them for failing to do so. Rather than reflecting shared values, the approach of the courts to sentencing the rioters, coupled with the then government's strong political support, appeared to exacerbate pre-existing feelings of social exclusion and discrimination. Arguably, the state's penal ideology, as reinforced through its sentencing approach, helped to intensify these negative perceptions (Henham 2014).

In what follows I want to explore the wider social significance of these assertions in the context of the reasoning and justifications given for the sentencing decisions that followed the riots, and draw out some more general conclusions about the relationship between sentencing policy and social justice for minority and socially deprived communities. More particularly, I consider the longer-term implications for social justice of retaining the present punitive neo-liberal sentencing framework should such serious public disorder reoccur.

The emotive nature of the debate surrounding the sentencing of those involved the English riots of 2011 has drawn attention to the complex nature of the relationship between punishment and social justice—in particular, the notion that social policies which exacerbate social inequality, poverty, alienation, and social exclusion are synonymous with penal discrimination against racial and ethnic minorities (Hall and others 1978). However, whilst racial and ethnic bias in sentencing has been, and continues to be, extensively debated among scholars (Shute, Hood, and Seemungal 2005, Tonry 2011), its wider normative significance for sentencing remains underdeveloped. Such a question is germane since this book is concerned with explaining how sentencing praxis can better reflect and reinforce shared values within and between different communities.

There is a tendency for debates about social justice to become decontextualized for political reasons. In the case of sentencing, this may manifest itself in the rationales judges use to justify their sentencing decisions when juxtaposed against the social reality of citizens' lives. Hence, the sentencing decisions of the English courts are often justified in terms that appear to echo the political rhetoric and symbolism of the state.[12] Such expressive symbolism was evident in the case of *R v Carter, Beswick, Boyd and Gillespie-Doyle*,[13] which was heard in the immediate aftermath of the 2011 riots by HH Judge Gilbart sitting at Manchester Crown Court. During sentencing, the judge was at pains to point out that the exemplary sentences he was imposing on the rioters fulfilled the expressive function of reaffirming the state's core governance role of upholding the universally accepted moral value of public protection. The court's instrumental role of acting as an arm of the state in defending shared moral values was emphasized. Furthermore, the nature of these values was discussed more specifically as expressing the appropriateness of the behaviour demanded of citizens within civil society, and the reciprocal notions of responsibility this should evoke. However, I would contend that the very notions of communitarian responsibility this invocation alluded to are beyond the purview of the existing sentencing regime.

Lacking advice from the Sentencing Council regarding how to treat the existing sentencing guidelines, and, since the events in question fell 'completely outside the usual context of criminality', Judge Gilbart felt at liberty to depart from them.[14] Nevertheless, The Court of Appeal in *Blackshaw* strongly criticized the judge's

[12] A rare exception at the time of the riots was the then Justice Secretary, Kenneth Clarke (Clarke 2011).

[13] *The Queen v Carter, Beswick, Boyd and Gillespie-Doyle*, Manchester Crown Court (16 August 2011), Sentencing Remarks of HH Judge Andrew Gilbart QC http://www.judiciary.gov.uk/Resources/JCO/Documents/Judgments/hhj-gilbart-qc-sentencing-remarks-r-v-carter-others.pdf.

[14] ibid para 14. See Cooper (2013) for further observations on this.

attempts to justify sentences outside the range of the existing guidelines as a recipe for chaos, emphasizing that it was completely beyond the remit of a sentencing judge to issue, or appear to be issuing, sentencing guidelines.[15]

It is worth noting that most of the appellants in *Blackshaw* were employed, some had family responsibilities and, typically, several maintained that they had been caught up in the general hysteria, or swept up in the events as they unfolded; in other words, they had not set out with any specific motive or intention to become involved in the serious public disorder that ensued. The various community impact reports cited by the Court of Appeal in *Blackshaw* did not appear to indicate that specific individuals or properties were singled out as targets on the grounds of race, ethnicity, or religion, although a mosque on London's Old Kent Road was destroyed. Hence, it was difficult to draw anything from the Court's deliberations which suggested that it had considered profounder questions about the possible social causes of the disorder, or how it developed, and the impact that this should, or might, have had on the sentencing decisions to be made or, indeed, whether such questions were relevant at all.

Academic commentators such as Mitchell (2011), Roberts (2012), Ashworth (2012), and Thomas (2012) similarly tended to focus on the difficulties caused by departures from the sentencing guidelines, concentrating on the problems of defining culpability, harm, and impact in terms of the exceptional circumstances involved. In other words, attention was firmly directed towards trying to rationalize punishment and the value that should be attached to it within the framework of the dominant neo-liberal paradigms of retributivism and deterrence. For example, Ashworth's (2012: 89) discussion of when upward departure from the sentencing guidelines might be justified in the interests of justice is couched entirely within the context of the possible repercussions for the existing sentencing framework, and what possible reforms to that framework might be needed to ensure

[15] *The Queen v Carter, Beswick, Boyd and Gillespie-Doyle* (n 13) para 20. See also *R v Blackshaw and Others* [2011] EWCA Crim 2312. Many of the exemplary sentences for theft and handling were subsequently overturned on appeal; see eg *R v Ursula Nevin* [2011] heard at Manchester Crown Court (*BBC News* 2011).

that the system retained its core principles of consistency and proportionality.[16]

Whether what took place was in some way a manifestation of deeper social unrest or tensions, possibly caused by racially oppressive policing or social policies that failed to deal with social deprivation,[17] or whether such factors served to conceal politically motivated, hedonistic, or gang-related violence, were questions that remained unaddressed by the courts.[18] Some academics and community leaders urged caution in the immediate aftermath of the riots, suggesting that the causal factors consisted of a toxic cocktail of economic and social tensions that would have erupted sooner or later. Others argued that Britain was 'broken' and on the edge of an abyss following widespread moral collapse.

More considered scholarly analyses have followed from a wide variety of disciplinary perspectives. Drawing on Wacquant (2009), Slater (2011) sees the state's punitive response as part of a neo-liberal agenda to reserve social welfare reductions together with penal expansion for those at the bottom of the class structure, with laissez faire attitudes prevailing at the top, as evidenced by the state's reluctance to punish those responsible for precipitating the 2008 financial crisis. Reference was also made to the fact that the looters had targeted consumer goods rather than symbols of the state, thereby confirming Bauman's (2011) characterization of 'defective and disqualified' consumers seeking 'prized items'. Slater usefully draws attention to the neo-liberal right wing's narrow interpretation of 'social justice', with 'family values' forming the cornerstone of welfare policies, rather than abstract notions of social equality and the more egalitarian distribution of resources favoured by so-called 'left wing and social democratic thinkers'.

[16] Lightowlers and Quirk (2015) regard the relatively insular nature of the criminal process as an important factor in encouraging the development of the punitive rationale for sentencing riot-related offending behaviour in the aftermath of the 2011 riots. See Pina-Sanchez, Lightowlers, and Roberts (2017) for further analysis based on the 2011 Crown Court Sentencing Survey data set.

[17] See the documentary film 'Riots Reframed' http://riotsreframed.com.

[18] Possible causal factors debated in the media immediately after the riots were legion; for example, welfare dependence, social exclusion, lack of fathers, spending cuts, weak policing, racism, gansta rap and culture, consumerism, opportunism, technology, and social networking (see *BBC News Magazine* 2011).

Cooper (2012) focuses on the policy response of the then Coalition government, particularly its failure to address the issue of disenfranchisement expressed by many young people engaged in the riots and the deeper political context of the events themselves, such as poor relations between black youth and the police (LSE/*Guardian* 2011).[19] Further collateral social implications of right-wing policy are highlighted, particularly the threat to social cohesion resulting from the withdrawal of welfare benefits from those convicted, or their families (Cooper 2012: 17). Arguing from a historical perspective, these sentiments are echoed by Frost and Phillips (2012), who suggest that there is sufficient evidence from which to conclude that the lack of any serious public and political engagement with deep-seated grievances was a major causal factor behind the riots.[20]

Ultimately, the complex inter-relationship of possible causal variables undermines the credibility of more generalized conclusions. For example, the first phase of the *Reading the Riots* project, which focused on London, Birmingham, Manchester, Salford, Nottingham, and Liverpool, cited opportunism, coming from a poorer background, perceived educational, social and economic 'injustice', and inequality as significant factors in riot-related offending behaviour (LSE/*Guardian* 2011). Particularly important, however, was perceived discriminatory treatment by the police, especially with regard to the exercise of their powers of 'stop and search'. The study confirmed that offenders came from a cross-section of local communities, with just under half being students. Of the remainder, some 59 per cent were unemployed. Significantly, the riots were not generally perceived as 'race riots', despite the fact that 47 per cent of interviewees identified themselves as black (see further Newburn and others 2015).[21]

[19] See also Riots, Communities and Victims Panel (2012).

[20] A similar conclusion was reached following a detailed investigation into the rioting on the Broadwater Farm Estate in Tottenham, North London in 1985 (The Broadwater Farm Inquiry 1986). For a historical and comparative overview see Newburn (2015).

[21] The second phase of the project concentrated on the Police, Courts, Crown Prosecution Service, legal profession, and members of the public affected by the riots.

Implications for change

Overall, therefore, a plethora of social and political causes have been cited for the 2011 riots, confirming the huge complexity of the task of producing a credible and politically impartial account of 'how' and 'why' they occurred and, more difficult still, then to translate this knowledge into credible social policies designed to ameliorate and address the identified causes. Thus, one might legitimately ask how all of this conjecture relates to sentencing. Furthermore, such complexities may prompt some to argue that sentencing policy should remain aloof and distance itself from areas of social policy that cannot be addressed without destroying the coherence and consistency required to sustain a morally credible and socially valued sentencing system.

One way of responding to such questions is to examine how the public's approach to sentencing riot-related offending compares to that of the courts, and then to consider the implications for sentencing policy. Roberts and Hough's (2013) findings suggest that the public would have supported a modest increase in the severity of the punishment for riot-related offending,[22] but was inclined to take a more lenient view than the courts had done when it came to sentencing non-violent, riot-related offending, where there was greater support for a non-custodial option. This would indicate that public opinion might support more restorative forms of penal intervention in the case of future riot-related offending (2013: 21).

Whilst this may signify a positive way forward for incorporating public opinion into the development of sentencing policy and guideline reform, it remains the case that the comparisons made by Roberts and Hough related to decisions that were made within the constraints of the existing paradigm for formulating sentencing principles and guidelines. Hence, Roberts and Hough (2013: 20) advocate a cautious approach to any greater reflection of community values in sentencing.

Yet, it may be argued that this posits a somewhat inflexible approach to sentencing reform. Roberts and Hough imply that

[22] Research in London by Hohl, Stanko, and Newburn (2013) suggests a significant increase in punitiveness among respondents with an average of 44 per cent favouring harsher sentences for rioters, coupled with a more authoritarian shift evidenced by a perceived decline in so-called 'traditional' values among the young, regardless of the level of disorder-related incidents experienced.

the contribution of public opinion research to sentencing should be limited to that of reflecting the boundaries of public tolerance, the subtext being that public opinion may be dangerously disruptive and to be resisted—policy-makers and practitioners should beware upsetting the public's penal sensitivities. Such an approach does nothing to change the system from within; rather, it keeps the whole issue of what society, and communities in particular, might regard as the social value of punishment at arm's length. All must be done, it seems, to protect the status quo of 'principled sentencing'.

But what exactly is 'principled' sentencing? This expression is open to several different interpretations, rather like the politically loaded slogan 'prison works'. 'Principled' sentencing is usually taken to refer to the need for sentencing decisions to be consistent and proportionate, but it might be argued that this is unhelpful, since one can remain principled within a system of laws that is morally abhorrent. No one is suggesting that the present sentencing regime is 'morally abhorrent', but many commentators have argued that it is in need of substantive reform because it does not engage with the social reality of many people's lives. Sentencing as presently conceived is to that extent deficient, since it does not consider how contexts shape social morality and, more particularly, the value citizens attach to various forms of state penal intervention. Becoming 'principled' in a truly egalitarian rather than procedural sense implies an engagement with ideology. Thus, to become so 'principled' the state must engage more effectively with those values that are likely to render sentencing policy more egalitarian and communitarian. As argued, this entails a complete reconceptualization of penal ideology.

Roberts and Hough (2013) found that the public and the courts both agreed that deterrence became more important as a sentencing objective when dealing with offences committed during a riot. The success or otherwise of such an objective is always hard to establish, and understanding the influence of complex social variables on desistance poses a major challenge. Analyses of the effects of deterrent sentencing often tend to be empirically focused and skewed towards promoting economic rather than rehabilitative goals. For example, Bell and others' (2014) analysis of the deterrent effect of the relatively severe sentences passed on the 2011 London rioters suggests a fall in riot-related behaviour in the six months after the riots, with the trend reversed for non-riot-related crime. Moreover, neither spatial displacement nor more intensive policing appeared to account for the fall in riot-related behaviour, this against the background of a general fall in crime in the immediate aftermath of the riots. The authors consider that a significant part of the post-riots decrease in overall crime rates was attributable to the general deterrent impact of tougher sanctions imposed by the criminal justice system. They also suggest that a major factor prolonging any such deterrent effect was the perception by potential criminals that the change was permanent rather than transitory.

However, I suggest that we should look again at the wider social context within which such debates about desistance and the general deterrent effect of sentencing take place. A small deterrent effect of some kind is typical in the aftermath of exemplary sentencing, but this tells us little about the social value of deterrent sentencing in such circumstances. Thus, the social repercussions of penal measures deployed against those convicted of riot-related offences are likely to remain obscure. So whilst the deterrent message might be described as public affirmation of how the state intends to fulfil its moral obligation to protect citizens, it is declaratory, designed to reassure citizens that the requisite degree of retributive censure will be inflicted on those who commit similar crimes in the future. In this sense, deterrent sentencing reinforces the sentiment that such behaviour is socially and morally reprehensible—that the penal state will not tolerate repetition. In effect, consensus is implied as to the perceived immorality of the behaviour in question, and, the nature of the state's penal response. However, this assumption is always open to conjecture, since broader social and moral questions are excluded from consideration, the narrow focus of penal morality being validated by the existing paradigm.

Although generally considered a consequential side effect of retributive punishment, such a diminished account of the relationship between sentencing and desistance, especially its moral and social significance, is misplaced (McNeill 2009). A complex inter-relationship exists between those variables that contribute to desistance, especially their configuration and subjective influence in any particular case (Bottoms and others 2004; Farrall and Maruna 2004). As McNeill (2009: 35) suggests, desistance is not simply about the development of human capital, it is also about creating the optimum social conditions, such as those aimed at promoting family ties or broadening supportive social networks, for human capacities and motivations to flourish. Hence, the deployment of scarce resources should be targeted at increasing the capacities of agencies such as the police or probation services to promote networks encouraging the development of feelings and beliefs related to reformation, reparation, and redemption, rather than the feelings of negativity commonly attached to retributive and deterrent punishment (2009: 36).[23]

Ultimately, of course, the deployment of scarce resources, whether or not directed towards the enhancement of human or social capital, is a matter for the state. Hence, as Piper (2011) points out, the nature of the relationship between the state and the judiciary is crucial in determining whether such resources are distributed fairly and proportionately. Therefore, where the elected government ignores or encroaches upon the discretionary powers of judges and magistrates, as happened in the immediate aftermath of the 2011 riots,[24] this poses a direct challenge to the independence of the judiciary (Ashworth 1990), and, more insidiously, undermines (what should be) their vital role in protecting citizens from abuse and oppression by the state—in other words, their moral credibility. I suggest that these dangers were multiplied in the case of the 2011 riots, since judges and magistrates were ill-prepared to respond swiftly and effectively to the sentencing challenges presented by such offending behaviour, the existing sentencing framework and the level of guidance afforded being substantially inadequate. In fact, one might argue that the state effectively capitalized (albeit inadvertently) on public mistrust of the judiciary by distancing itself from what some portrayed as the dangers of possibly idiosyncratic or eclectic sentencing, adopting instead the moral high ground of advocating rapidly dispensed exemplary 'justice' in the name of public protection. Thus, the judiciary was rendered powerless to resist the political and social pressures for exemplary punishment, amplified by a vociferous media,[25] from a position of authority, moral or otherwise.

[23] See Marchetti (2015) in the context of sentencing indigenous offenders for intimate partner violence in Australia.

[24] Evidenced by ministerial exhortations that offenders would be dealt with swiftly and severely, and that magistrates should disregard existing sentencing guidelines when dealing with offenders convicted of riot-related behaviour.

[25] See further *BBC News* (2011).

The exact nature of this 'authority' bears further comment, because it is not simply a question of legal authority (Bingham 2011). One may argue that the long-standing constitutional convention of judicial independence, if taken as an abstract principle, should permit sentencing judges to use their discretionary powers to protect individual freedoms where appropriate, thereby enhancing social capital by promoting social values of equality and non-discrimination.[26] Instead of being perceived as a threat to proportionality and consistency, the individualization of sentences through the principled exercise of discretion, when expressed within the framework of an appropriated ideology, could become a useful mechanism for promoting outcomes that have social value, so reducing the excessive use of imprisonment. Better this than the gradual elimination of discretion and its replacement by a bureaucratic, inflexible, and symbolic version of 'justice' unable to respond to moral and social change and its impact on human behaviour.

Regrettably, following the Criminal Justice Act of 1991, the incremental erosion[27] of the principle of judicial independence in England and Wales by successive UK governments has significantly reduced the capacity of the judiciary to defend the interests of citizens. In my view, this has diminished the judiciary's practical ability to resist punitive policies through individualization in the everyday practice of sentencing, more particularly in pursuing restorative and reintegrative solutions, thereby damaging the perceived legitimacy of sentencing and its development as a key element of criminal justice governance.

Social, historical, and cultural factors not only shape public order offences and public attitudes to offending behaviour but also the extent to which state attention is focused on causal factors and prevention rather than the nature and appropriateness of the penal response (Jarman 2006). Furthermore, the downward delegation of 'justice functions' to local communities during

[26] The exact limits of the principle of judicial independence and its implications for the future development of sentencing policy are discussed in the final chapter. Evidently, the impartiality, representativeness, and training of the judiciary and magistracy are crucial to the principled exercise of discretionary power in sentencing.

[27] Notable examples were the Crime (Sentences) Act 1997 and the Criminal Justice Act 2003.

periods of social instability may obfuscate the search for 'truth' and accountability (McEvoy and McGregor 2008a). In short, decontextualized arguments about the relative gravity of riot-related offending behaviour are unhelpful in shaping constructive sentencing responses. Rather, they serve to illustrate the serious limitations of the current paradigm in taking account of social value. As pointed out earlier, much of the academic discussion has focused on advocating technical adjustments to the way in which judges and magistrates should respond to issues of culpability and harm within the existing sentencing paradigm. Key questions concerning the social value of punishment are largely ignored.

Fundamentally, my argument concerns the nature and sources of the moral authority that underpins the justification for punishment, and how that authority is exercised. du Bois-Pedain (2017) argues that: 'the humanistic and political commitments on which life in a liberal political community is based require a reintegrative conception of punishment that rules out the severance of relationship as a response to crimes.' However, punishment is only justifiable to 'preserve conditions of equal freedom, not to make people better people as such'. I suggest that social conditions maximizing equal freedom are more likely to exist in societies where values of equal freedom are shared and respected by the state through penal policy and practice: cf Durkheim's moral individualism. Accordingly, the state should identify, reflect upon, and determine an appropriate moral framework for operationalizing such a shared value system, with policy fixing the institutional parameters for regulating the penal relationship between citizen and state. Thus, ideology may be justified through its social impact, as monitored consistently over time.

The moral basis for holding citizens to account for their failure to respect the existing social order should suggest values that maximize the virtues of equality and fairness through penal practice. However, the political terms that determine the framework for maximizing equal freedom among citizens are unlikely to address the social reality that shapes their capacity to achieve equal freedom. Rather, as argued, neo-liberal justice has so far marginalized questions of inequality, discrimination, and poverty in justifying punishment, whether perceived or 'real'. Addressing the social morality of punishment would, I suggest, add a new dimension to sentencing, enabling the penal state to respond with greater social sensitivity to events that challenge the existing social order. Such a move would alter the parameters of penal accountability, thereby allowing decision-makers to fashion morally coherent and socially constructive responses to offending behaviour.

In summary, I have argued that the penal ideology underpinning the state's response to the rioting that took place in 2011 severely restricted the ability of courts to explore the social value of the sentences passed for victims, victim communities, and wider society.[28] Ultimately, the social value of any penal intervention is likely to be measured against the values underpinning that intervention. For state morality to be shared by citizens requires a common belief in its virtue and, in normative terms, a shared belief in the impartiality of the institutions, agents, processes, and outcomes of sentencing. Punitive and deterrent justifications could be re-evaluated and take on more socially relevant meaning if underpinned by a morality of core values, as identified in the BA Report (2014). Policy responses would then draw upon a shared morality committed to socially constructive responses to crime. That the state's reactive and punitive response to the riot-related offending of 2011 was facilitated by neo-liberal values rather than values committed to social justice represents both an ideological and institutional failure.

Changing the predominant driver for sentencing so that its moral foundations become more communitarian, thereby reflecting the 'core' social values identified in the BA Report (2014), would give decision-makers the requisite moral (and so normative) authority to engage with broader social concerns when justifying penal interventions on behalf of citizens, particularly in response to offences committed during periods of potentially destabilizing social unrest. So conceived, sentencers would be obliged to pay far greater attention to the collective social impact of penal measures on offenders, victims, and victim communities.

[28] It is worth noting that the majority of prosecutors questioned during the second phase of the *Reading the Riots* project (LSE/*Guardian* 2011) supported the punitive sentencing stance of the courts, although the then DPP Keir Starmer suggested that the speed of the sentencing response rather than its punitive nature was key to re-establishing state control in the immediate aftermath of the riots (Bawdon, Lewis, and Newburn 2012).

Accordingly, the following conclusions are drawn:

- In terms of ideology, the values promoted by the penal state in sentencing the 2011 rioters did not appear to mirror the morality shared by many citizens living in the socially deprived communities where the rioting took place. I have therefore suggested that the exemplary sentences imposed by the courts tended to inflame social tensions and so undermined social cohesion. In this sense, the punitive rhetoric of neo-liberal retributive justice rendered the moral value of sentencing harder to justify.
- Changing the ideology underpinning sentencing as proposed to facilitate a more inclusive and socially sensitive approach would allow less punitive and more restorative interventions to be readily explored in such cases. Retributive and consequentialist solutions could be effectively justified and integrated within such a paradigm.
- So conceived, sentencing is less likely to be perceived as unfair and discriminatory, since the norms, ethics, and structures for its delivery would provoke a more profound engagement with the everyday *reality* of life for offenders and victims and, more particularly, the communities where the offences are perpetrated. Hence, harm and culpability would be evaluated within a broader communitarian context of accountability, suggesting ways in which the penal response might foster social repair rather than social division.

The current sentencing paradigm and the approach it demands, even with appropriate guideline adjustment, is a blunt instrument with which to confront the complexities of social unrest, or the motivations for offences allegedly perpetrated during episodes of violent disorder. Whilst sentencing is clearly not the place for resolving social conflict, the uniquely public platform occupied by the criminal process suggests that the deliberations, pronouncements, and outcomes of the sentencing court are the primary and most visible means the state has of conveying its own sense of moral outrage, or otherwise reflecting what it perceives as shared moral sentiments. Hence, the publicly perceived openness and impartiality of the process and the moral credibility of the policy informing it is crucial if sentencing decisions are to avoid inflaming what may already be significant social tensions.

The changes advocated should also strengthen the capacity of sentencing courts to resist the kind of political pressure and adverse media attention evidenced in the immediate aftermath of the 2011 riots, pressures that lent 'credibility' to those who believed that the courts were ostensibly acting as an arm of a repressive penal state. Furthermore, the prescriptive nature and inflexibility of the sentencing guidelines, when coupled with diminished discretion, left judges and magistrates with little or no room to manoeuvre. Sentencers were ill-equipped to respond proportionately or consistently to widespread riot-related offending behaviour and the range of complex and interrelated causal variables and motivations presented. This failure indicates an ideological flaw, one reflected in the inability of the current guidelines system to incorporate socially significant information. An ideology for sentencing that reflects shared social values should produce policies that are, as Roberts and Hough's (2013) findings suggest, more in tune with the public's nuanced approach to dealing with riot-related offending rather than the punitive stance adopted by the courts in the wake of the 2011 riots. Such a paradigm shift would ensure that the courts have the deliberative space to explore the restorative potential of alternative penal interventions for both victims and victim communities.

3

The Relevance of Globalization and Notions of Transition

Introduction

This chapter considers the global and comparative dimensions of sentencing and explains their significance for developing a more positive relationship between sentencing policy and social justice. The globalization of certain forms of crime exerts a significant influence on the purposes and practice of sentencing within domestic settings. This influence has a bearing on the value attached to the punishment of such crimes and reduces the ability of states to control factors that influence penal legitimacy.

I begin by assessing the influence of globalization on the formulation of sentencing policy more generally in England and Wales, before focusing on the wider problems of drawing comparisons and policy transfer in the sentencing field. I then reflect on sentencing as a transitional concept, drawing upon the justifications, concepts, and practices of various transitional justice settings and examining their relevance in the domestic arena. I argue that notions of transitional justice offer some valuable insights into how one might conceive of sentencing policy's relationship to social justice, particularly in situations where the state lacks a coherent moral mandate for criminalizing and punishing offenders.

Finally, and by way of illustration, I consider whether in the aftermath of global recession the juxtaposition of communitarian values with those of global capitalism has influenced the approach taken to the sentencing of financial crime in the domestic context. I conclude by explaining why and how the proposed changes to ideology and practice are more likely to enhance the moral credibility and social value of sentencing in this area.

The Impact of Globalization on Sentencing Policy

Certain scholars have suggested that globalization tends to universalize crime problems and generalize control responses (Findlay 2008). Whereas the definition and control of crime was once the sole concern of nation states, it has also increasingly become the responsibility of regional and international agencies, with the strategic direction of that control being shaped by international and bilateral agreements forged between nation states.

Given this scenario, the response of the penal state is often reactive and punitive, its relevance to the social welfare of citizens seemingly of rhetorical rather than social significance. For example, the punitive penal response of many states to the global phenomena of mass migration has resulted in what Pickering, Bosworth, and Aas (2014) describe as a 'criminology of mobility', whereby states have deliberately sought to use punishment as an essential tool of social engineering, discrimination, and social exclusion to regulate and control the social order (Zedner 2010). As discussed in Chapter 1, such reactive and negative policies, characterized by the demonization of external influences and events perceived as politically threatening, have proved an increasingly prevalent feature of the late modern neo-liberal state. Thus, one may argue that the social exclusion of migrants has been achieved at the symbolic level through media induced public stigmatization and denigration, whilst the overzealous use of incarceration, coupled with wholly disproportionate collateral sanctions, has had a direct and 'real' effect on subjective notions of identity, status, and citizenship, particularly in the case of migrant prisoners (Kaufman 2014).

Yet, as Garland (1990: 260) argues, historically, symbolism and partial rhetoric have always been paramount in shaping the institutional practice of state penal policy. In the case of rehabilitation, for example, this has drifted from communitarian ideals and moral education to the more administrative and economic concerns of the neo-liberal state. However, I would argue that the strategies which states have adopted to deal with the social, economic, and political problems posed by the globalization of crime and its control have magnified the already tenuous connections that exist between penal ideology and the promotion of social justice in sentencing. As a reactive response to globalized forms of crime, penal norms borne out of political compromise often have more to do with appeasing the hierarchical relationships of international politics and global economic power than they have with local mechanisms of accountability and the institutions of state punishment. As Bauman (2000) suggests, global and local contexts tend to suggest contrary values that lead to conflict, wherein paradox and disharmony are disguised, submerged, and ignored.

The failure of retributive and just deserts sentencing to confront contradiction and relativity between the global and the local often conceals and obfuscates the rationales for punishment, and also accentuates the gap between the rhetoric and the reality of sentencing practice within the nation state. In the case of international crimes, for example, the penal response may be left grounded in the rhetoric of international accords aimed at drawing the world's attention to the seriousness and need for universal condemnation of the activity in question, but failing to provide the normative direction needed for individual states to operationalize penal aims as principles of distributive justice in a coherent and consistent manner (Henham 2003). Thus, community-based interventions with a restorative or rehabilitative focus aimed at fulfilling an important transitional role may be compromised at the national level where, as in England and Wales, state penal ideology is insufficiently conditioned to respond to communitarian frameworks of accountability. Hence, essential components of restorative justice, key to promoting social justice, such as diversion, mediation, apology, forgiveness, 'truth-telling', compensation, restitution, reparation, reconciliation, and reintegration may be obfuscated by the politicized context of global penality and the resulting distortion of domestic praxis this produces. Thus, the disconnected rhetoric of domestic neo-liberal penal policy may reinforce distorted notions of accountability and polarize competing value systems.

It is also important to recall that the relationship between the global and the local is reciprocally constituted so far as globalized crime and penal governance is concerned. It is not simply a question of how the local interprets or translates the moral and legal imperatives set by globalized crime and the policy directives or protocols established by external normative frameworks of accountability. Sentencing policy at the local level reflects back on to the global governance framework and, in so doing, strengthens its moral authority. This is socially significant in suggesting that, to retain moral credibility, models of accountability for global forms of crime should also possess social value at the local level.

Paradigms of accountability as between the global and the local should therefore be conceived as mutually interdependent. To gain legitimacy they should reinforce shared values and norms postulated for accountability, so that what takes place at the local level is consistent with the penal ideology developed on the global platform. Therefore, communication structures should facilitate the reliability and predictability of relevant information at all levels of accountability. Processes should be transparent and inclusive in a democratic sense, and the nature and exercise of legal, institutional, and operational responsibility should ensure conformity to norms for their effective enforcement. In turn, forms of global penal governance should then move towards the development of flexible pluralist regulatory regimes that engage more effectively with diverse cultures and contexts, so helping to depoliticize the hegemony exercised by powerful global players over the control of globalized crime (Findlay 2008). These issues are explored further in the next section.

Whilst the politicized rhetoric of global crime invariably centres symbolically on the victim, the moral character of victimization is largely ignored in the framing of domestic penal ideology. Therefore, there is little sense in which the state's penal response mirrors a shared morality of how to respond to suffering and social deprivation; rather, it struggles to establish a meaningful relationship with the moral subjectivity of victimization in its social context (Boutellier 2000). Little wonder therefore that it is difficult to discern a sense of shared moral purpose centred on 'core' social values when sentencing is detached from any meaningful engagement with the moral and social dimensions of crime. Since states have difficulty in dealing with the diffused accountability globalized forms of crime engender, sentencing policies correspondingly fail to engage effectively with the socio-political forces responsible for shaping the moral climate of accountability, as with human-trafficking or drug-related crime.

In England and Wales, neo-liberal values underpin what counts as individual and collective penal accountability. However, the globalized nature of crime belies the social value of local accountability. Accordingly, the state is faced with the difficult task of discriminating fairly and meaningfully between penal measures on the basis of desert at the expense of any profounder engagement with the social value of criminalization and punishment on the ground. Thus, the presumed universality of the values underlying globalized forms of crime and punishment may be displaced by the state, with local perceptions suggesting different forms of accountability from those envisaged at either the state or global level.

Problems of Comparison and Policy Transfer in Sentencing

Since the globalization of crime and crime problems draw the international and domestic dimensions of criminal and penal justice closer together, state institutions should take proper account of the complexities of these relationships in the development of domestic sentencing policy. England and Wales is no exception to this. Indeed, vertical relationships between global and local structures and processes, as well as horizontal relationships between nation states, are significant in this respect.

More generally, many areas exist where, on the face of it, comparisons could usefully be made between the juridical practices of different nation states. The conventional rationale for drawing such comparisons is that lessons might usefully be drawn from elsewhere, with practices adopted or transplanted from other jurisdictions.[1] In the present context, for example, the following comparative questions may arise:

- What is the constitutional position of the judiciary in matters of punishment and sentencing?
- How independent is it of the executive?
- How accountable is it to the legislature?
- To what extent is the judiciary criticized for being 'out of step' with public opinion when it comes to sentencing?
- To what extent is penal policy dictated by political objectives?
- How responsive are the courts to the needs of victims and communities?
- What is the relationship between the aims of punishment and the principles for their distribution?

[1] See Findlay and Henham (2007) for a comprehensive analysis of the disadvantages of this approach.

- To what extent is the exercise of judicial discretion in sentencing influenced by legal and social constraints?
- To what extent do the aims of punishment and sentencing practice reflect shared values about 'justice'?

Distinctions between common and civil law paradigms may also be relevant, for example—as to pre-trial and evidentiary procedures, rules regarding standard and burden of proof, the judicial role in the admissibility of evidence and the questioning of witnesses, relevance of related civil proceedings, trial by jury as opposed to judicial determination, and, as to sentencing, divisions between verdict and sentence delivery, appeal rights, the degree of judicial discretion, and differing rights for victim participation.

Needless to say, the above list is not exhaustive. Yet it is difficult to see how criminology, or social science more generally, can provide meaningful comparisons, so enabling policy-makers to develop more equitable and socially relevant penal policies. As Cotterrell (2002) suggests, comparisons might more profitably focus on common conceptual themes, such as social values, moral action, citizenship, community, reintegration, and exclusion, to facilitate a better understanding of how concepts of justice translate from one location to another.[2] However, such comparisons do little more than point to what is an extremely difficult and complex area for social theory and methodology (Melossi, Sosso, and Sparks 2011).

I have argued elsewhere that the moral imperative for comparison should be that of advancing a more ethical practice (Henham 2012). Where globalized forms of crime and control are at issue, the state has the additional task of ensuring that sentencing policy provides a basis for accountability that resonates with its core values. However, in reality, domestic sentencing policy can only engage with social values in so far as they represent some sort of politically acceptable accommodation between the interests of citizens and the exercise of state power.

[2] Cotterrell (2002) also makes the important point that the integration and differentiation of law involves a continuum of comparisons. The debate is further complicated by the fact that disagreement persists about the validity of sociological insights in the interpretation of legal ideas (Cotterrell 1998; Nelken 1998).

Cotterrell (2002) suggests that, if the instrumental claim for law's moral authority is based upon an appeal to shared values and beliefs, then the value of comparison and differentiation lies with the export, reception, or transplanting of fundamental values and beliefs in legal form. Hence, law may be seen as a means of protecting and symbolizing various forms of collective identity in different ways. Although it may be difficult to disagree with the fundamental values that underpin the control and punishment of globalized forms of crime, it may be more difficult to translate them into norms valued equally by the citizens of nation states. The problem lies, not in the values themselves, but in their enabling structures, and, more particularly, their relative perception by citizens as 'legitimate' sources of moral authority. The reasons for this disjunction differ according to time and place and, most importantly, as between states.

Thus, in the case of the EU, for example, the moral authority of its institutions, and so the extent to which it is perceived as protecting or symbolizing some kind of collective identity, is determined by complex socio-cultural and historical variables that not only differ enormously within nation states, but also between them. If, as may well be the case, citizens of member states question the EU's moral authority over certain aspects of criminal justice policy, nation states are faced with the challenging task of converting this moral conjecture into penal rationales and norms that engage with competing domestic interests and values. This demands policies that are grounded in a profound sociological understanding of how the norms and practices of sentencing interrelate, and the collective impact of this on the social value of any suggested reforms.

Sentencing guidelines should therefore contain normative indicators that assist sentencers in accommodating and promoting credible responses to communitarian demands for justice. Yet much of the material for comparison is inadequate. Most measures of penal severity and the judicial practices of different jurisdictions are of little assistance since they ignore or marginalize social contexts (Frase 1998, Albrecht 2001). Since, as with all statistics, comparative sentencing statistics are easily manipulated for ideological or political reasons, developing a convincing comparative methodology for deconstructing the dynamics of trial decision-making in terms of the relationships between ideology, structure, process, and outcome becomes critical (Findlay and Henham 2005).

Scholars have long argued that the simple juxtaposition of conclusions drawn from research carried out in different jurisdictional settings is flawed (Nelken 1997; 2000, Nelken and Feest 2001, Harding and Orucu 2002, Legrand and Munday 2011). As argued in Chapter 6, comparative contextual analysis of normative processes such as sentencing requires a methodology that is capable of deconstructing the broader social contexts in which discretionary decisions are made. This suggests a form of socio-legal inquiry that focuses explicitly on actual decision-making practice within states, and the significance of this and each outcome for citizens and communities. Whether particular jurisdictions share similar juridical foundations and styles of trial process, or represent hybridized or transitional forms of justice delivery, is a matter for scholarly debate. Although common issues and themes arise from the social function of the trial and jurisdictional responses to it, this commonality cannot be assumed in terms of shared meanings, values, and beliefs.

Notwithstanding, empirically grounded descriptions of different trial contexts can reveal how 'real' understandings of decisions and procedures are constructed (Rogers and Erez 1999). Comparative knowledge about the way judges approach the more subjective aspects of discretionary decision-making, such as the individualization of sentences, is crucial for policy-makers. For example, Henham and Mannozzi's (2003) comparative contextual analysis of victim participation and sentencing in England and Italy gauged the potential effects of control mechanisms on the judicial capacity to implement particular sentencing strategies through discretionary decision-making. Their research suggests that, where it is proposed to transplant structures from different trial styles and legal cultures into existing or novel jurisdictional forms, it is necessary to provide detailed accounts and understandings of the trial contexts from which these transplants have come, in order both to comprehend what they historically and currently represent, and to speculate how they might develop in the future.

In addition, developing knowledge about trial dynamics, especially ways in which professional relationships influence sentence decision-making in different contexts, provides important indicators of how the purposes chosen for sentencing are likely to find expression, and what potential exists for their transformation

(Kirby 2014). Henham and Mannozzi's (2003) study highlights that failure to develop rational justifications for sentencing, other than through reaching some accommodation with pre-existing philosophical positions, may prove counterproductive in terms of successfully integrating processes and structures transplanted from alien jurisdictions. Thus, changes in structure and form without a corresponding re-evaluation of the overall purposes for prosecution, trial and sentence, beyond a basic need to remedy procedural deficiency, produce penal structures whose philosophical justifications are impossible to reconcile with the stated aims of punishment and the legislative model that embodies them. This insight confirms that policies advocating new or alternative penal interventions should be rationalized within a coherent penal ideology, and validated contextually through normative practice.

It may prove valuable for policy-makers to draw comparisons between jurisdictional trial forms (local, regional, or global), where, despite differences in legal and cultural context, there are cogent reasons for examining how and why the quality of justice is constructed in certain ways. For example, where trial justice is measured in terms which suggest the integration of retributive and restorative aspirations, knowledge of how professional and lay relationships in different trial contexts accommodate these tensions in decision-making, and the reasons for this, can provide a legitimate platform for examining how these experiences might relate to the processes and purposes of domestic criminal justice.

Meaningful generalizations can therefore be made about the exercise of discretion in different social contexts by deconstructing specific sites of decision-making within the sentencing process. However, it is important to understand how tensions between fact and value are resolved in discretionary decision-making in order to capitalize on the instrumental power of judicial discretion for developing constructive outcomes and strategies. Whilst empirical research alone cannot reconceptualize, rationalize, or reposition the justifications for sentencing, what it can do is to explore the different social contexts for achieving particular penal outcomes (Henham 2005).

It is difficult to speculate about specific sites or aspects of decision-making relevant to sentencing, but these are likely to include pre-trial decisions, communication structures, prosecutorial and defence discretion, and inter-professional dynamics, in addition to judicial and post-trial decision-making. Within this framework, critical areas for research are:

- how notions of accountability are formulated and facilitated during the trial and sentencing
- the nature and role of the evidence deemed necessary to bring this about
- how processes and procedures are operationalized in the everyday routine production of sentencing
- the subjective interpretation of relevant information by legal professionals, and
- perceptions of the sentence by the 'relevant' audience (see further Chapter 6).

Recognizing the Relativity of Value

The gap between the rhetoric and the reality of universal declarations of intent is normally bridged by states through the political accommodation of competing interests. This shapes norms of implementation, including the degree of judicial discretion allowed for interpretation or deviation from what is legally prescribed. However, any assumption that social values are perceived in similar ways is especially tendentious when it comes to questions of criminal accountability and punishment.

Recasting state penal ideology on the basis of shared social values should provide a context where the state's penal response to globalized forms of crime or criminal justice policy is able to take greater account of values at the local level. However, the most difficult question to answer is not so much whether states should take account of social values to inform such decisions, but rather, how they might go about explaining what such values actually signify as a matter of empirical fact. Social values must be recognized by states, before they can be identified. The empirical task is then to describe and explain their existence as a social fact, particularly whether or not values are shared and why. Having done so, a judgment has to be reached as to whether particular punishments are effective in realizing state values. Judgments about the social value of specific punishments should reflect the degree to which state values are being realized.

Taking account of social value requires an empirically informed focus on collective accountability to ensure that the legitimate interests of relevant victims *and* victim communities are protected. However, such an engagement requires the identification of much broader realms of accountability than the current narrow focus on individual censure. It demands a process that empowers decision-makers to allocate responsibility through ethics and norms validated by shared social values. The extent to which such decisions are linked to wider considerations regarding punishment's potential contribution to social harmony is fundamental to the legitimacy of penal governance. Accordingly, empirical evidence as to the meaning and significance of 'collective accountability' is vital in defining which social goals ought to influence sentencing policy. Such understandings are not only essential in establishing contextually meaningful rationales and practices within states, they are also important in promoting social cohesion between states, and effectively realizing globalized forms of penality at the local level. Finally, the reinforcement of such social goals through practice is important for embedding rights of access and participation in sentencing.

In order therefore to grasp the significance of criminal justice as a core element of governance, it is necessary to appreciate vertical and horizontal relationships of influence between systems (Baker 2013). Although there will necessarily be system differences, my argument for focusing on synergy rather than diversity transcends debates about differences of form and process, or their particularly exclusive cultural manifestations. As indicated, the drive for synergy and unity in penal governance is based upon a belief that, for criminal justice to transcend mere symbolism (at whatever level), requires a new kind of penal ideology where the rationale for action is social legitimacy, for sentencing outcomes especially. The move towards further synergy between national and globalized forms of criminal justice cannot easily be dismissed. However, the social implications of such relationships, whether in terms of form, process, or influence, are not necessarily beneficial. The reasons for this are complex, but I would argue that the question of legitimacy, in terms of *how* 'justice' is perceived as fair and appropriate, is a crucial factor (Bottoms and Tankebe 2012).

I argue instead that sentencing policy should embody certain 'core' values, more specifically those identified as desirable by the BA Report (2014), with sentencing decisions rationalized in these terms. However, as suggested, taking account of overlapping networks of crime and community, and the need for penal aims and outcomes to respect cross-cultural values and recognize common interests is hugely problematic. The value attributable to a specific sentence—its social value—is a morally informed judgment made in the light of subjective experience. Understanding how such judgments are made in different jurisdictions, and their sentencing implications, poses complex comparative, moral, and ethical questions for social theory and methodology.

Sentencing and the Notion of Transition

The notion of transition suggests a fluid conceptual space wherein different structures and processes are able to merge, transform, or be rejected. It therefore offers an important framework for developing insights into the way social values might be accommodated within a changed ideology for sentencing. More particularly, 'transition' conjures up visions of movement and change; in this case, changes in social values. Hence, transition is driven by ideology and values. Whilst at one end of the transitional continuum values may appear to favour social conflict, social harmony might characterize values at the other extreme. Within the framework of criminal justice governance, I argue that sentencing policy has an important role to play in effecting a transition from neo-liberal values to social justice values. In this sense, sentencing may be conceived as implicated in a transitional discourse between the state and citizens aimed at promoting restorative and reintegrative rather than retributive solutions to crime problems.

More specifically, this perspective suggests that sentencing practice could help to maximize values of social harmony, particularly in situations where the state is perceived as lacking a coherent moral mandate for criminalizing and punishing certain offenders (McEvoy and McGregor 2008b: 6). It also highlights the dangers of imposing 'top down' criminal justice solutions and the need to address the question of relativism:

> [t]he attempt to apply values uniformly across cultures and societies, where the possibilities for peoples in those societies to participate, influence and impact upon that process are confined and delimited, is in essence a negation of those values by the very means of their supposed implementation.
>
> (Lundy and McGovern 2008: 102)

Hence, 'transition' may be an important concept for envisioning how sentencing constructs particular (possibly false) narratives of crime and criminality over time; for example, narratives favouring retributive rather than reintegrative penal solutions, particularly where the former exacerbate social disharmony. Thus, to view sentencing in transitional terms is to acknowledge that it could have an important role in promoting values favouring social coherence, alongside other agencies and structures concerned with delivering criminal justice. In this context, 'transition' is a useful lens for conceptualizing how elements involved in the social (re)-construction of criminal justice governance might work together for the common good. The practical benefits of this speculation include the undoubted social value of increasing the effectiveness of sentences for offenders and the wider community, as well as the empathy of sentencing courts to the diverse social contexts of criminality and victimization.

The notion of justice as embedded in a contested and constantly changing social setting is key to developing an understanding of the relationship between social morality and punishment. This conception suggests that 'justice' is anchored to social contexts in a transitional sense, obliging the state to respond directly to changes in social morality to maintain credibility. Within complex social contexts and competing value systems this response must be based on accurate information. Thus, for sentencing to make a useful contribution towards diffusing social tensions, rather than exacerbating them, as did the exemplary penalties imposed on the 2011 rioters, judges and magistrates need to be in a position to respond to a different set of penal objectives; objectives that foster values of community, such as mutual awareness, respect, and social responsibility. Such an approach empowers citizens and communities by maximizing their moral stake in decision-making and in shaping the boundaries of accountability.

Accordingly, outcomes should be evaluated against measures of satisfaction that go far beyond those designed to maintain confidence in deserts-based offence proportionality. Instead, judicial sensitivities as to the 'appropriate' penal response should extend beyond conventional understandings of procedural 'justice' to engage with the emotional consequences of crime and victimization for victims and communities over time (Flynn 2014), particularly since the emotions are intrinsically linked to moral judgments (Prinz 2006). This opens up the possibility that penal policy could be reconceived within the context of a fresh vision wherein retributive and deterrent responses are viewed as part of a morally accepted and socially relevant mechanism for conflict resolution, rather than symbolizing an unresponsive, divisive, and oppressive arm of the state. Here it is important to note that social values infer individual and collective as well as vertical and horizontal dimensions of accountability. This insight is significant for envisioning a penal paradigm that explores how changes in social values relate to the diffusion of social conflict. Thus, notions of 'transition' can stress the benefits of positive intervention over time in response to social change. For sentencing, this suggests its broader social implications, particularly its relationship to social values, and the need effectively to realign penal policies in times of rapid social change or significant social unrest.

As suggested, criminal justice may be implicated in constructing false accounts of victimization (Lea and Young 1984). So conceived, the processing of false victim identities is enabled through the normative framework of the criminal trial and sentencing. Under the adversarial system, the focus is on constructing the penal identity of the individual offender (Starmer 2014), rather than reflecting on the collective nature of victimization and the accountability this engenders. As argued, law's propensity to distort value relationships and social reality is validated through the value-related dimension of sentencing, as justified by the prevailing penal ideology (Ewald 2006)—a tendency exemplified in the punitive sentencing of female offenders. Thus, consistent false labelling also amounts to social victimization where it systematically promotes distorted deviant identities.

Whilst trials manufacture a form of 'truth' and provide 'legal' closure, this kind of 'truth' may be regarded as distorted by the limited rationales and objectives set for trial justice, and the closure provided as falling far short of 'managing' the emotional demands of victims and victimized communities (Flynn 2014). In transitional terms, one may view such justificatory boundaries as delineating the 'appropriate' moral terrain for penal intervention, so limiting the potential for devising reintegrative solutions. Such a narrow, one-dimensional view of trial justice's instrumental capacity mirrors conventional retributive and deterrent concerns, ignoring the fact that transitional elements—the structures and institutions charged with delivering reform—must not only be identified, balanced, and coordinated (Boraine 2004), but also engage meaningfully with relevant social contexts. Accordingly, to become a more effective and constructive force within penal and social policy more broadly, sentencing needs to be evaluated against measures of satisfaction that resonate with victims, victim communities, and society at large, especially in terms of emotional engagement.

Thus, although retribution and deterrence might be deemed essential to social reform, assessing the basis upon which individuals or groups attribute greater satisfaction to one kind of process over another is problematic. Satisfaction may ensue because a process is inclusive and participatory, or because of feelings about its intrinsic social value. However, satisfaction is only likely where processes are inclusive and participatory in 'real' terms, or because of genuinely held feelings about sentencing's potential value in promoting social cohesion through reintegration. Further, in terms of timing, the window of opportunity and impetus for restorative solutions to be exploited by the state may quickly dissipate. Moreover, since transitional impacts vary as between cultures and communities, by coordinating ideological and institutional reform transitional approaches to managing penal change can help to justify and bring coherence to the governance framework.

In transitional terms, reforming institutional structures with the aim of achieving a greater measure of social justice may be seen as more pressing than pursuing the conventional goals of neo-liberal justice. However, to realize this objective, policy-makers require methods for understanding how values relate to social contexts, since it cannot be assumed that values correspond to any preconceived notions of governance, or the roles and structures needed for its realization. Whilst the state may seek to justify harsh punishment for serious public disorder and riot-related criminal activity on the basis of 'democratic' values, such responses may instead increase social tensions and so prove counterproductive. 'Representative' democracy does not guarantee equality of treatment, nor freedom from discrimination under the law. Understanding how social contexts shape the moral value of punishment, particularly in terms of the relationship between penal intervention and social change, may therefore be seen as a critical first step towards achieving the ideal of a more inclusive kind of justice for citizens and communities (Findlay and Henham 2010).

Social Values and the Sentencing of Financial Crime[3]

Following the global financial collapse of 2008, one might have expected the value system underpinning the sentencing of financial crime to become more punitive in its orientation than that which had existed hitherto, either as a reflection of perceived public opinion, or to counter the hegemony of capitalist values, or both. Yet, whilst these events have not heralded widespread change, they have prompted a concerted search for more restorative solutions, alongside a more general trend to find credible alternatives to trial intervention, such as deferred prosecution agreements or negotiated settlements (Mazzacuva 2014). The discussion that follows considers the extent to which perceived changes in social morality may have influenced the approach taken in England and Wales towards developing sentencing policy and practice in this area, and whether this forms part of a broader reappraisal of the kinds of values that should inform the sentencing of financial crime.

It is reasonable to assert that since the 2008 financial crisis the climate of hostility towards banks, the bonus culture, and corrupt practices in the banking and financial sectors such as the Libor and foreign exchange rate fixing scandals, has increased exponentially (YouGov-Cambridge 2013). Yet, it may be argued that vested economic and political interests continue to ensure that the institutions, structures, and practices of powerful elites remain largely untouched, as Chambliss and Seidman (1971), Quinney (1980), and Box (1983) forewarned. Set against a background of increased media scrutiny and state regulation, one may argue further that much of this is simply illusory, a symbolic nod in the direction of transparency. In truth, it often conceals a reality where what needs to take place to maximize profits, will take place, regardless of its moral virtue. Accordingly, where individuals are singled out, the status quo is (re)-legitimized by reassurances from state agencies that offenders will 'feel the full force

[3] The expression 'financial' crime includes crimes committed by corporations and individual perpetrators (*contra* Box 1983).

of the law', so satisfying (apparently) what is deemed necessary politically to stigmatize 'corrupt' practices publicly.[4]

Undeniably, there are many problems in successfully prosecuting crime in this area, including its global reach, evidential complexity and a lack of juror comprehension (Findlay 2001). Indeed, the sheer complexity of the law and its interpretation sustains a vast array of corporate lawyers, accountants, and advisers. Hence, what one can (or should) reasonably expect of sentencing policy and practice in this context remains unclear. To begin, one may ask whether the state's penal response correctly identifies and reflects any kind of shared morality or shared value system. This poses a hugely problematic task for policy-makers. To provide a morally acceptable response the state must determine exactly where the 'public interest' lies; essentially, whether there exists an identifiable and shared social morality requiring protection, and, more purposefully, whether the courts can realistically be expected to engage with such values when punishing these offences.

Some may question whether, in reality, alternative forms of intervention such as deferred prosecution agreements (DPAs) form part of an elaborate stratagem intended to divert conventional criminal justice processes away from those suspected of serious financial crime. Introduced in 2014 by the Sentencing Council in its definitive guideline on Fraud, Bribery and Money Laundering, negotiated agreements between the prosecution and commercial organizations require crown court approval in the form of a declaration that the DPA is in 'the interests of justice' and its terms 'fair, reasonable and proportionate' (see Bisgrove and Weekes 2014; Padfield 2016). Whilst allowing judges a considerable degree of discretionary latitude in making these determinations, considerable uncertainty inevitably persists as to whether potential criminality comes to light, particularly where such behaviour is endemic to the business culture of a particular organization or industry. Furthermore, legal judgments as to what constitutes 'the interests of justice', or what is 'fair, reasonable and proportionate'

[4] The Governor of the Bank of England, Mark Carney, recently signalled the need for a tougher approach and longer prison sentences for market abuse (*BBC News* 2015b). However, changing the ingrained culture of impunity and providing socially meaningful corporate accountability in the financial industry remain distant goals.

are notoriously opaque and may be subject to legal obfuscation. More pertinently, DPAs are made within the overarching climate of neo-liberal retributive penal ideology and, as with so many other diversionary mechanisms, may be seen to represent yet another addition to the penal armoury whose 'real' social value is neither identified nor addressed by the decision-making process. Rather than relying on such 'criminality' coming to the attention of the prosecutor, even through prosecutorial initiative, a penal policy grounded in shared social values seems far more likely to be successful in prioritizing, or at least adequately recognizing, communitarian rather than corporate interests in DPAs and their subsequent judicial approval.[5]

Sentencing policy for financial crime in England and Wales over the last twenty-five years has developed from a predominantly just deserts model underpinned by neo-liberal retributive values. Thus, for individuals, penal aims have been advanced within narrowly defined principles to determine offence seriousness and culpability. However, as Braithwaite and Petit (1990) argue, there are difficulties with the notion that just deserts actually leads to more justice in such cases, since offenders are easily able to minimize elements of intent and culpability, and punishment cannot readily be equated with the harm done where offences are perceived as less serious, especially if there are regional variations in prosecution and enforcement practices (Croall 2001). Both Braithwaite and Pettit (1990) and Hudson (1987) argue convincingly that the criminal process and the just deserts model in particular are likely to perpetuate class-based and ideologically constrained definitions of crime seriousness, thus reinforcing cultural perceptions that white-collar crime and related forms of legal non-compliance are less serious than crime committed by the 'working class'.

Deserts rationality is further compromised in the case of regulatory offences by the doctrine of strict liability and selective prosecution policies. Braithwaite and Geis (1982) and Braithwaite (1989) argue in favour of selective policies of rehabilitation or incapacitation in appropriate circumstances, based on grounds

[5] So-called 'SOCPA' agreements made between prosecuting authorities such as the Serious Fraud Office (SFO) or the CPS and defendants may also result in significant sentence discounts (ss 73 and 74 of the Serious Organised Crime and Police Act 2005).

of public protection and prevention. Braithwaite (1989), in particular, has long argued that effective self-regulation can only be achieved through a combination of preventative and other sentencing approaches. His original call for a radical departure from traditional approaches based on reintegrative shaming, advocated combining effective social control for corporate offenders by encouraging moral disapproval for non-compliance with appropriate reinforcement through conventional forms of state punishment. However, the general consensus has favoured deterrence as the most effective penal response on the assumption that, since financial crime is economically motivated, it is more likely to be subject to a rational calculation of the risks involved. Unfortunately, deterrence has traditionally been undermined by low rates of detection, prosecution, and conviction, and the limited impact of the sentences imposed, factors compounded by financial crime's inherent complexities.

Corporate punishment and the development of more effective notions of criminal responsibility and appropriate accountability for companies, such as corporate manslaughter, have, until recently, languished at the bottom of the political law and order agenda of successive United Kingdom (UK) governments. The adoption of United States (US) style penal and other initiatives such as corporate inquiry reports, tighter inspection regimes, larger corporate fines and corporate probation have all been questioned on economic grounds, for example, the imposition of excessive burdens on management, financial impact on shareholders, deterring investors, and so forth (Slapper 1994). The only argument that appears to carry any weight is the reputational one, namely, the likely deterrent effect of a loss of market share resulting from the adverse publicity that would inevitably accompany a corporate conviction. Paradoxically, whilst potential loss of reputation and market share has proved to be the most effective response to corporate wrongdoing, this cannot simply be attributed to the introduction of more effective penal remedies.

More recently, the advent of a new form of corporate accountability in the form of corporate social responsibility (CSR) has transformed the behaviour of companies and the role of penal sanctions in securing compliance (McBarnet 2007). Social responsibility has now become directly linked to profits and market share in ways that could not have been envisaged in the 1990s. However, this trend owes little to the 2008 financial crisis, although this undoubtedly heightened corporate awareness and investor sensitivity to the impact on profits of any possible reputational issue. Rather, it represents a broader cultural shift in public awareness of the environmental and social consequences of corporate activity, this having developed alongside the public's growing distaste for purely financial wrongdoing and corrupt practices. Thus, the exponential growth of self-governance by corporates, which began as a largely voluntary movement, has now become a firmly entrenched and widespread part of business policy. McBarnet's (2007: 4) most important conclusion for present purposes is that securing effective business compliance with CSR through penal law is only a small part of the picture—corporate compliance is hugely complex and affected by a wide range of variables, such as NGO activity, human rights challenges, competitor activity, market pressures, insurance, civil actions, and other extra-legal means of enforcement, individual and collective, aimed at generating adverse publicity, protests, and boycotts.

McBarnet (2007: 18) observes how the complex interplay between market forces and the law has not only generated new legal forms and voluntary CSR compliance, it has also spawned a varied assortment of indirect enforcement mechanisms, as well as the creative use of pre-existing legal rights and remedies, so that 'the art of creative compliance' has now become a growth industry for lawyers and allied professionals. Yet law suffers from a lack of contextualization that puts it at a severe disadvantage in terms of its capacity to engage with both ethical and non-ethical forms of business activity and in foreseeing how market trends and corporate behaviour are likely to respond to new legal compliance devices and challenges.

Notwithstanding, the parameters of corporate accountability have undoubtedly shifted. The old argument that companies are unlikely to spend shareholders' money on social goals has been replaced by a renewed focus on social values. Business and investment choices are now positively allied to socially relevant values and outcomes (Vogel 2005).[6] Nevertheless, penal law and sentencing policy has been slow in catching-up with these developments. Although the Sentencing Council has been proactive

[6] The morality of the market and capitalism has provoked extensive theological debate (see Williams 2012a: 219 and ch 18).

in promulgating definitive guidelines for environmental offences (Sentencing Council 2014a) and fraud, bribery, and money laundering guidelines for corporate offenders (Sentencing Council 2014b), it is doubtful whether the Sentencing Council or the general law of sentencing are presently able to engage with the wider socio-political contexts of such criminality or take into account the social value of particular penalties through conventional forms of guidance. For example, at the lower end of the spectrum of seriousness, one may convincingly argue that the level of investor and creditor protection provided against the (often) adverse social consequences that frequently result from the strict application of the limited liability principle remains morally indefensible. The narrow interpretation of this legal construct severely limits the ability of courts to provide 'real' accountability for victims. Hence, courts are unable to effectively sanction the wider social harm caused to communities through the proliferation of 'phoenix' companies[7] that consistently allow wrongdoers to evade personal responsibility for negligent, reckless, and fraudulent trading activities over many years (see Fuller 2013).

For environmental offences, the Sentencing Council followed the lead of the US Sentencing Commission in allowing mitigation where a company is able to demonstrate that it has introduced a code of conduct and activated a programme for its dissemination and enforcement. However, aggravation of offences located near, for example, housing, schools, livestock, or environmentally sensitive sites, or where there is established evidence of wider community impact, is considered within the framework of an overarching injunction for the court to review 'whether the sentence as a whole meets, in a fair way, the objectives of punishment, deterrence and removal of gain derived through the commission of the offence'. Proportionate fines based on turnover aimed at removing any economic benefit remain the order of the day.

The Sentencing Council's definitive guidelines for fraud, bribery, and money laundering do refer to 'substantial harm (whether financial or otherwise) suffered by victims of offending or by third parties affected by offending' as significant aggravation. However, since there is no further elaboration as to what might

[7] For a discussion of government policy see House of Commons (2009).

amount to 'substantial harm', one must conclude that this falls to be interpreted within the existing just deserts rationale. In other words, the interpretation of 'harm' remains tied to the immediate concerns of directly identifiable victims and third parties, whilst more communitarian considerations, such as the broader social impact of the offending behaviour on the lives of ordinary citizens within affected communities, are unlikely to count as aggravating factors. Significantly, considerable emphasis is placed on the notion of 'substantial harm' being caused by offending the markets and local and national governments through loss of integrity and confidence.

Similarly, when it comes to the imposition of fines, considerations of social harm are restricted to individual factors, such as the offender's ability to make restitution to victims or implement effective compliance programmes. As for direct impact, the guidelines refer to the employment of staff, service users, customers, and the local economy and, whilst this expressly excludes shareholders, it is clear that the emphasis here is on how the court should go about satisfying the requirements of proportionality without doing too much damage to the local economy. Hence, the primary focus is whether or not the fine fulfils the objectives of 'punishment, deterrence and removal of gain', but the calculation of social harm is very firmly tied to economic considerations.

Thus, the question remains as to whether the current sentencing regime is 'fit for purpose' in the context of widespread financial crime. Regarding gravity, one may argue that, if measured in terms of their social consequences, some of these offences are at the very highest end of the spectrum—equivalent perhaps to a crime against humanity.[8] But, of course, 'society' does not equate the two, although financial crimes can and do cost lives, whether directly or indirectly. Arguably, such potentially catastrophic consequences indicate that 'top down' state or global solutions to corporate wrongdoing do little more than reinforce social distance and polarize competing moralities (Braithwaite 2009). A more nuanced engagement with social values appears to be the best way forward, not simply paying greater attention to the minutiae of sanctioning companies and individuals, but finding better ways of reconciling corporate and communitarian

[8] Certainly a convincing argument in the case of catastrophic environmental crimes such as the Bhopal disaster of 1984.

interests in developing sentencing policy for financial crime (McBarnet 2013).

Until recently, so-called 'value economics'[9] has characterized a tendency to decouple the idea of social morality from considerations of profit on the basis that the free market and a light-touch regulatory system are for the common good. This philosophy is now largely discredited in favour of the reverse proposition that the morality of economic and business activity should be more aligned to what citizens 'as consumers' value. Whereas value economics recognizes that economic relationships are as integral to good governance as other social relations, a tendency to prioritize individualistic goals over notions of social accountability persists in the sentencing of financial crime. However, the aim of promoting social justice necessitates some accommodation between economic priorities and citizens' pluralistic needs, expectations, and values. I suggest that a change of focus in penal ideology would allow courts to redress this moral imbalance by ensuring that the ideology, structures, and practices of sentencing engage with social morality.

In dealing with financial crime, the sentencing policies of successive UK governments have failed to reflect and keep pace with changing social values as measured against public perceptions of the seriousness of such crimes and the social harm that they cause (see further Chapter 6). There is no evidence of any fundamental change in penal practice being precipitated by the global financial crisis of 2008 to reflect these changed perceptions, so that concepts of participation, accountability, and the overall governance framework for dealing with such crimes remain the same. Failure to ensure effective compliance through the criminal process is facilitated by the narrow retributive focus of penal law and the constraints this imposes on the court's ability to take account of social value when imposing custodial or non-custodial measures. It also acts as a severe limitation on the court's ability to exploit other forms of penal intervention linked to shaming or community reparation.

[9] Economic theories proliferate as to what determines the value attached to the provision of goods and services and the mechanisms that bring this about. The late modern trend towards privatization of the penal estate has focused attention on these debates and prompted much empirical evaluation (see eg Matrix Evidence 2009).

However, I would argue that, by expressing values and moral disapproval through public denunciation and condemnation, sentencing courts have an enormously important role to play in helping to ensure that penalties for financial crime resonate with contemporary social morality; in so doing, strengthening the moral authority of the 'rule of law' and establishing credible penal governance in this area. The advent of longer sentences in individual cases where large-scale market abuse has occurred, as recently exemplified in the case of *R v Tom Hayes*,[10] may herald the beginning of a moral and cultural shift in the fundamental values that govern the daily operations of financial markets and corporations.[11] But this has yet to establish itself as financial orthodoxy, so a similar realignment of penal ideology seems unlikely in the near future.

As for the case itself, in sentencing Hayes to fourteen years imprisonment, the maximum possible under the relevant sentencing guidelines, Cooke J emphasized the defendant's high culpability and the enormous harm caused by his offences to the financial sector and the banking industry as a whole. Evidently, the sentence was intended to be exemplary, signalling the need for greater probity, honesty, and trust within the banking industry. But changing the collective morality that facilitates the commission of such offences may prove problematic.[12] Thus, there is little

[10] The case involved the systematic manipulation of the Libor or interbank lending rate, which determines the cost of borrowing on the international money market.

[11] See *R v Tom Hayes* Southwark Crown Court (3 August 2015), Sentencing Remarks of Mr Justice Cooke https://www.judiciary.gov.uk/wp-content/uploads/2015/08/r-v-tom-hayes-sentencing.pdf, paras 6 and 12 in particular (see *BBC News* 2015b, 2015c). Hayes' sentence was subsequently reduced to 11 years on appeal on the ground that Cooke J had failed to take sufficient account of certain mitigating factors in setting the starting point for determining the sentence (see *R v Tom Hayes* [2015] EWCA Crim 1944). However, the Court of Appeal was otherwise unequivocal in its support for the judge's reasoning, his general approach to determining culpability, and the need for a deterrent sentence (see, in particular, paras 95–99 and 109).

[12] The shelving of plans by the Financial Conduct Authority (FCA) to conduct an inquiry into the culture and behaviour of the UK banking industry may be seen as symptomatic of these difficulties (*BBC News* 2015d). The Banking Standards Board (BSB) established in 2015 to improve the standards and reputation of the banking industry in the wake of the Libor scandal published its first report in 2016 (Banking Standards Board 2016).

sense in which policy-makers are moving towards developing new and more socially relevant notions of individual or collective responsibility and consequential accountability, or broadening the prospects for achieving greater social legitimacy in practical terms, for example, by giving judges more discretion to dispense a wider range of alternative interventions, perhaps combining civil, criminal and restorative measures. In short, despite the advent of CSR, the state has been slow to appreciate changing social values in this area, or in providing an adequate ideological and normative framework for their realization.

On appeal, a key aspect of Hayes' case was that his culpability should have been judged against the background of the pervading culture of dishonesty prevailing within the banking industry at the time. However, the Court of Appeal held that Cooke J had been correct in directing the jury that the standard to be applied was that of reasonable and honest people, not the standard of the market in which the defendant operated (para 24). The defence contended that the judge's direction had precluded the admission of further evidence relating to prevalent market practice under the first limb of *R v Ghosh* [1982] 1 QB 1053, by which the jury must satisfy itself as to the objective standard to be applied in determining dishonesty.[13] This contention was firmly rejected by the Court of Appeal, which emphasized that it had an important role to play in correcting standards of behaviour that deviated from the norms of 'honest and reasonable people' (para 32).

Although juries determine the objective standard to be applied in such cases, decisions do not necessarily equate with contemporary social morality and are constrained by narrowly circumscribed legal and processual norms. Hence, there is no guarantee that sentences for financial crime accurately reflect shared social values, particularly in cases where the 'accepted' boundaries between deviance and crime remain equivocal. The present individualistic focus limits the prospects for admitting evidence of broader social or cultural relevance. Moreover, judges are further precluded from exploiting the potential benefits of alternative or mixed interventions, or involving trial participants and

[13] The second limb in *Ghosh* concerns the defendant's subjective dishonesty, given that the offences alleged are judged to be (objectively) dishonest according to the standards of 'reasonable and honest people'.

representatives from the financial sector or, indeed, the wider community, in their design and implementation.

Changing the ideology that underpins sentencing policy as suggested would provide the necessary normative flexibility for sentencing courts to contribute more effectively to cultural change and a transition of values within the banking industry, and the financial sector more generally. Although demands for individual retribution and deterrence must be satisfied where appropriate, broader notions of collective responsibility and social accountability also need to be addressed by interventions capable of maximizing rehabilitative and restorative prospects (Braithwaite 2002). Encouraging interventions that challenge conventional cultures and practices and engage more effectively with the social reality of financial crime would also satisfy the broader moral imperative of engaging with social values that resonate with offenders, victims, and the wider community, enabling courts to integrate individual and collective interventions more convincingly. Furthermore, as explained in Chapter 6, the direct participation of offenders, victims, and representatives from the financial sector in devising pre-trial programmes and assisting in their implementation should provide a more effective platform for devising solutions that challenge entrenched values than the present system of negotiated settlements or conventional trials.

The proposed ideological and policy changes would result in enhanced discretionary power, giving judges greater freedom to direct the timing, nature, and form of penal intervention, whether restorative or otherwise. This might include combining criminal and civil remedies, or trial-centred penalties with alternative forms of intervention involving institutional reform or community reparation. Safeguarding equality of access and participation for the various participants would also form an intrinsic part of the intervention process. In essence, the nature and extent of penal intervention would be informed by socially relevant values with dependent norms.

Further reform is necessary to integrate individual and corporate forms of penal accountability, encourage more proactive corporate responses to risk and wrongdoing, stimulate a greater engagement with victims and increase transparency. Ensuring that sentencing policy reflects shared values that inform practical interventions is key to changing the culture of responsibility within the banking industry, and in broadening notions of corporate accountability. Such values are much more likely to become embedded through consistent and principled enforcement, thus complementing the formal accountability associated with trial justice. Establishing a framework of shared values that has moral credibility and provides effective accountability for financial deviance is also crucial to the development of corporate governance. Realizing such values within a reconceived sentencing process should strengthen the moral credibility of penalties and bolster the effectiveness of internal compliance regimes within corporates generally.

4

Engaging Sensibilities and the Common Good

Introduction

This chapter discusses two interrelated concerns. It begins by explaining why sentencing should engage more directly and effectively with the emotions and sensibilities of its relevant audiences before considering the broader question of how it might better serve the 'public interest' by contributing more effectively to the 'common good'. Both issues are seen as fundamental to the aim of promoting social justice through sentencing.

Trust and attachment are increasingly important in shaping contemporary morality about punishment and the purposes of sentencing. Whereas Durkheim stressed the collective power of religious morality in fostering social solidarity, such assumptions have long ceased to have universal application in modern industrialized societies. More recently, as the moral credibility of neo-liberal penal policy has declined, so belief in the viability of therapeutic interventions has correspondingly increased. Emotional empathy and engagement are now recognized as having a central role to play in building trust and boosting the moral credibility of penal policy. However, there is little sense of how such an enhanced moral engagement might coalesce around the kind of social values discussed in the BA Report (2014). I have argued that this goal can only be achieved if the ideologies, structures, and practices of sentencing, and criminal justice in general, are committed to realizing such values in a concrete way, so that state values resonate with citizens in their everyday lives. Whilst the emotions influence value judgments, adherence to particular value systems, religious or otherwise, posit additional dimensions of attachment and commitment. Current penal ideology lacks moral credibility because these dimensions are delineated by neo-liberal and retributive imperatives. Accordingly, it fails to promote sentencing contexts that are capable of exploiting the potential of emotional engagement by developing a commitment to shared values.

Understanding how the emotions and sensibilities of citizens relate to institutionalized activities such as sentencing is therefore important in explaining how concepts such as trust and legitimacy are socially constructed, and meanings shared. This is significant in building a complete picture of what values signify and their attachment to the purposes and practice of punishment within different social settings. However, the realization of 'common good' values depends upon their adoption and reflection as shared values through the development of sentencing policy.[1] Crucial to this endeavour is social theory's capacity to explain the importance of attachment and how commitment to such values can influence conduct. The discussion that follows aims to explain why an ideological commitment to shared social values is considered pivotal in encouraging adherence to penal norms and influencing conduct. More specifically, for sentencing policy, this commitment means moving away from neo-liberal values and retribution as the main drivers justifying intervention towards ideological foundations which are more attuned and sensitive to today's rapidly changing moral climate.

Sentencing as Therapy

This section begins by examining the extent to which the emotions and sensibilities of social actors are linked to their perceptions of punishment and sentencing (see Doak 2011; Loader 2011). It then considers whether these factors ought to exert a greater influence in the shaping of penal ideology and, if so, how such a move might influence sentencing policy and practice (Roberts and Hough 2002, 2005; Tyler 2008; Loader 2011).

The role of emotions recently came to the fore in discussions of criminal justice processes as part of the therapeutic jurisprudence

[1] 'Common good' values are not necessarily the same thing as 'shared' values. Values may be shared for reasons that do not benefit the good of all; to further hegemonic ambitions, for example. Common good values are values that benefit all members of society.

movement (Karstedt, Loader, and Strang 2011).[2] One aspect of this is the notion that institutionalized social activities like sentencing can play a constructive role in enhancing the psychological well-being of individuals and, by implication, that of the groups and communities in which they live. This raises philosophical questions about the 'appropriate' role of the emotions in shaping our reaction to wrongdoing, as well as sociological difficulties in terms of theorizing and developing the methodological tools needed to comprehend the links between emotional experience and social action. Both aspects are touched upon here.

A crucial issue in the present context is how the emotions and notions of emotional repair attached to sentencing connect to individual values and norms and, beyond that, to shared values and norms. If emotional experiences are related, either directly or indirectly, to perceptions of what is just and fair, then this is likely to have a significant influence on values and norms governing social interaction, and consequently the degree of social harmony or cohesion within a given society. The key questions in developing sentencing policy are whether, and to what extent, issues of emotional redress and repair are relevant to enhancing the moral credibility of penal governance.

The conventional terrain for exploring these issues is the discourse of restorative justice (see further Rossner 2013). In that context Doak (2011) lists the possible benefits of a greater engagement with the emotions in terms of: account-making, apology (particularly important in relation to shaming), forgiveness (closely linked to apology, but difficult to understand in terms of its emotional significance), and procedural justice. As regards the latter, Doak (2011) argues that the collapse of the public/private divide has focused attention on the role of the emotions in the public sphere, with the emotional impact of the criminal process most evident in the sphere of procedural justice (Tyler 2008). Here, evidence suggests that the perception of processes as fundamentally fair may produce some therapeutic benefits. Hence, it would seem that the capacity of criminal justice processes to deliver therapeutic benefits bears a direct correlation to how fairly victims feel they have been treated, and vice versa.

[2] Problems of definition and understanding how the emotions work are noted by Doak (2011: 441).

Yet one may question whether these presumed benefits are restricted to restorative forms of justice. Doak (2011) proposes three main reasons for presuming such a linkage. First, in helping to rebalance the detriment of victimization; secondly, by public affirmation of the wrong suffered, and, thirdly, by making it easier for victims to accept what might otherwise be unpalatable (Wemmers 1996). However, one might equally argue that these same rationales are, or should be, deployed to characterize 'conventional' forms of trial justice. The current fragmented approach to justice reform tends to hinder prospects for broadening the therapeutic reach of penal interventions beyond restorative forms of justice, so diminishing the governance potential of sentencing policy. Currently, restorative forms of justice are better at account-making, apology, forgiveness, and procedural justice than conventional forms of adversarial resolution. Far from integrating the institutional response, the juxtaposition of top-down adversarial/retributive and bottom-up restorative approaches only serves to highlight differences in justice delivery and polarize already diverse emotional responses, thereby promoting very different perceptions about the morality of the 'justice' the state offers its citizens. Restorative justice is more likely to be driven by emotions that favour reconciliation and social harmony. Hence, retribution and deterrence may be valued equally alongside other justifications for penal intervention within a facilitative ideological context.

The governance point merits further comment. In addition to specific therapeutic benefits for victims, Doak (2011: 450, 451) argues that the emphasis placed upon procedural justice by restorative justice schemes has the potential to reinvigorate democracy by creating new community bonds and strengthening existing ones, and concludes that: '[o]n many measures, [restorative justice] has been shown to outperform the conventional criminal justice process'. Whilst this may (or may not) be true, one might counter that following such a path will not necessarily lead to a more 'democratic' or socially engaged form of criminal justice. Rather, the creation or strengthening of community bonds attributed to restorative justice schemes will do nothing to rectify the present incoherence and fragmentation of justice delivery, nor correct the failure of the criminal justice process as a whole to engage with a broader moral constituency.

Of course, one may argue that criminal justice delivery need not, and should not, be conceived in terms of a dichotomy between adversarial and restorative forms of justice. Indeed, as Doak (2011: 452) points out, some scholars see law itself as a means to communicate a more participatory form of justice for those who have traditionally felt alienated from established legal processes and institutions (Braithwaite 2002; Mathiesen, 1990)—'a dyadic process that facilitates dialogue between community and transgressor', which should allow communities to acknowledge their differences and identify transgressions as disputes among members (Cordella 2006: 201). Sadly, this does not represent the reality of conflict resolution in the late modern world.

Nevertheless, the idea of law as a communicative mechanism has long been recognized (Duff 2001), but its capacity to communicate something having far reaching individual (and social) consequences (such as desistance from crime) is quite another matter, let alone its ability to provide a context for promoting social reform. Accordingly, if restorative justice norms must be contextualized before practice can engage effectively with social reality, so should the norms and practices for penal resolution more generally. So conceived, the emotional engagement of criminal justice interventions ought to derive from a holistic and inclusive penal ideology. All penal processes should be involved in the business of communicating the social values underlying punishment, albeit that the way each institutional mechanism is set up, and how it might go about achieving this overriding goal, differ considerably.

The need for some pre-existing, underlying, and profound emotional connection between the rationale and the type of punishment is borne out historically.[3] Therefore, rather than ignoring the essential linkage between the emotions and social values, we should, as Loader (2011: 355) suggests in his 'Redirection Model',[4] concern ourselves with the moral direction of the

[3] An English example is the gradual but intractable shift away from the excesses of capital punishment prevalent during the era of the Bloody Code to its replacement by transportation for life and penal servitude for all but the most serious offences.

[4] 'The aim is to subject the arbitrary and the irrational to the power of reflection by means of institutional devices that routinely allow voice to, and seek engagement with, the wide range of affects—anger, fear, resentment, disgust, pleasure, but also shame, remorse, pity and compassion—that are aroused or mobilised in social life by problems of crime and punishment' Loader (2011: 356).

emotional response to punishment. If the emotions are the basis of any penal response, the question then is how do we re-engage with them (2011: 356).[5] As argued in the next section, of concern here is the notion that the state's apparent lack of moral authority to punish is in some way attributable to a secularization of morality, and a failure to establish a common moral platform for realizing the social values that should justify punishment.

At the micro-level, emotional reactions to sentencing vary as between individuals and depend upon the degree of personal involvement or attachment to particular events. The exact relationship of these variables to perceptions, attitudes, motivations, and social behaviour is for social psychologists to determine, but it seems reasonable to suggest that a connection between the emotional responses of individuals to sentencing and the value choices that govern their social behaviour does exist (Franklin and Ramamurthy 2006).

Accordingly, the role of the emotions in strengthening bonds of community is likely to be considerable. However, as Cotterrell (2012: 10) points out, 'bonds of community' of varying degrees of stability or fluidity, transience, or permanence, arise from: common or convergent interests, shared beliefs or ultimate values, co-existence in particular cultural or physical environments,[6] or emotional allegiances. Regrettably, the diversity and polarization of moral values characteristic of late modern societies, coupled with increased secularization, may well have increased suspicion of, and alienated, groups and communities (religious and secular) with divergent moralities (Siddiqui 2012).

Sparks (2011: 321) draws attention to Hume's observations concerning the relationship between our feelings about what we experience in our everyday lives and the role these factors play in our reasoning processes and the moral judgments we make. Thus, emotions such as sympathy are important in defining how the interests of others are defined and the extent to which we

[5] See Canton (2015) for further detailed commentary. Coverdale (2014) explores the morally problematic nature of conventional definitions of harm in punishment and how the application of principles drawn from care ethics might be used to secure the more equal treatment of offenders.

[6] This includes racially distinct or ethnic minority communities, multicultural environments, areas of social deprivation and poverty, and areas of social transition.

identify with them. Further, the sharing of experiences helps shape our reactions to processes such as the criminal justice process and contributes to the formation of a collective moral memory that influences determinations of its future social value. Thus, Sparks (2011: 326) observes that emotional predisposition influences strategic decisions about whether or not to engage or reject opportunities for dialogue about such matters as apology or forgiveness that might lead to reconciliation. More broadly, one might reasonably conclude that the accumulated passions aroused by a penal system that discriminates unfairly against certain groups or minorities infuses the collective memory of the oppressed and predisposes them to withdraw and reject the state's moral authority to punish its members.

Moral fragmentation, polarization, and the alienation of communities have had a significant impact on the state's moral authority to punish its citizens, both in terms of identifying a commonly accepted moral discourse about the social value of punishing them and, more specifically, in hindering the reintegration of offenders within society, as McNeill (2013) points out. The important point here is the state's inability to fulfil its moral duty to reintegrate offenders and, more generally, the moral responsibility it shares with all citizens to deal with social injustice, especially circumstances that give rise to offending behaviour. In this sense, the state's moral duty might be discharged more effectively if it were able to encourage empathy between communities about the appropriateness of penal responses and the kinds of interests it is trying to protect.[7]

Notwithstanding, I would argue that the moral obligation to reflect social values should not be judged merely in terms of a state's ability to secure normative compliance with the law (Hough, Farrall, and McNeill 2013). The problem is rather to identify the moral basis for securing compliance: how to identify 'relevant' social values. In other words, decision-makers should think more carefully about the nature of the social bonds that bind communities together and then ensure that the interests of those who have a 'legitimate' stake in society are represented in penal policy (Brooks 2012).

[7] See further Dubber (2006) who defines the sense of justice in terms of empathy as 'the emotional capacity that makes law possible by giving us vicarious access to the experiences of others'.

Hough, Farrall, and McNeill (2013) argue that the state's vision of the positive goods brought by sentencing to support constructive citizenship and the building of community capacity and cohesion must be expanded. Thus, the social value of punishment, and so the costing of penal policy, should be judged by the extent to which it makes a positive contribution to the well being of other members of society. However, top-down evaluations of funding priorities should be based upon a clear identification and understanding of their moral foundations, more especially, how goals of 'constructive citizenship', 'community capacity', and 'well-being' are to be defined, and by whom.

Certainly, building 'social capital' is vital in fulfilling the state's moral duty to promote community cohesion, but an identifiable moral connection is needed between what the state regards as 'social capital' and the measure applied by citizens. Simply extending the reach of criminal justice by justifying interventions on the basis of perceived economic necessity is morally problematic. The building of emotional allegiances between individuals, groups, communities, and the state will only come about where the state is able to nurture a deep inner conviction among its citizens that upholding certain moral values is for the common good of society as a whole. As Loader (2011: 358) suggests: '[f]eelings of collective national belonging and solidarity are ... important cultural prerequisities for creating and constraining the power to police and punish in liberal societies'.

Human rights discourse similarly confirms the need for contextualized understandings of social morality in different governance settings. Legal pluralism and increasing value pluralism within and between states pose a constant challenge to the universality of human rights. Whilst the values that underpin rights may be described as fundamental, rights lack cultural authority unless they engage with the multiplicity of contextual settings and multi-dimensional process relationships that give them meaning (Provost and Sheppard 2012, Douzinas and Gearty 2014). Effective human rights regulation in different social contexts increasingly depends upon the capacity of regulatory bodies to gauge how relevant legal processes can best engage with multiple, overlapping, and often competing, value systems. Cultural shape is given to human rights norms at the intersection between formal and informal sources of law, yet this knowledge alone does not guarantee the effective reconciliation of competing values.

Hence, prior cultural validation is necessary if rights are to be realized in a normative sense.

For human rights protection to become a social reality depends upon some agreement being reached about the basis upon which competing social moralities may be drawn together for the common good. There is an added complexity here, since the values underlying punishment, although possibly rational and justifiable in the abstract, may *not* be constitutive of the common good; unlike human rights values they do not necessarily proclaim the integrity and dignity of all human beings.[8] Yet, the legitimacy attached to both human rights and penal norms depends upon their cultural authority. One might then argue that penal values and human rights values reflect opposite, but closely-related facets of state moral obligation—one is concerned with justifying deprivations of human liberty, whilst the other is concerned with ensuring that such deprivations are not excessive or disproportionate.[9] Nevertheless, both are meaningless in a social sense unless they are able to draw upon common understandings of what punishment and human rights are for. Consequently, penal policies that fail to engage with questions of value and social justice undermine efforts to find a common language and platform for expression and compromise. I argue that the diminishing capacity of the state to define the common good, let alone articulate it effectively, stems from a fundamental failure of moral ideology.

Rights alone cannot be expected to correct the immorality of state punishment, or infuse the criminal justice system with common good values, although they can go some way in changing attitudes, expectations, and future outcomes. As rights need to be socially embedded to be effective, so, ultimately, must the values that sustain the punishment practices of the state. Their

[8] Retributivist and consequentialist aims may contravene individual and social rights, since such aims are not intrinsically constitutive of the common good. The universality of rights derives from our common humanity. Thus, in theory, such rights apply to all citizens in equal measure. So they *are* intrinsically constitutive of the common good.

[9] That the intrinsic nature of the justifications chosen to validate punishment will serve to restrain the practical excesses of eclectic or disproportionate sentencing cannot be guaranteed. Such an outcome depends upon the interests such justifications are deployed to defend, essentially a contextual and empirical question.

interdependence is crucial in sustaining penal legitimacy. State values and rights values cannot operate fairly where conflict and competing interests continually destabilize their relationship.

Public Perceptions of Sentencing

Creating a political or public discourse of empathy relating to justice is problematic where the moralities and motives of minority populations are misrepresented or distorted by the media. The importance of the emotions in creating moral panics and influencing political and judicial responses is well documented, as is the role played by the media in shaping perceptions of what constitutes morally acceptable behaviour (Young 1974; Chibnall 1977; Cohen 1985). Consequently, where the polity has no commonly accepted moral stance upon which to base its penal response to publicly perceived deviance, resort to penal populism may be inevitable (Bottoms 1995; Pratt 2011). Despite such potentially catastrophic implications for social cohesion, the prevailing approach of state penal policy in recent years has been one of limited engagement with the social contexts of emotional intelligence. Rather, it has pursued what Loader (2011: 348) describes as a 'cognitive deficit model', whereby the answer is perceived to lie in supplying the public with increasing amounts of 'robust' information about every conceivable aspect of the criminal justice process in the name of transparency and better regulation. As Loader (2011: 350) points out, this approach is regarded by its proponents as sufficient to counter the distortion of penal policy resulting from the interplay between the government, media, and public opinion (Roberts and Hough 2002, 2011: 10). Loader (2011) rightly criticizes this model on the basis that it incorrectly assumes the prior existence of a rational crime and penal policy and invests the information supplied, and the manner of its delivery, with an unjustifiable presumption of neutrality.

Notwithstanding, other scholars have advocated a more inclusive approach for incorporating public opinion into sentencing. Brooks (2014a), for example, proposes a form of 'stakeholder sentencing', whilst alternative approaches rely on contextualized empirical justifications for penal intervention (Robinson 2013), or direct public participation via mechanisms such as jury sentencing (Dzur 2012), as part of a broader movement to 'democratize' punishment (Roberts and de Keijser 2014).

Yet none of these approaches address Loader's (2011: 358) point concerning the public's need for order and security as, in part, an expression of a desire for solidarity and compassion towards strangers. The challenge lies in giving effect to Loader's conclusion that the state should focus on 'designing democratic systems that acknowledge the legitimacy of how people feel towards matters they care deeply about'. Realizing this aspiration requires more profound thinking about the nature of the values deemed necessary for promoting the common good, and about the role of sentencing policy in realizing this goal. But, before doing so, more effective ways of understanding the role of social morality in sustaining networks and relationships of community need to be developed. It is to this question that I now turn.

Sentencing Policy and the Common Good

I would argue that a system of values which embodies the common good is one that reflects 'core' social values, such as those identified by the BA Report (2014). However, to realize such values for the common good the state must ensure that they are shared between the citizens of different communities. In terms of punishment and sentencing, such values should therefore represent an identifiable and shared morality. Accordingly, the closeness of that connection should be consistently monitored, and taken into account in the formulation of sentencing policy. It has a crucial function in penal governance, as a measure of the extent to which the values promoted by sentencing policy retain moral credibility in the eyes of the majority of citizens. Hence, I suggest that embedding and sharing values within and between communities is more likely where the state takes a positive role in encouraging the development of reciprocal notions of awareness, mutual respect, and responsibility, both individual and collective; notions that have moral credibility and practical relevance. Sentencing policy has a small, but nevertheless important, role to play in achieving this objective.

Unfortunately, as currently conceived, social theory falls short of explaining how the fundamental links that exist between the ideology underpinning sentencing and the outcomes of that process act as normative guides to conduct. Understanding how a shared belief in the value of penal intervention actually translates into socially meaningful (i.e. credible and effective) outcomes in individual cases is vital. Coherence between ideology and practice is key to achieving this objective. In order to highlight the point, I consider the contribution made by Durkheim's notion of moral individualism, elaborated more recently in the BA Report (2014),[10] against the backdrop of recent discussion about social values and punishment by Rowan Williams (Williams 2012a).[11] The discussion explains why I believe it necessary for sentencing policy to be based upon a coherent ideology that enables punishment's social value to be realized in a practical sense.

'Moral individualism' and the common good

There are, I would suggest, important parallels between religious and secular notions of the common good, providing insights that bear directly on sentencing policy's role in promoting social justice. With this in mind, this section draws attention to the religious concept of the common good and, more particularly, how religious values give coherence to its theory and practice. As suggested, the purpose of this exercise is not to advocate religious morality, but to consider how insights provided by religious notions of the common good might inform the debate about the legitimacy of punishment and its relationship to social inequality and social justice. Such insights have received scant attention from criminologists and socio-legal scholars when discussing penal policy.[12]

[10] The BA Report (2014: 70) invokes moral individualism as denoting a system of values that aims to maximize the autonomy and dignity of each individual member of a given society. It suggests an overarching moral system that works against discrimination on any ground. This is more likely to be achieved where there exists a certain level of social integration within society. Moral individualism therefore favours penal practices that foster social inclusion and social solidarity.

[11] See, in particular, ch 21 'Reforming Punishment' in Williams (2012a). See Chaplin (2012) for a critical review of the book itself.

[12] By contrast, with the more recent exception of hate crime, most criminological attention has been devoted to religion and the social bond, as with control theory, or to religious perspectives on the use of the death penalty. However, the connection between religious values and the exercise of political power is well documented (see eg Parry 1986; Smith 2007).

The coherence of religious value systems is crucial to the legitimacy of their theoretical and practical methodology, something noted long ago by sociologists such as Durkheim (2008). In fact, it was an important theme in Durkheim's functionalist theory concerning the significance of the collective sentiments in changing contexts of social solidarity.[13] One might argue further that the religious idea of values derived directly from God is replaced by the secular value of moral individualism in Durkheim's writing.[14] However, equality of treatment is threatened where societies are characterized by competing moralities. Thus, the moral foundations of state governance may be seriously undermined unless public policy is informed by some vision of why and how competing values can be reconciled.

Although empirically incontrovertible, the notion of moral individualism lacks the spiritual dimension of belief necessary for the coherence and practice of religious values. In other words, something more than simply recognizing the social value of humanity is needed to ensure that the laws designed to protect and respect the integrity and freedom of human beings within a given society are socially just. Thus, one might argue that, in a secular world, the possibility of social justice should be based upon a belief system analogous to religious notions of the common good. According to such a belief system, citizens would need to feel that the values they regard as essential prerequisites for the common good are reflected in some way in the ideology and penal practices of the state. To achieve this, the moral foundations of penal policy and practice should derive from a deeper understanding of how individual and shared experiences shape social values, especially those concerned with mutual awareness and collective responsibility. Knowledge regarding the extent to which such profound beliefs are constructed, shared, and reinforced over time should provide the dimension of belief and moral authority necessary to underpin the exercise of state penal power.

[13] See Cotterrell (1999: 53) for further discussion of Durkheim's thinking on the relationship between law and morality.

[14] Moral individualism asserts that the common humanity linking all human beings has a social value. However, social conditions determine the degree to which this value is shared and the extent to which the law respects the autonomous right of all human beings to life and liberty.

The central religious credo of the 'common good'[15] highlights respect for human dignity in maintaining social harmony and working towards social improvement for the benefit of all citizens as core values. An important aspect of this conception is the notion that respect for human dignity and the life and security of the individual are values which intersect one another. For Williams, this intersection highlights the moral responsibility each individual has for the welfare of others. Since discriminatory and oppressive penal policies contravene this moral principle they detract from the social value of punishment and so cannot be regarded as constitutive of the common good.

Religious teachings and practices that foster values of mutual awareness and responsibility for others are more likely to encourage the development of notions of civic identity that cross social and religious divides (see further Lichterman 2012; Siddiqui 2012). It follows that a mutually inclusive conception of the civic identity of the individual is a key factor in promoting the moral and social cohesion of society and, therefore, a morally justifiable penal policy. Williams describes such mutual relations of responsibility in the following terms:

> Responsibility *for* – speaking up for, defending and enriching the lives of others
>
> a Liberal-plus approach – the idea of individuals growing into a better mutual awareness – speaking for each other, but also taking on the task of another's welfare (ibid: 252–253)

Respect for human dignity is also central to Durkheim's sociological conception of moral individualism. As Cotterrell explains:

> The modern value that underlies penal law and punishment is the value of human dignity and the protection of the security of persons and their property (ibid: 79).
>
> Thus the value of individual worth and dignity becomes a social value because it demands respect for all other individuals. It embodies concern for others, not the desire for gratification of the self. It is the value par excellence that can provide a secure basis for flourishing social relations of reciprocity and interdependence (ibid: 112).

[15] The notion of the Common Good forms an important aspect of Catholic moral teaching and methodology (see further, Catholic Bishops' Conference of England and Wales 1996), and has become a focal point for mobilizing contemporary religious concern about social justice; see eg 'Together for the Common Good' http://www.togetherforthecommongood.co.uk.

Hence, the importance of Durkheim's approach lies in his assertion that moral individualism is an expression of social conditions, rather than an intrinsic quality of individual human beings. Durkheim sees moral evolution, and hence the significance attached to moral values such as individualism, as the result of the interplay between social and personal forces. Punishment therefore reflects shared sentiments that the wrongdoer has offended in the particular context of the offence. It also has the wider social function of reinforcing the social value placed upon those shared sentiments by society at large.

As Cotterrell (1999) explains, Durkheim's functionalism leads him to argue that punishment, as crime itself, is morally useful because it encourages adjustment to society's moral code, rather than addressing the moral significance of the offender's conduct. Unfortunately, Durkheim's positivism also prevents him from taking proper account of the subjective experiences and meanings of solidarity and, crucially, of the fact that group relationships may not be organized for the common good.[16] Therefore, beyond alerting us to the fact that legal rights are culturally authorized as an expression of popular morality, Durkheim does not engage with some of the more significant questions concerned with developing a shared morality to promote the common good.

The source of moral values, and how individuals within society should best nurture and develop them for the benefit of all, is, of course, central to the religious credo. The subjective experience of belief is beyond sociological explanation, yet the existence of shared values favouring the common good, and the extent to which such values might actually influence penal policy are matters to which both religious and sociological perspectives can make a significant contribution.

Notions of 'responsibility' and the common good

Developing mutual awareness and reciprocal notions of responsibility, both individual and collective, is at the core of Williams' thinking about the common good, for example:

[16] Cotterrell (1999: 224) develops the point that Durkheim fails to distinguish theoretically, or explain, the connections between the diverse kinds of relationships that characterize different forms of social solidarity—one of the most important being relationships of 'community'.

> So when talking about developing 'appropriate' forms of responsibility this means extending our understanding of a genuinely collective responsibility fully-owned by the state—a properly common moral discourse about crime and punishment—one where the state is committed to penal policies which address the offender's personal conscience and changes their moral compass.
>
> (Williams 2012a: 258–259)

But what might 'extending our understanding of a genuinely collective responsibility fully-owned by the state' entail? What are the 'common good' values that might engender such a sense of responsibility? If regard for the welfare of others is the only value that will make society 'work', in the sense of inducing social harmony, to that extent, one can see the merit of Durkheim's functionalism. Yet, aligning penal policy with what ordinary people regard as justice more generally, or in a particular case, may induce the opposite; it may be a recipe for anarchy unless it promotes the common good.

Thus, one might argue that the 'correct moral balance' in penal policy should be taken to mean whatever it takes to promote the common good. A significant role for sociology here is helping to explain why and how a society comes to define what is 'common' and what is 'good'. Aiming at 'social justice' may well be for the common good, but sociological insights can only seek to explain the normative implications of adopting particular moral values when formulating sentencing policy; what kind of morality should inform those values will always remain a question of belief, and philosophical speculation.

Yet, understanding the normative implications of a particular penal ideology implies an appreciation of what it is that influences and motivates thoughts and actions, and it is in this area that sociological methodology can make a vital contribution in deconstructing the subjective dimensions of human experience. These include social influences on morality, social explanations for moral diversity and the sharing of moral values, the extent to which social morality influences understandings and experiences of the penal system, and how such experiences influence the moral value attached to punishment within particular social environments.

The common good of social values in penal policy

The problem of how one might reflect social values for the common good in penal policy remains a major challenge. Williams

(2012a: 2–3) argues against what he calls programmatic secularism, as in the French model, on the grounds that it represents a potentially dangerous form of 'exclusive public orthodoxy'. A counter argument might be that it does at least provide a template that sketches out the moral relationship between citizen and state. If this template has a moral mandate, in the sense that it reflects shared values for the common good, then, in theory at least, it should engender the formulation of principles for a secularized version of the common good in the administration of justice. Arguably, this is preferable to the moral uncertainty of competing values characteristic of neo-liberal western democracies, where disagreement invariably persists about the limits of the state's moral authority to penalize populations who are consistently oppressed by policies of social exclusion (see Howard 2013).[17]

Danger also lies in the juxtaposition of individualistic or secular values against vaguely defined values favouring moral diversity and pluralism. This is not to favour programmatic secularism. Rather it suggests that the social instability that may result from a lack of agreement about which values are for the common good is equally dangerous. Something more than mere functional necessity is needed to bridge the gap and regulate tensions between the individualistic morality of globalization and those who believe in promoting common good values within the confines of the 'nation state'.

As Sandel (2010) suggests, a debate about which values are for the common good is long overdue. This should precede the formulation of policy and the establishment of institutional structures to carry it into effect. Penal policy should be underpinned by a morality that aims to draw the individual and the state together; one where the moral values validating punishment are seen by the majority of citizens as existing for the common good. If such a course is deemed desirable, the next question to explore is the extent to which social values for the common good might be identified.[18]

[17] The English courts often appear to obfuscate important moral issues; for example, the suspended sentences imposed on four Muslim girls at Leicester Crown Court in 2011 (see further Pitt 2011).

[18] Empirically the task is complex due to the overlapping nature of the social networks and relationships that exist within and between diverse 'communities'.

Identifying social values for the common good

Certain courses of action may militate against the adoption of values favouring the common good.[19] A useful illustration is the relentless privatization of criminal justice driven by expectations of the 'market state'. As Williams (2002) argues, it must always be for the common good that key functions affecting human life and liberty should remain in state control. Another contemporary example is the unjustified infliction of harsh punishment, exemplified by increased penal severity as a response to low-level offending. Rather, one might argue that the common good lies beyond the moral confines of retributive justice. It involves raising the awareness of citizens and communities alike to their shared responsibility for each other's welfare. This includes a sharing of responsibility for crime problems and how to deal with them.

Identifying which values should inform a more parsimonious approach to sentencing forms a core theme of the BA Report (2014) discussed earlier. In particular, the Report confirms the need for a practical, but above all, meaningful engagement with social value at the point of sentencing. Whilst greater engagement with the emotions and sensibilities of trial participants may be important for developing trust and credibility in the process itself, this is inconsequential unless the values that are being pursued have wider moral credibility.

This debate has heightened significance given the proposed widespread adoption of restorative values and practices within criminal justice and the professed cathartic value of engaging with the emotions and sensibilities of victims and offenders (Karstedt, Loader, and Strang 2011). Focusing on the extent to which procedures, rules, and processes engage with the emotions has become a primary measure of the legitimacy of criminal justice, as well as many other key governance functions of the late modern state (Tyler 2006; Jackson and others 2015). However, measures of 'procedural justice' largely ignore questions of social value,[20] particularly how procedural experiences and outcomes

[19] For Weber (1971: 217) the progressive alienation of religious ethics was an inevitable consequence of the patterns of relationship and economic rationalizations demanded by the pursuit of capitalism.

[20] The only ideals considered by Weber as a sufficient ideological foundation for law were the consistent patterns of values to be derived from the various forms of natural law, including different religious influences. However, such considerations

contribute to the common good. Such questions are not answered by simply focusing on the cathartic impact of criminal justice, or the emotional responses of individuals. These factors, and similar associated measures of institutional performance, are easily manipulated for pragmatic or opportunistic political purposes.

Penal practices and procedures should be evaluated within their relevant social contexts before conclusions are reached as to whether or not they are for the common good.[21] A crucial factor in sustaining the legitimacy of punishment is that citizens believe in its social value, so that any changes in the moral authority this confers on penal policy are taken into account (Henham 2012). As with religious values, belief in the moral virtue of punishment is in essence a question of faith, the 'truth' of which may, or may not, have empirical justification.

Community justice and the common good

Policies that devolve responsibility for crime to communities may be viewed as an abdication by the state of its moral obligation to ensure that the values underpinning punishment are consistently enforced for the common good of society. The state's continued emphasis on 'empowering' the victims of crime, and the apparently ad hoc creation of pre, out-of-court, and other diversionary mechanisms, may conceal the disturbing fact that the rationale underpinning the state's actions lacks either empirical justification or moral credibility, or both. In such circumstances there is little sense in which the policy of decentralization to communities can be viewed as part of a coherent and morally justifiable strategy for promoting the common good. Rather, the state's moral terrain is effectively vacated in favour of what is claimed to be the more representative and therefore appropriate alternative of community resolution.[22]

were eclipsed by the need to rationalize formal law to meet the demands of the modern capitalist state, resulting in increased bureaucratization and legal domination of the politics and economics of 'justice' (see Cotterrell 1995: 157).

[21] An important example is the gradual development of restorative justice practices for young offenders in Northern Ireland (see O'Mahony and Doak 2007).

[22] This issue may be subsumed within a much larger political debate about devolution (see eg IPPR North 2014).

The problem with this notion is that the moral vacuum left by decentralization is not necessarily filled satisfactorily at the community level. Where the state's moral mandate is lacking, the void may simply be replaced by conflicting local moralities. Thus, instead of a local moral consensus being forged, vested and powerful interests may attempt to secure their own advantage, leaving the disempowered increasingly alienated and frustrated. More broadly, moral credibility in the body politic is likely to diminish unless localism forms part of an inclusive social agenda aimed at restoring trust and credibility in democratic institutions. Ultimately, the absence of any convincing moral mandate for decentralization may prove socially divisive, undemocratic, and as having the potential for damaging community cohesion. To that extent it may be counterproductive of the common good.

Vested interests and the morality of the market tend to predominate in such situations. Furthermore, as Weber (1954) suggests, the legal rationality of the market place changes incrementally, helping to entrench the bureaucratic and administrative machinery needed to facilitate partial decision-making processes at the local level. Such processes may conceal corruption, perpetuating practices that pay lip service to the interests of those whose moral values differ from those of vested concerns, and who have no intention whatsoever in allowing such views to hold sway.[23] Hence, the legitimate interests of ordinary citizens may be ignored but, worse still, policies that exacerbate prejudice, exclusion, and social injustice at the community level may increase. Consequently, the moral divisions created by policies of decentralization may be reflected back towards the centre, so compounding the moral bankruptcy of state policy.

Such consequences raise difficult questions concerning the moral authority of state law and, more particularly, the source of that authority. Williams' (2012a: 252) relational view of personhood suggests that the state has a duty to promote policies which maximize the human potential of all individuals. In the context of late modern value pluralism, this implies the provision of structures and mechanisms to facilitate the exchange of opinions and beliefs derived from diverse and possibly competing value

[23] 'All politics is oriented to the material facts of the dominant interest of the state, to realism, and to the autonomous end of maintaining the external and internal distribution of power' (Weber 1954: 235).

systems, as is consistent with Williams' notions of interactive pluralism and procedural secularism (2012a: 2, 3). The public platform that Williams envisages is therefore one that prioritizes notions of freedom and responsibility in terms of the intersecting relationships of human beings, so that the role of the state may be seen as one that encourages the healing of conflict and brings communities together:

> The law of the state is what provides the stable climate for all first-level communities to flourish and the means for settling and enforcing 'boundary disputes' between them (ibid: 50).

Williams implies that in promoting community justice the state should 'engender in the offender a sense of believing that he or she is the object of someone's responsibility' and so increase the offender's belief that they have a stake in society (2012a: 256). However, Williams criticizes the localism and decentralization of government policy for failing to promote a clear vision of what this might mean in terms of the common good (2012a: 272). Notwithstanding, Chaplin (2012) takes Williams to task for not providing a more convincing account of the state's role in realizing this vision, suggesting that notions of 'adjudication' and 'justice' need to be directed to 'doing justice to the particular normative designs of the plural communities of society' (Williams 2012a: 13, 14).

Williams' argument suggests that the kind of managerial or administrative tendencies identified by Weber can only be countered effectively if the state takes the reality of human diversity and the three-dimensional character of other human beings more seriously. Hence, the state should promote a shared vision of what constitutes the common good, particularly since so many human activities require cooperation. Localism in criminal justice will not of itself deliver 'the right kind of balance between statutory provision and local initiative' without first identifying 'public interest' values (Williams 2012b). Pushing back the dependency culture and centralized state provision is an important step towards establishing a mutual taking of responsibility and mutual recognition of the three-dimensional character of human existence at the local level.

Yet, without a priori religious morality, we are left with a secular moral plurality that lacks the common attachment and commitment of the former. The moral autonomy that Durkheim identified as essential to escape the constraints of religious morality looses its creative potential when there is nothing to replace it but an uncertain struggle between the individual and society. Thus, social interaction as a source of moral values replaces the religious moral discourse. This breaks free from the discipline and constraints of religious morality but, at the same time, replaces it with a contingent morality that fails to recognize the relational dimensions of personhood identified by Williams.

The contingency and content of moral values may be driven by powerful vested interests and so produce social injustice rather than a morality of respect for the welfare of others. Suspending for one moment a belief in God's creation, one might argue that Williams' theology otherwise identifies accurately core aspects of the human condition that help to expand Durkheim's functional and, ultimately, incomplete account of the human experience of social interaction. This is Williams' notion of the unconditional interdependence of human existence; that one only exists as a person through the subjective experience of our intersecting relationships with others. The task of sociology is surely that of explaining the phenomenology of these intersecting relationships from the perspective of the self and others. For a shared morality in a secular world, such a phenomenology might reveal that the meanings human beings attach to the relationships and interactions that determine their social identity bear a close relationship to Williams' account of the contingencies that shape our identity as human beings. Ultimately, common understandings based upon shared experiences shape social morality. This determines how state values are perceived, and the value attached to the policies and practices the state adopts to realize them.

The courts and the common good

The discussion so far has highlighted the contingent nature of the 'common good' and the difficulties of providing moral or empirical support for its reflection in sentencing. The resolution of this problem has become more urgent in the face of increasing secularization and the impact of moral diversity on the perceived legitimacy of sentencing decisions.

The value pluralism of contemporary English society means that judges can no longer mediate between church and state as custodians of a 'public' morality. Rather, they must tread a difficult path, showing no favour towards any particular religious (or political) doctrine, nor seeking to define the moral limits of the law they apply, but ensuring that equal respect is accorded to religious and other philosophies that are 'worthy of respect in a democratic society' and otherwise not incompatible with human dignity.[24]

Notwithstanding, whilst this is not the place to explore the nuances of legal expression, assertions that the courts are properly equipped to act as *impartial* moral arbiters on behalf of the state raise concerns. In a recent lecture, Sir James Munby stated that:

> The court recognises no religious distinctions and, generally speaking, passes no judgement on religious beliefs *or on the tenets, doctrines or rules of any particular section of society*. All are entitled to equal respect, so long as they are 'legally and socially acceptable' and not 'immoral or socially obnoxious' or 'pernicious' (Munby 2013) (emphasis added).

A difficulty with this assertion is that it sets forth an untenable aspiration, and possibly a naive one, in suggesting, first, that the judges themselves are capable of such impartiality,[25] and, secondly, and perhaps more importantly, that the courts inhabit some kind of moral vacuum—what meaning, for example, should be attached to words such as 'socially acceptable, immoral, socially obnoxious, or pernicious'? The answers to these questions remain contested. Although legal positivists may posit law's intrinsic integrity, others argue strongly that law, and the courts and judges who apply it, are very much part of the moral world, in the sense that legal systems reflect particular moral values that vary according to time and place.[26]

It is difficult to argue convincingly that judges are able to 'suspend' completely the partiality of their attitudes, feelings, and emotional responses when deciding individual cases, particularly when the norms and institutional framework for their delivery are shaped by a specific penal ideology. Rather, it is often argued that judges adopt a particular frame of mind, or 'judicial' approach,

[24] See Article 9 of the ECHR and *Campbell and Cosans v United Kingdom (No 2)* Application No 75 No 751/76 (1982) 4 EHRR 293. The nature of the relationship between law and morality continues to be a subject of fierce debate in legal theory. See Lacey (2008b) for a recent evaluation.

[25] See Hutton (2006) for an insightful analysis.

[26] See Cotterrell (2003) for a useful overview, and further Cotterrell (2008) for arguments supporting the sociological analysis of law and its functions.

that aims to neutralize the inevitable influences of social background and possible bias. Of course, extending judicial discretionary power also facilitates the kind of 'creative' decision-making designed to frustrate the intentions of state penal policy, so indirectly undermining its core values. However, this may be deemed a positive attribute, since discretionary power can be deployed effectively as a protective device to defend human rights and hinder the oppression of disadvantaged minorities.

That being so, one might argue further that the 'unjustified' statutory control of sentencing through various forms of regulation or 'guidance' may work against the common good. However, this argument only holds where there is no reason to question the partiality of the judiciary. Such an assumption is problematic in cases where the sentencing norms judges and magistrates have to apply are called into question, as occurred in the immediate aftermath of the English riots of 2011. I suggest that courts are more likely to have the moral authority to use sentencing discretion for the common good where penal policy and practice are based on a coherent framework of shared values.

Taking account of how the policy framing the law and ethics of sentencing is influenced by moral ideology is therefore crucial to the legitimacy of trial justice (Henham 2012). The judgments reached by judges *do* reflect a particular moral position: that of the values that have informed the making and content of the law, and the penalties that Parliament has decreed should follow if citizens break that law. This morality then influences the normative reach of the sentences judges pass, and so may reinforce, either negatively or positively, the moral climate within which the law and the criminal process sits.

Thus, the courts address moral questions in the light of categories established by Parliament or regulatory bodies, such as the Sentencing Council, or they may be forced to create new categories, or reinterpret old ones,[27] to deal with novel social and moral contingencies.[28] The difficulty faced by judges is therefore to reach beyond the moral parameters set by existing penal ideology

[27] Such was the guiding principle of the liberal reforming judge, Lord Denning (1979).

[28] A difficulty faced by the sentencing courts in the aftermath of the English riots of 2011.

to engage with everyday social morality in all its diverse forms, be it religious or secular.

Where the morality in question is that of individuals or communities that have suffered social injustice as a result of state policies the question that arises is not so much whether judges can act impartially in 'balancing' competing moral demands within the parameters set by law. Rather, it is how to design a more egalitarian penal system that gives greater weight to shared values, so that sentencing policy addresses the common good, irrespective of whether that good has religious or secular origins.

To this end, one might argue that building social capital to give excluded or oppressed individuals and communities a greater stake in society is morally equivalent to the religious imperative of 'giving back to God what God created in you' through your thoughts and actions. The religious morality of the common good is staked in God's creation, whereas the secular morality of greater social justice is staked in a similar quest to respect the human dignity of all citizens. In this, the courts, and judges in particular, have a crucial role to play.

Conclusion and Implications

The unconditional nature of faith or religious belief implies that that there will be occasions when the extent of that belief is tested to the full. The circumstances provoking any such test, the form of the religious response and that of the individual concerned, will all vary according to time and place. Unless the events in question provoke an abandonment of belief, the religious individual must rationalize what has occurred in terms of a particular value system. Fortunately, where values for the common good are challenged by events, the religious citizen is already equipped with a set of moral prescriptions. Furthermore, contemporary religious teaching is committed in its response to the injustices of oppression and social injustice.[29]

Nevertheless, for many, the moral certainty of religious values has been eroded or suspended, and, for the majority of citizens, despite a concerted evangelical mission, the morality of a

[29] See eg the Catholic Church's Social Teaching (1996: para 73).

life governed by religious orthodoxy has all but disappeared.[30] Therefore, when tested, most citizens fall back on a plurality of disparate values to inform their thoughts and actions, drawn from a vast array of social, cultural, and spiritual influences and experiences. These values may, or may not, engage with those of the state and its penal policies, or those of other citizens, and possibly bear little relationship to what the tenets of religious or secular thinkers conceive as common good values. Thus, it is not surprising that this lack of connection between the values espoused by the state and those of citizens is increasingly mirrored in criminal justice and penal policy (Henham 2012: ch 1).

Criminologists, in common with religious commentators, have long recognized the normative implications of competing value systems and the shortcomings of 'democratic' processes in addressing social injustice (see Tonry 2011). Loader and Sparks (2011: 122), for example, acknowledge that there is a need for much greater involvement in politics and public life on the part of criminologists, more particularly to influence the policy-making process. Furthermore, philosophers such as Wolff (2002) argue that public policy can only effectively address issues of social inequality by first identifying and defining what 'injustice' means within a given society, again emphasizing the need for contextualized understandings of value.[31]

Religious, philosophical, and social thinkers have therefore come to recognize that greater knowledge about the social contexts of morality and its normative implications is crucial in developing socially just public policies for the late modern state. Whether or not such values are for the common good remain philosophical and religious questions. However, social theory can prompt unique insights for understanding how individual and shared experiences shape feelings, emotions, and beliefs about the value of punishment. I have argued that these understandings should ultimately determine what is defined as the 'common good'. Such knowledge is vital for informing criminal justice policy and mediating between competing values, particularly in societies characterized by overlapping networks and relationships of community.

[30] As have the moral certainties of the paternalistic state (Loader 2006).

[31] This view reflects Sen's concern with human capability as a measure of value to enable public policy to deal more effectively with structural inequality.

Since religious conceptions of the common good and the coherence of the value systems they offer have little resonance for the majority of citizens in contemporary democracies, states are unlikely to adopt them as foundations for penal ideology and policy.[32] Furthermore, Durkheim's account of social solidarity falls short of providing a credible alternative explanation of the origins and content of social morality and takes no account of how values are shaped by social experiences.[33]Whereas moral individualism retains importance as a unifying thread, it has no tangible existence in the real world. The extent to which citizens actually share values of respect for human dignity is seen predominantly as a function of social conditions.

Notwithstanding, there is some merit in exploring further Durkheim's notion of moral individualism, particularly the suggestion that its social significance depends upon the way individuals reflect upon their conditions of existence. In this sense, therefore, the degree to which values of respect for the humanity of others are shared may be viewed as a function of social experience. However, a crucial gap in our understanding concerns the way in which experiences of criminal justice, and sentencing in particular, shape individual and shared perceptions within particular social contexts.

Yet the problem of identifying a particular system of penal values that embodies the 'common good' remains. One answer might be to develop or modify certain religious approaches,[34] but drawing together and reconciling the insights and values of different religious systems is hugely problematic and not feasible. A more realistic alternative is to develop principles from universally recognized 'core' values, as does the BA Report (2014). However, as argued, such values need to be sufficiently grounded in social contexts. Pre-determined evaluations of social value, citizenship, or other 'objective' criteria by which to measure social morality

[32] Notwithstanding that the content of religious moral values may be replicated as secular values.

[33] Durkheim's account would, in any event, need further refinement to make it relevant for explaining the phenomenon of social solidarity in the era of late modernity.

[34] A compromise position might be to adopt a belief system along the lines of Comte's religion of humanity (see further Wernick 2001).

should be rejected as self-serving in terms of explaining the relationship between subjective experience and perception.[35]

Further developments in social theory and methodology are required if policy-makers are to understand how values are socially constructed and shared—more particularly, what makes it socially acceptable and morally desirable for certain values such as those associated with moral individualism to flourish, and which social conditions might maximize values identified as common good values. Such knowledge would then provide the basis for promoting a coherent vision of the common good—one that reflects the social reality of shared values.

[35] Furthermore, conceptions of legal individualism do not necessarily accord with those of moral individualism (Ramsey 2006).

5

Bridging the Gap between Political and Penal Legitimacy

Introduction

Penal policy in the late modern era has been acutely affected by the rapidly changing relationship between politics and economics, a phenomenon that has increasingly shaped the morality of criminal justice (Bauman 2000: 2013). Thus, one may argue that the social impact of sentencing has been evaluated primarily against criteria that reflect economically driven politicized judgments, rather than values reflecting some clearly defined moral consensus about the role of punishment. It may be argued further that the exigencies of political realism have narrowed the moral case for penal intervention to one that tends to enhance social exclusion, the major concern being to promote a populist agenda and a pragmatic morality designed to placate those whose support is deemed necessary in order to gain electoral advantage. An additional complication is that global economic forces and market driven forms of transnational crime pay little attention to the penal policies of individual nation states, or their social priorities.

So conceived, the political morality of criminal justice has become the morality of economic determinism rather than social justice, a political survival strategy where the social value of punishment is judged against measures of satisfaction that fall far short of any 'real' engagement with social reality. Rather, penal policy seemingly reacts to the perceived demands of a deeply mistrusting citizenry, whilst in reality prioritizing powerful national and globalized economic interests. Hence, according to this view, public policy delivers what is determined economically, but judged politically, as the bare minimum necessary to appease the increasingly disenfranchised poor and socially excluded, whilst

Sentencing Policy and Social Justice. First Edition. Ralph Henham. © Ralph Henham 2018. Published 2018 by Oxford University Press.

effectively assuaging the moral sentiments of the remaining population.

More recently, scholars such as Cavadino and Dignan (2006) and Lacey (2008a) have provided a salient additional perspective, by explaining how differences between nation states in the degree to which the management of crime depends upon the political economy vary according to a wide range of cultural, macroeconomic, and institutional factors, especially the nature of the democratic process.[1] Developing a deeper understanding of why these differences exist, and the role they play in shaping the cultural and political climate of penal policy within states, can provoke useful insights into the kinds of political and institutional reforms that might be necessary to minimize harsh and discriminatory penal policies, so achieving a greater measure of social justice.

This chapter probes the veracity of this proposition and the implications for sentencing policy of developing a deeper understanding of the relationship between the political economy and penal legitimacy in England and Wales. In particular, it examines Lacey's (2008a) contention that communitarian justice requires the adoption of a conception of 'consistent pluralism' through which the values each society places on the goods in question are given equal prominence in criminal justice practice, so that fundamental community values and interests are consistently reinforced.

Evidently, the practical realization of this imperative through sentencing depends upon its capacity to reflect pluralistic conceptions of the good in a non-partisan fashion. An important aspect of this is the nature and quality of the 'truth' about the social reality of crime that sentencing relies on, and its public perception. I argue that the capacity of sentencing policy to engage with this social reality in a meaningful way necessitates a recasting of penal ideology. To achieve this entails something more than institutional reform, or a greater engagement by policy-makers with the cultural and political determinants of crime and its penalization. Rather, it requires a profound understanding of the value citizens attach to sentencing and its outcomes, and what this actually signifies in terms of their everyday social experience. The

[1] See also Lacey and Pickard (2015a) for a contextualized approach to understanding the social construction and meaning of proportionality.

greatest challenge then lies in establishing coherent links between penal ideology and practice to encourage forms of sentencing that are sensitive to changes in social value.

To illustrate these issues in the domestic context, the chapter concludes by explaining how the ongoing tensions between neo-liberal retributive ideology and utilitarian values continue to define the approach taken by the courts of England and Wales to the sentencing of women. This tendency works against developing a socially relevant policy commitment to a 'consistent pluralism'; rather, it encourages sentencing outcomes that exacerbate the social exclusion of women and reinforce existing divisions in social morality.

The Legitimacy of Sentencing and the Political Economy

I begin by posing a number of questions about the relationship between the political economy and sentencing policy that are considered central to the project of enhancing the legitimacy of sentencing. The notion of moral attachment is significant in this context, not simply because it refers in an abstract sense to some form of identifiable common bond or agreement between citizens and the state about the moral value of punishment, but, more importantly, because the 'validity' of that evaluation requires social context to give it meaning.

How does the notion of a 'consistent pluralism' relate to sentencing policy?

In the individualistic world of late modern neo-liberal politics, penal ideology is likely to be driven by market forces that pay little heed to the social consequences of policy (Cavadino and Dignan 2006). Indeed, as Cavadino (2013a) suggests, neo-liberal retributive policies may determine economic legitimacy, a view that differs sharply from the economic determinism of Marxist theorists such as Rusche and Kircheimer (1939).

The communitarianism of conservative corporatist states such as Germany, or the egalitarianism of social democratic nations such as Norway, is informed by different cultural and ideological factors. However, as discussed in Chapter 3, this assumption provides insufficient justification for supposing that the legitimacy of penal policy in England and Wales could be increased simply by adopting or modifying more communitarian approaches for dealing with offenders that have succeeded elsewhere. Hence, Lacey (2008a: 205) argues that institutional reforms alone are unlikely to produce the desired cultural shift. Rather, a fundamental reappraisal of how the state can better fulfil democratic ideals is a necessary precursor to reform, informed by a deeper understanding of the cultural and macro-economic conditions of existence for citizens.

Yet the moral value of the ends law seeks to achieve through neo-liberal policies continues to remain elusive in the face of the increasing 'moral blindness' of late modern penal ideology (Bauman 2013), and the absence of any practically realistic means for citizens to achieve common goals except through direct intervention. Furthermore, it is unclear how the notion of 'consistent pluralism' relates to criminal justice practice without a better understanding of social values, and, more controversially, how the latter are to be identified and explained where law is implicated in their social construction (Lacey 2008a).[2]

There are a number of complex interrelated issues here. First, as discussed in the previous chapter, it is by no means clear how values for the common good might be identified within a morally pluralistic society, state, or community, and who should have the responsibility for producing an impartial assessment of what they are. Secondly, greater clarification is needed of what might amount to a 'convincing account' or the 'truth' of the social reality one seeks to identify. Thirdly, where law is central, as in sentencing, how one conceives of the relationship between law and morality needs to be made absolutely clear; more specifically, is law to be conceptualized in positivist terms as having its own intrinsic moral validity, or, within the natural law tradition, as a collection of norms whose moral value depends upon their social context (Lacey 2008a). Finally, and perhaps the most difficult question is how to ensure that social values identified as 'common good' values are given equal prominence in criminal justice practice.

A popular approach to the first question of identifying values for the common good is to focus on the idea of reducing

[2] See Lacey (2012) for a valuable discussion of 'neo-liberalism' in the context of punishment.

disadvantage and valuing those actions which might have that effect (see Kaufman 2014). The implications are that, rather than adopting the 'top down' categorizations of administrative criminology, penal policy should become more integrated with other social interventionist strategies in promoting crime prevention and rehabilitation.[3] Indeed, similar notions are explored in recent philosophical discourse.

Wolff and de-Shalit (2007), for example, favour a pluralist account of well-being, arguing that to identify the least advantaged in society is less problematic if the state focuses on how to 'decluster disadvantage' within social groups rather than adopting reductionist top-down categorizations of poverty or social disadvantage to inform policy. Hence, identifying and tackling clusterings of social disadvantage, so-called 'corrosive disadvantages', for example, the multiple victimization of women in poorer areas, is the key to preventing the further disadvantage. This is achievable by encouraging 'fertile functionings'; in other words, functionings that reduce risk and enhance security because they are more likely to enhance equality.

From a sociological perspective, social theory and methodology is key to identifying and explaining the social significance of so-called 'fertile functionings'. Indeed, one may view this as a primary task for any social theory that seeks to fully comprehend the relationship been social factors and criminality. Whilst the resulting conclusions might inform policy and so help the state to discharge its moral obligation of promoting equality and reducing social disadvantage, conventional approaches do not suggest non-partisan methodologies that might help to promote policies for 'declustering disadvantage'. Hence, I would propose a more socially interventionist stance for theory in these circumstances, one aimed at extending its capacity for explaining why and how 'fertile functionings' might work in particular social contexts.

This suggestion does not seek to narrow the scope for state intervention. On the contrary, it would offer policy-makers a more detailed understanding of those factors that shape social morality within clusters of social disadvantage; a sentencing

[3] These may, or may not, be community-based. The now closed North Liverpool Community Justice Centre, which opened in 2005 with a view to offering a more holistic and therapeutic solution to address the kinds of problems afflicting many women offenders, is a case in point (see post).

policy that engages with social justice. What it cannot do, however, is provide the state with reasons for choosing between areas where disadvantages cluster. I would argue strongly against the idea that moral choices *emerge* from any external assessment or prioritization of what the social priorities or capabilities of disadvantaged populations are presumed to be.[4]

The problem with all such approaches for prioritizing values is, and always has been (Box 1983), how to obtain impartial accounts of which values are for the common good where this 'truth' may be manipulated by the ruling elite (Quinney 1980: 17). Accepting that the state has a fundamental moral obligation to promote the welfare of its citizens at least implies that policy-makers must do their utmost in a practical sense to ensure that ideology and policy are consistently aligned with values shared by the majority of citizens.

Therefore, although rights may be necessary to ensure that social values are given equal prominence in criminal justice practice, as credible moral injunctions, rights can only inform practice to the extent that they relate to what citizens *actually* value. As argued in Chapter 7, giving practical shape to the values that inform sentencing in England and Wales should become part of a wider remit for the Sentencing Council. However, this presupposes that the argument for reflecting social values in sentencing is accepted. No amount of sociological theorizing or philosophical debate can induce that decision. The morality underpinning sentencing policy can only strive to keep pace with the value citizens and communities attach to sentencing practice, howsoever expressed. That is an empirical question.

Can sentencing policy give equal prominence to pluralistic conceptions of the good?

In this context, one might begin by reflecting upon Weber's (1958) ideas concerning law's rationality, especially its implications for establishing a truly pluralistic system of criminal justice.

[4] The globalization of economic value systems and the morality that underpins the global regulation of risk management strategies by financial institutions under the Equator Principles also illustrates key concerns in the relationship between the political economy and law (see further Sobel-Read 2014; Worsdorfer 2014).

Law per se does not have a rationality that allows *it* to distinguish between what may, or may not, be for the common good (see further Perez 2003).

Weber argues that law tends to develop its own rationality and so generates values that are inherently legal in their source, nature, and moral authority. As such, one might expect that the inherent morality law develops from within as an independent functioning system of rules and procedures is for the common good where law emanates from a fully-fledged democratic process. However, that proposition does not represent social reality, particularly where penal law is manipulated by powerful elites for hegemonic purposes (Hudson 1993).

Seen in this light, law, as a moral system, appears inherently exclusory. Furthermore, law's rationality tends to serve this purpose. This would certainly be true if law were simply to remain a body of rules, but, evidently, that it not the case. Rather, as Fuller (1969) argues, law engages with a social world that determines its moral credibility, and thus, its moral authority. Where moral pluralism increases there is a corresponding tendency for law's rationality to become embedded, so enhancing and entrenching existing moral and social divisions rather than engaging with them, unless contrary values are somehow injected into penal policy and its normative framework.

For Luhmann (2013), however, law's rationality ensures its survival as a closed system of rules and is reflected in the processes of sentence decision-making. Thus, the self-fulfilling nature of law and legal processes in complex industrial societies is actually accentuated because law itself excludes the threat posed by competing normative systems. Law is seen as actually creating the conditions for securing its own legitimacy in that the influence of human agency is minimized by the way in which legal systems prioritize communication inputs (see further Wandall 2008).

Weber's more instrumental view of the relationship between law and society recognizes its key role in providing the stable conditions necessary for political and economic advancement. Hence, although Weber believes in the systemization of rules and procedures, he acknowledges the fact that forms of legal domination require empirical justification. However, Weber does not see rules as requiring moral validation by citizens, but rather as an inevitable consequence of the exponential growth in regulation and bureaucratization arising from the economic and political complexities of advanced capitalist societies. Moral certainty comes through the prosperity of the regulated market and the economic growth of capitalism,[5] not through any kind of moral consensus or collective sentiments of the kind described by Durkheim.

Yet, despite Weber's (1958) ambivalence about the source of law's moral authority, unlike Luhmann, he does at least acknowledge the transitory nature of law's authority and the need for its rationality to respond to the social forces that threaten the economic and political stability of the state (see further Spencer 1970). Thus, the entrenchment of legal formalism is tempered by social change and the capacity of law and legal processes to resist those challenges to the state's power that threaten existing forms of authority. As Blau (1963) suggests, the likelihood of retaining a particular type of authority may depend upon the ability of that authority system to retain the traits that make it unique and reject the traits that make it more conducive to another authority type.

Whilst moral contingencies such as 'justice' or 'fairness' sit uneasily with the rationales that underpin economic legitimacy, modern commentators now recognize that the capacity of the state to successfully manage economic growth depends upon its ability to engage with social values and norms and to develop ways of understanding the meanings individuals and groups attach to their everyday experiences and behaviours. However, as Habermas (1998) confirms, the rationality of consensus formation and its true reflection in law is crucially dependent upon the political relationship between law and democracy, since this determines the extent to which communicative rationality can find true expression through law.[6]

Paradoxically, the onset of human rights discourse and its increasing influence over penal law and practice has materially affected the state's power to control the rationality of law and its

[5] However, it cannot be assumed that such a morality will be reflected empirically.

[6] The concepts of 'deliberative space' and 'communicative rationality' are useful in drawing our attention to the fact that the rationalities of relational justice cannot simply be superimposed or otherwise transplanted into predominantly retributive penal ideologies if they are to develop successfully.

development.[7] Coincidentally, the late modern state's diminished moral authority has hindered its capacity to engage with value pluralism and its impact on the perceived morality of penal law. These combined pressures on legal dominion and the rule of law have gradually weakened the state's ability to rationalize penal norms in terms of their social impact. What policy-makers now perceive as legitimate social purposes for penal law can no longer necessarily be rationalized as common social goods.

Does sentencing policy currently take account of social value?

The politicization of penal policy determines the social value of punishment and imbues it with a morality that may bear little resemblance to intuitive notions of the common good, particularly where economic criteria are employed to measure value, or where political motives influence the nature and extent of the rights accorded to citizens in the criminal justice process.

Recent policy pronouncements usefully illustrate the point. First was the UK Coalition government's 2014 proposal to introduce prison sentences of 100 years for those convicted of murder and other serious offences in an attempt to circumvent the original ECtHR ruling in *Vinter* (2013).[8] Arguably, this strategy was linked to the wider political agenda of resisting EU interference in domestic criminal justice policy, whilst simultaneously appealing to neo-liberal rhetoric favouring harsh punishment. Similarly, one might argue that the possibility of 10 year prison terms for benefit fraud,[9] and the consequent repositioning of benefit fraud with other forms of financial crime, such as money laundering or banking fraud, was an economically motivated policy move. Its political credentials were established by aligning benefit fraud

[7] The Supreme Court and the European Court of Human Rights (ECtHR) have been instrumental in frustrating the penal policy ambitions of successive UK governments. Another important influence is that of the sentencing laws and practices of different countries, particularly where the human rights of the state's own citizens are concerned; see, for example, the Irish Supreme Court Decision in *Minister for Justice and Equality v Kelly aka Nolan* [2013] IESC 54.

[8] *Vinter and Others v United Kingdom*, Application nos 66069/09, 130/10, and 3896/10 (9 July 2013).

[9] For the CPS charging guidance see http://www.cps.gov.uk/news/latest_news/director_of_public_prosecutions_sets_out_charging_standards_for_benefit_and_tax_credit_fraud/.

with offences normally committed by more affluent offenders, and, in so doing, placing sentences for such fraud above the average range for serious offences such a murder or rape. The ferocity of the political rhetoric deployed against benefit fraud was hardly matched by that accompanying the prosecution of tax evasion or financial crime in the banking industry, or more generally. Whilst there may well be a compelling moral case for acting against *all* those who deliberately set out to defraud the taxpayer, the politically attributed social value that dictated the 'appropriate' punishment for benefit fraud was clearly shaped by retributive considerations. Thus, the political rhetoric of neo-liberalism effectively precluded any meaningful discussion of state or communitarian responsibility for addressing the wider social causes of benefit fraud, let alone its social consequences.

Furthermore, Ashworth's (2013b)[10] polemic against the continued detention of offenders convicted of theft or fraud appeared timely, not so much in terms of the utilitarian calculus that prison was failing to rehabilitate such offenders, but rather, the more politically attractive rationale that huge economic savings for the taxpayer would follow such abolition. Whilst Ashworth's argument failed to convince the neo-liberal political right wing, this belies a certain paradox, since he was not advocating a radical departure from the existing status quo of penal ideology, but rather defending the system through principled argument against losing further credibility by needlessly imprisoning those convicted of particular crimes. Thus, without further detailed consideration of the possible social causes or harm caused by such crimes, the value placed upon Ashworth's suggested reforms was directly influenced by the extant neo-liberal penal discourse, consummately fuelled, as always, by the right wing media.

The political reaction to the way in which judges and magistrates utilize their discretion when sentencing depends upon the type of crime involved, as much as it does upon how the offender is characterized. A straightforward illustration of this is where the exercise of discretionary power offends common sense notions of proportionality and consistency for offences that readily fit the

[10] See also Ashworth (2014a) for an assessment of the wider effects of prison overcrowding during a period of economic stringency, especially for prisoners serving short and indeterminate sentences.

retributive paradigm of 'tariff' calibration; for example, driving offences involving fines or disqualification, such as speeding.[11]

Similarly, whilst there appears to be minimal 'political' risk in establishing specialist courts to fast-track traffic offences, economic arguments in favour of giving the police the discretion to fast-track cases of criminal damage and other 'minor' offences where the accused pleads guilty may be viewed as controversial. This and other proposals for extending the discretionary powers of either the CPS or the police over offence choice and method of disposal,[12] whether at national or community level, are problematic in terms of their legitimacy because they largely ignore questions of social value.[13]

Alternatively, one might argue that contextual evaluations of the social harm caused by a wide range of less serious offences are gradually being replaced by mathematical models and economic regulators that take no account of social value or the promotion of more egalitarian forms of criminal justice; rather, they exist to fulfil self-serving bureaucratic and system goals (Cicourel 1968). Cultural sensitivities and the scrutiny of social factors related to longer-term goals aimed at strengthening bonds of community (such as the criminality of migrant workers or the relationship between social deprivation and theft) are more likely to be ignored where the social value of sentencing is measured largely in terms of narrow political advantage and economic gain.

The state has a pivotal role to play in deciding whether, and on what grounds, 'deviance' attributable to poverty should be criminalized. For example, when the police suspended a project in Stoke-on-Trent aimed at giving food bank vouchers to shoplifters in an attempt to deter food theft (see *BBC News* 2013), little attention was devoted to the causal factors that might have been responsible for driving people who were desperate for food to commit such crime. In other words, one might legitimately have asked—which social values did the penalty endorse, or indeed, wherein lay the social value of criminalizing those in need?

[11] For example, the reported failure of magistrates to disqualify from driving some 7,300 motorists with 12 or more penalty points on their driving licence (see *BBC News* 2014a).

[12] See the policy commitment given in the 2012 White Paper (Ministry of Justice 2012a).

[13] Notwithstanding that they also diminish fair trial rights.

Unquestionably, this should have been viewed as a social policy rather than a penal policy issue.

Arguably, the most socially detrimental of the UK government's recent privatizations of the criminal justice estate is the 'Transforming Rehabilitation' agenda first launched in 2013.[14] The centrepiece of this policy was the disestablishment of the Probation Service and the creation of a completely restructured and market driven National Probation Service (see Travis 2014; Garside 2014 for criticism). As McNeill (2013) observes, the policy's adoption of risk as the main predictor of desistance was misguided because it ignores the complex and unpredictable nature of desistance at all levels. Loss of trust and disengagement is also likely to be compounded and accelerated by the introduction of a purely target driven market culture (McNeill 2013: 85).[15]

As argued in the preceding chapter, adequate social theory and methodology is crucial for understanding the degree to which social values are shared, especially where, as in the case of rehabilitation and desistance, adherence to such values may be constitutive of the common good. However, the sharing of common good values is an ideal; it does not represent social reality. If values of humanity are in fact shaped by social experiences, then it seems reasonable to conclude that criminal justice and sentencing policy should play a role in realizing them, more particularly by promoting outcomes that engage as holistically as possible with the impacts of social diversity and value pluralism. Sociological inquiry can also help to predict which social conditions might promote the realization of shared values, such as those associated with rehabilitation and desistance, and account for their individual and social significance.

Can sentencing policy consistently reinforce fundamental community values and interests?

A preliminary answer to this question might begin by exploring the meaning of the expression 'fundamental community values and interests'. Certainly, values might be regarded as fundamental

[14] See the British Journal of Community Justice 2013 for a detailed critique. Provisions in the Offender Rehabilitation Act 2014 relating to extended supervision, sentencing, and release came into force on 1 February 2015.

[15] See McNeill (2013). See also ch 8 for further discussion.

if they serve to bind a particular community together in a way that is crucial to the survival of that community and the individuals within it. The extent to which such values are perceived as fundamental to the common good of society as a whole is problematic.[16] Hence, the relationship of 'fundamental' values of community, even if they are identifiable, to the values that the laws of the penal state appear to represent is problematic.[17]

Wacquant (2009) has argued that penal values allied to politicized agendas for economic prosperity are socially unjust since they consistently discriminate against the poor. However, arguing for a more socially inclusive and integrated agenda for penal policy assumes that the state is able to engage in a meaningful dialogue with 'communities' regarding which values are perceived as 'fundamental', and, beyond that, whether notions of maintaining consistency at the state level are useful when contemplating policy engagement with community values.

Such difficulties return us to a key issue discussed in the previous chapter concerning the capacity of the state to take the moral lead in identifying values for the common good, and what should guide its identification of shared values. Whilst economic prosperity might be a prima facie good, its social value is shaped politically. Inevitably, perceptions of the morality of economic policy and its relationship to sentencing policy will vary considerably as between the constituent communities of any society.

A disconnect often exists between what the law states and what might be regarded as morally appropriate. Increased value pluralism may therefore have the effect of moving the state further away from engaging with what ordinary citizens regard as necessary for the common good of society. I suggest that the solution lies in developing far better channels of communication with offenders, victims, and citizens within 'victimised communities' to understand how sentencing's social value is related to community values more generally.

Thus, a politically credible strategy for strengthening bonds of community should recognize that the key to understanding how social values reflect normative change is essentially a sociological

[16] Crucially, values shared and recognized as common good values should promote the welfare of *all* citizens.

[17] In this, it should be remembered that networks and bonds of community may be global as well as local. See Cotterrell (2014).

question. As a moral injunction, the state has a duty to reflect these understandings in formulating penal policy. However, in reality, in order to maintain power and political legitimacy, the moral values and cultural practices of particular groups or communities are often compromised, negotiated, or simply ignored.

How should the social reality of crime be conceptualized in sentencing policy?

The idea that state morality should draw upon 'bottom-up' evaluations of social needs and aspirations within different communities is problematic because it appears to ignore the problem that penal law, as with any other body of law, does not exert equal normative force for *all* communities and citizens within a given society. However, as Brooks (2014b) points out, the claims that citizens make on law are not reducible to a single moral view; rather law is morally pluralistic in the sense that it may simultaneously satisfy a variety of moral claims. Hence, the normative force of law depends upon how the practical consequences of legal claims are valued within different social contexts.

The ongoing debate about the relationship between law and morality is particularly prescient here. However, abandoning the positivist notion that legal morality is distinctive in favour of the idea that law has moral force and a social function detracts from what I regard as the more important practical question—the notion that the state-sponsored sentencing has a moral obligation to promote social justice. Viewed purely as a normative system, law may become self-serving in the Weberian sense of adapting to whatever allegiances of politics and economics fulfil the moral claims made upon it by citizens, regardless of social class or status. However, recognizing that law and morality are intimately connected suggests that the state should attempt to ensure that law has the capacity to satisfy the moral claims of *all* citizens.

Can sentencing policy promote 'justice' in a socially meaningful way?

There is another sense in which one might view sentencing as having distinctive moral and normative dimensions. The purposes it seeks to fulfil, whether retributive or utilitarian in nature, are declaratory; they express, and are designed to convey, some kind of moral message about how the state, and citizens at large, feel about the behaviour in question, and the way in which the offender should be dealt with (Duff 2001).

However, as a social phenomenon, the credibility of any moral message is contingent upon time and place. The state's interpretation of what constitutes the 'truth' about social conditions and its relationship to crime does not of itself invest sentencing law with any moral authority. Rather, as Gardner (2012: 131) argues, the morality of law comes from what policy-makers claim as the purpose of law *and* how that purpose will be achieved. Thus, although policy-makers shape the moral contours of penal policy rather than validate the law itself in terms of its moral authority, investing law with a morality whose purposes cannot be achieved, or are achievable only at the expense of certain individuals or communities, is morally suspect and likely to prove politically problematic.

The idea that law itself has a role to play in *enforcing* social morality has recently been revisited by Green (2013). Green argues that there are three aspects to law's role as a possible enforcer of social morality, based on the assumption that there is a pre-existing social morality to be enforced; that social morality changes and law may play a part in this; and, finally, that using law to shape our morality is a good thing. Green (2013: 479) makes the point that a tolerant society is one whose social morality is sensitive to deviations from what ideal morality requires but that, for structural reasons, law tends to lag behind what is perceived as popular morality. Changes in law are unlikely to change the social morality of particular groups or communities, although the use of law to implement social policies designed to improve the conditions of life for poorer citizens might induce changes in social morality and so have a longer-term impact on neighbourhood criminality.

Certainly, the unwarranted criminalization of behaviour by the state is more likely to polarize than reconcile competing social moralities. As Green (2013: 488) suggests, crime control becomes an important penal goal only where it is appropriate to criminalize the behaviour in question in the first instance, irrespective of whether or not penal laws are formulated in response to any perceived public need or aspiration, empirically justified or otherwise (see Robinson 2013). Hence, the moral credibility of penal law depends upon its capacity for tolerance and its ability to respond in such a way as to maximize its moral credibility by matching social morality, which Green (2013) argues, 'should be an independent general aim'. As argued, social research should play a greater role in identifying and explaining the contextualized meanings of social morality so that sentencing practice can become more sensitive to changes in social values. Establishing this kind of moral credibility requires an understanding of the values involved, and the extent to which they are shared.

Law's capability as a communicative mechanism is crucial to establishing its normative credibility. Thus, Cotterrell (2013) argues that an appreciation of how law operates within its social environment entails a profound understanding of its relations with 'networks of community', many of which are dominated by economic rather than social or legal relations. In other words, Cotterrell views the relationship between economics and law as embedded in the social fabric or environment of any society, so that the values citizens hold about law are part of a shared network of values, allegiances, and customary practices (2013: 51). The idea that law can be instrumental in influencing the nature and direction of social relations depends crucially upon the degree to which law and legal institutions are regarded as *integral* to maintaining relationships of community. This is essentially a question of how the law works to promote relations of mutual interdependence and trust, rather than the way community relations might be configured or overlap in particular ways.

Although law is crucial in influencing the shape of social relations, the significance of law in promoting bonds of community remains a matter of conjecture (Cotterrell 2013). The fluidity, transience, and overlapping nature of community relations in late modern society makes it more difficult to argue that law has an instrumental role in reflecting a particular moral consensus in terms of 'core' social values. Certainly, the apparent interdependence of individuals or communities is no indicator of a shared social morality. Yet, this does not imply that the state cannot develop penal policies based upon shared social values. As Cotterrell (2013: 63) suggests:

> [s]ociology can reveal empirically and theoretically the social structures and conditions in which moral ideas become meaningful for people in particular times and places, and in which moral arguments become

urgent. It can also identify conditions that foster solidarity, and those that threaten its existence.

Hence, leaving aside what might be valued as promoting social solidarity, the task for social theory and methodology may be seen more fruitfully in terms of explaining the role and meaning of moral ideas in relation to law, and, more importantly, focusing attention on the changing relationship between social morality and the law and practice of sentencing, a central concern for achieving a greater measure of social justice. As pointed out earlier, the important issue here is not simply the heuristic value of sociology, but the fact that it allows policy-makers to evaluate politically judged presuppositions about the social impact of sentencing, and the route designated for its realization. This includes appraising the 'truth' about the social reality of crime and its causes, evaluations that shape the normative parameters of penal measures.

Achieving Greater Recognition for Social Justice in Sentencing

If, as has been argued, the state has a fundamental moral obligation to promote the welfare of its citizens,[18] this extends to ensuring that the values underpinning sentencing policy are consistently aligned with values that are generally accepted as being for the common good. The practical implications of this imperative are the provision of:

1. A normative framework that allows knowledge about the social value of penal measures to inform the decision-making process.
2. A system to monitor changes in the social value attached to penal measures at the community level.
3. A system to ensure consistency of practice at the state level.
4. A mechanism to ensure that sentencing policy, and penal policy in general, is consistently aligned with changes in social policy.

[18] A sentencing policy which promotes social justice *is* for the common good because it values all individuals as equal members of society. It is therefore consistent with values of equal respect for human dignity and the realization of rights. Law has an instrumental role in promoting such a morality.

One of the greatest obstacles to achieving a meaningful link between penal ideology and sentencing policy in England and Wales lies in the fact that there is no clear articulation of the social values that the state is trying to promote. The BA Report (2014), discussed earlier, suggests that certain 'core' social values should inform penal policy. However, it does not recommend a reconceptualization of penal ideology to bring this about—the position adopted here. I argue that this is required to effectively realize the aim of promoting social justice in sentencing. Adopting 'appropriate' values signifies the first step in what represents a complete paradigm shift.

The conventional aims of retributive and utilitarian sentencing, or variations and combinations thereof, are usually discussed in terms of their philosophical orientation, or as principles of distributive justice (Hart 1968), the latter invariably focusing on the relative merits of individualization (Hutton 2014). The notion of penal ideology as a 'representative' collection of values designed to underpin, or in some way providing the moral authority for the state to punish its citizens in prescribed circumstances, has, until recently, provoked limited debate. What has been debated extensively, however, is the economically and politically pertinent question of how scant penal resources may be allocated more efficiently by manipulating the normative framework for delivering justice.

Hence, in its current manifestation, sentencing policy does not appear to concern itself with the notion of 'justice' in a social sense. Rather, policy focuses relentlessly on the economic management of social priorities, in which the allocation of resources to address the social causes and consequences of criminality is given a very low priority. Thus, for the cynical observer, the concept of 'social justice' remains somewhat opaque. Promoting it is a long-term, politically controversial, and, therefore, potentially risky electoral strategy. Paradoxically, the goal of 'justice' is often addressed retrospectively through the pragmatic deployment of human rights norms in individual cases. However, rights are not integral to a penal ideology aimed at realizing 'core' social values (Doak, Henham, and Mitchell 2009).

The UK government's enthusiastic promotion of community justice centres in several larger conurbations in England and Wales usefully illustrates how failure to account for social value at the local level can frustrate policies aimed at promoting social justice.[19] Regrettably, it proved difficult to quantify the benefits offered by such centres in terms of the criteria devised by the Ministry of Justice, attributable in part to the complex links that existed between the focal points of their work. In the case of the Liverpool centre, this was characterized by an individualized problem-solving approach, community engagement, multi-agency partnership working, and a unique role for the judge (Mair and Millings 2011; Booth and others 2012).[20] Certainly, the driving force behind the creation of these centres and the ultimate reason for their demise was economic in terms of reducing crime and speeding up the 'justice' process, rather than their much-vaunted social value in increasing community participation and local justice resolution. The impact assessment carried out by the Ministry of Justice in 2013 that pre-empted the closure of the Liverpool centre left no room for doubt (Ministry of Justice 2013b). Described originally as a 'model court' and 'lean beacon office' [sic], and, despite the fact that it had been agreed in 2011 that the centre should remain open 'even though its particular problem-solving approach had not made it any more successful than other courts in relation to reducing re-offending', the centre was promptly closed in 2014. Closure came notwithstanding the known adverse impact this would have on vulnerable groups, such as the oddly classified 'turnaround women', who would no longer benefit from the centre's outreach activities. Such events illustrate that, where social priorities and political agendas diverge, economic concerns are more likely to predominate and determine the value of penal interventions. Notions of 'participation' and 'greater community access to local criminal justice' are thus consistently redefined in terms of costs savings and greater transparency for crime victims and the wider public through the publication of 'robust' information about court 'results' and sentence effectiveness (see Ministry of Justice 2011; Newlove 2015).

Furthermore, one may argue that, where neighbourhood justice panels or neighbourhood resolution panels have been introduced, economic goals have impeded their effectiveness as social

[19] Between 2005 and 2007 community justice centres were opened in North Liverpool, Salford, Nottingham, Bradford, Middlesbrough, Hull, Leicestershire, Birmingham, Devon and Cornwall, Merthyr Tydfil, and London.

[20] It is worth noting that the issue of how to improve community awareness and engagement was not explored by Booth and others (2012: iv).

interventions concerned with crime causation and desistance. Thus, instead of infusing penal justice with a tangible sense of social value, such outcomes may be viewed as symbolic of the state's failure to assume primary responsibility for the implementation of penal policy, and a broader failure to accept moral responsibility for the social consequences of penal intervention. Not only does this tendency weaken penal governance, it conceals a significant detachment of state values from their social context, suggesting that present policies remain constrained by narrowly circumscribed, politically-defined neo-liberal values, rather than values shared by communities and civil society for the common good.

Penal policy should instead be instrumental in promoting 'core' social values as the BA Report (2014) suggests,[21] with the project of identifying 'core' social values for trial justice and other state sponsored penal interventions conceived within the framework of a reformed penal ideology. Moreover, far greater integration of penal policy with social policy is seen as fundamental for realizing such values and promoting social justice through sentencing.[22]

Communitarian Values and the Politics of Sentencing

In recent years the notion of deliberative justice has emerged as an important strand of thinking in political philosophy (Bohman 1998; Saward 2002). As an alternative to traditional forms of democratic theory that take account of citizens' expressed preferences as the basis for resource allocation, notions of deliberative justice focus on choice as emerging from diverse processes of practical deliberation. The most important difference between deliberative forms of democratic authority and conventional forms of representative government is that the former relies on preferences emerging from the deliberative discourses of citizens, whilst the

[21] See Clamp (2014) for a discussion and critique of the notion of community justice and its deployment as part of the rhetoric of a political law and order agenda.

[22] Such a mission is central to Social Platform which represents NGOs working in the social sector across the EU http://www.socialplatform.org/who-we-are/.

latter closes off further debate. In practical terms, this partial exercise of political power may therefore lead to certain minorities, groups, or communities being excluded from effective participation in the political process. Deliberative democratic theory favours collective reasoning and common agreement about goods and ends as more likely to ensure human liberty and freedoms for all citizens, rather than conventional top-down democratic forms of authority that provide a single template or policy framework to resolve conflict in all social contexts.

Although the plurality of justice is widely recognized by philosophers and political theorists, there is considerable debate about what may be required in a practical sense to realize these aspirations, given that different meanings and priorities attach to goods relative to social context. Hence, as Dryzek (2013: 330) suggests, dialogue is needed to determine what justice means in particular contexts. However, the form that such a dialogue should take is by no means clear. Sen (2010) argues that knowledge of the basic capabilities and requirements of different groups should present decision-makers with a range of social value options, but he is vague in describing how to identify shared meanings; the institutional mechanisms necessary to prioritize expressed preferences; how the representatives of particular interests might be chosen; and the criteria for resolving moral disagreements.

For Ostrom (1990), realizing what different constituencies regard as 'shared values' would depend upon how economic resources are identified and prioritized. Weale (2011) favours an empirically informed account of deliberative rationality for the practical realization of such values based upon a deliberative conception of democracy—a kind of empirically informed social contract. However, the degree of citizen participation and the boundaries that might regulate excessive or inconsistent policy outcomes requires further debate (Crawford 2002). More recently, these ideas have found some resonance in discussions of the role of democratic theory and public opinion in sentencing policy (Dzur 2012; Robinson 2013; Bennett 2014).

Whether or not greater public participation in criminal justice increases the likelihood of fairer or more egalitarian decision-making is a different question from that which asks whether such a course is desirable, or which 'core' social values should inform such a penal policy. One could argue that insulating policy from the vagaries of public opinion is essential to protect sentencing from the vicissitudes of party politics, especially the adverse social consequences of penal populism for democratic governance (Lacey 2008a). Yet this approach posits a diminished form of democratic participation that appears at odds with the notion of increasing the deliberative space for justice. Alternatively, one might argue that greater democratic representation results from increased public participation, even if the outcome lessens inclusiveness in practice (Bennett 2013: 5). But then there seems to be little social value in a democracy that values representation but fails to deliver policies that satisfy the justice demands of its citizens, or only gives the appearance of doing so.[23]

Resolving this question partly depends upon how the state perceives the relationship between individual and social morality across different social contexts. For example, the moral value each individual places upon public participation may be based upon a more widely held belief that 'participation' is the moral duty of every citizen. Such a shared morality signifies common agreement about the social value of public participation which should therefore be reflected at the policy level. However, the problem remains of how to ensure that the state's perception of this shared morality reflects social reality.

Hence, Dzur's (2012: 104) suggestion that the jury ought to be viewed as a platform for moral development wherein a public sense of justice might be forged remains illusory if the democratic framework for delivering fair and egalitarian criminal justice policies does not exist.[24] Collective and collaborative responses to common problems in criminal justice are harder to achieve without some reconfiguration of the moral foundations of penal ideology. This should be based upon values that resonate meaningfully with citizens. Unfortunately, the potential for realizing shared values is distorted by the current sentencing paradigm.

[23] Bennett (2013: 6) suggests that greater democratic value might be achieved through more effective public control of representatives, education, and lay regulation of professional decisions.

[24] This critique is supported by Hindman (2013) who argues that the democratic potential of Dzur's argument is diminished by his failure to address core concerns of race, class, gender, and inequality (see also Roberts and de Keijser 2014 and Feeley's 2014 review).

Social Justice and the Sentencing of Women

Considerable divergence exists between social morality and the rationales that inform the sentencing of women. This deficiency impacts significantly on the ability of sentencers to engage with issues that impact on the everyday reality of women's lives. Moreover, since access to justice for women is essentially linked to communitarian interests in ways that differ from those of men, arguably, one should acknowledge the communitarian nature of the public interest in criminal justice by giving greater recognition to values favouring social coherence (Lacey 1988: ch 8). In the context of women's sentencing, this should mean a more direct engagement with the social reality of crime on women's lives and those of their children, families, and communities. Such a communitarian reflection of the public interest does not currently resonate with the rights accorded to women sentenced in England and Wales (Player 2013).

To illustrate these issues more specifically in a domestic context this section examines how the ongoing tensions between neo-liberal retributive values and consequentialist values continue to define the approach taken by the courts to the sentencing of women, explaining how these effects are compounded by the continuing domination of the adversarial trial paradigm. Such tendencies work against the development of a relevant policy commitment to a 'consistent pluralism' in the sentencing of women (cf Lacey 2008a). Rather, they encourage sentencing outcomes that exacerbate the adverse effects of social deprivation and victimization, as well as reinforcing existing divisions in social morality.

I argue that the debate about penal legitimacy and the sentencing of women should pay much closer attention to social impact. By ensuring that penal ideology is more sensitive to the changing values, expectations, and needs of women, policy-makers should be better placed to develop principles of consistency and fairness for sentencing that are practically meaningful and socially relevant.

The impact of the retributive paradigm

The predominant retributive paradigm continues to operate against the interests of women. Neo-liberal discourse tends to emphasize traditional gender roles within the family, especially the economic dependency of women, ignoring causes and patterns of victimization (Gelsthorpe and Sharpe 2015: 129). In most neo-liberal democracies, retributive justice or variations thereof shape the practical context in which sentences are implemented (Tonry 2012). The current approach grossly underplays the role of contextual factors in constructing social identities and the impact on criminality, so influencing what should be the appropriate response to female offending by the penal state (Hudson 2003).

Since retributive justice is essentially backward looking and chiefly concerned with assessing the seriousness of the offence, difficulties persist in contextualizing previous convictions and behaviour that may add to desert. This may lead to the abandonment of humanitarian and reformative considerations which prove advantageous to women through the individualization of sentences. It also means that aggravating and mitigating factors have to be assessed within the rationale of narrow deserts-based definitions of harm and culpability (Player 2013: 284), thereby precluding broader considerations of social harm and social responsibility. Hence, the scope for restorative interventions and more contextually-related solutions relevant to women is diminished.[25]

Consideration of other sentencing aims may also be reduced, as conflicting goals tend to undermine deserts principles. Such has been the experience with community penalties, although advances have been made more recently in reconceptualizing and adapting community penalties to meet the needs of women (Gelsthorpe 2010; Brooks and others 2014). However, assessments of seriousness and culpability continue to focus disproportionately on fixing individual responsibility at the expense of collective and relational contexts of accountability, thereby ignoring crucial aspects in the social construction of women's identities, roles, and actions.

The introduction by the Sentencing Council of the new definitive guideline for theft offences in February 2016 raised a number of serious concerns in relation to women's sentencing which, I suggest, could be addressed more effectively if the changes proposed herein were adopted (Sentencing Council 2016). Such

[25] A particularly important aspect is the social context of multiple victimization and the relative powerlessness of women to resist.

concerns were cogently articulated in the Prison Reform Trust's (PRT) response to the guideline consultation, which highlighted the disproportionate and rising numbers of women being given custodial sentences for theft and handling offences in England and Wales (Prison Reform Trust 2014 and see Sentencing Council 2015b).

The PRT stressed the following:

1. The absence of any gendered analysis of sentencing decisions for theft given the disproportionate impact on women, especially those from black and ethnic minority backgrounds, and the failure to address this concern in the equality impact assessment. This point was not addressed by the Sentencing Council.
2. Gender specific sentencing options should form part of the sentencing guidelines. In addition, the Sentencing Council should be responsible for the systematic collection of data from magistrates' courts, which is where the majority of women offenders are sentenced, to ensure that women are not disadvantaged by guidelines designed to respond to male sentencing patterns. This issue was not addressed by the Sentencing Council.
3. Although required to do so, the courts find it difficult to balance the rights of dependent children with those of the mother, despite primary care responsibilities being taken into account in mitigation; this should be monitored and evaluated by the Sentencing Council. Again, no specific direction was given by the Sentencing Council.
4. Given the government's commitment to increase access to restorative justice, the Sentencing Council should ensure that the availability of restorative justice interventions is widened and not restricted to cases close to the community sentence or custody thresholds; evidence of capacity to engage successfully with alternatives could then be more effective—the Sentencing Council did not believe that a reference to restorative justice was appropriate, since the guidelines deal only with the sentencing of offenders. Restorative justice is considered pre-sentence, the provision of restorative justice services is not fully available nationally and, for those successfully completing restorative justice activities, this could be taken into account as mitigation (Sentencing Council 2015b: 6). The Sentencing Council also noted that the victim personal statement is not

within the remit of the sentencer or the sentencing guidelines, since it is the responsibility of the police (Sentencing Council 2015b: 16).

5. Given recent increases in thefts from shops committed by women following changes in benefit entitlement and the general economic downturn, the PRT recommended that the Sentencing Council should include an additional factor at Category C taking account of offences committed in the context of exceptional financial circumstances or destitution. The Sentencing Council considered that mitigation on the grounds of *exceptional* financial hardship would be sufficient to cover cases where offenders had been driven to steal food in order to feed themselves and/or other family members.
6. The proposed treatment of previous convictions was unacceptable, particularly since community-based multi-agency interventions with persistent low-level offenders,[26] including programmes developed for persistent shoplifters, had reduced reconviction rates. Nevertheless, the Sentencing Council decided that recent relevant previous convictions involving 'significant' persistent offending would merit an upward adjustment in sentence beyond that appropriate for the instant offence, although custodial sentences should be kept to the necessary minimum (Sentencing Council 2015b: 16).
7. An additional mitigating factor of 'not motivated by personal gain' should be included in shoplifting cases where the threshold for 'exceptional' financial hardship had not been met, and this factor had not been taken into account in determining culpability at Step 1. The Sentencing Council concluded that it was not appropriate to include this as a specific mitigating factor. Since the list was non-exhaustive, a court would be able to take this factor into account if relevant (Sentencing Council 2015b: 7).

The Sentencing Council's response to the concerns expressed by the PRT is revealing. Beyond its continued failure to take account of gendered patterns of sentencing when formulating guidelines,

[26] Section 176 of the Anti-social Behaviour, Crime and Policing Act (2014) provides that offenders pleading guilty to shop theft of goods valued at less than £200 no longer have the right to elect for crown court trial, nor can they be sent to the crown court for sentence. This is significant in that the vast majority of shoplifting cases involve property valued below the £200 threshold.

the Sentencing Council also appeared reluctant to encourage greater use of restorative justice interventions, a development considered of particular benefit for dealing with women offenders, primarily because restorative justice is currently not a fully-integrated, universally available sentencing option. Similarly, the Sentencing Council's approach to persistent offending behaviour fails to acknowledge significant advances in the development of community-based alternatives for women offenders. Thus, it seems reasonable to argue that the Sentencing Council's approach does little to address the increase in the number of women offenders receiving custodial sentences despite assurances to the contrary, a trend noted by McIvor and Burman (2011) in their analysis of female imprisonment in Scotland.[27] Tombs and Jagger (2006) suggest that this punitive turn may be attributable to the perception by sentencers that women offenders are more likely to access rehabilitative services within prison. This finding reinforces the need for better education and training for sentencers, a point recently emphasized by Gelsthorpe and Sharpe (2015).

These conclusions highlight an urgent need to develop sentencing guidance which draws attention to and enhances the court's capacity to access community-based and other restorative justice interventions more generally. Neo-liberal values and the predominant retributive paradigm are chiefly responsible for the continuing failure to integrate restorative justice into mainstream sentencing, more especially through the marginalization and treatment of restorative justice as an adjunct to the conventional formal criminal process (Henham 2014). This is partly due to concerns, never adequately addressed by policy-makers, that restorative justice is a consummate threat to consistent and proportionate sentencing. Thus, according to this view, despite its undoubted successes, restorative justice must not be allowed to undermine such core principles and destabilize the status quo of 'principled' sentencing.

Deserts arguments for proportionality and consistency depict an essentially closed and unresponsive criminal process based upon a narrow conceptualization of individual culpability (von Hirsch and Ashworth 2005). Ultimately, whether one considers this approach to be fair in any meaningful sense is a question of

[27] Women over 30 years of age were thought to be particularly vulnerable in this respect.

moral conviction. As argued in the previous chapter, increasing the moral credibility of sentencing by engaging with social value empowers citizens and communities because it takes account of local moralities, sensitivities, and social realities, thereby accessing communitarian dimensions of accountability. This suggests that collective support for reintegration and the kind of accountability likely to enhance social harmony requires a profound local understanding of social morality and its impact on perceptions of female offending behaviour.

Thus, the changed ideology advocated herein recognizes that promoting social value is fundamental to effective sentencing. Consequently, as explained in the following chapter, the rationale for penal intervention requires transformation far beyond the narrow goals of retributivism and the adversarial process. Instead of being seen as a route into one justice paradigm, sentencing would become crucial to the integration of restorative outcomes, with significant impact on the nature and admissibility of evidence throughout the trial. Hence, sentencing guidelines, and sentencing guidance more generally, would more readily incorporate gender-related sentencing options. This would include mediation, diversion, and other restorative departures from the conventional sentencing process, and the consequences should such interventions fail, extending to a merged sentencing and enforcement phase. Findings from contextual analyses suggesting disproportionate racial or ethnic impact would also feed into this process. More generally, such changes would also address the PRT's suggestion of integrating the court's power to defer sentence, currently exercisable under section 1 of the Powers of the Criminal Courts Act (2000), within the Theft guideline. Compliance with the activity requirements of gender-specific, multi-agency programmes, including supervision and support, might then be monitored and factored into the guideline decision-making strategy.

Furthermore, the Sentencing Council's failure to heed the PRT's warning that the Theft guideline's approach to previous convictions would not address the causes of offending or prevent similar offences is disappointing; a missed opportunity for the court to pause and explore the benefits that might result from intensive gender-specific community interventions. Replacing the existing paradigm with one that takes more account of social impact should not weaken the imperative for punishment provided there is prior agreement about what counts as harm—thus, not punishment *for* recidivism in the narrow sense, but punishment *because* recidivism damages the community. Offender culpability would therefore need to be judged against broader communitarian interests following contextual evaluation, particularly the social value of continuing to penalize persistent female offending behaviour. More importantly, such knowledge would establish the 'appropriate' parameters for community-based interventions, encouraging parsimony rather than punitiveness with a focus on reintegration. The deliberative space needed for this approach to succeed does not exist within the current paradigm.

The exigencies of adversarial trial

Retributive justice facilitates the political control of punishment because it favours the centralization of discretionary power. This supports the continuation of gendered justice and weakens the moral argument that criminal justice should provide democratic accountability through equal treatment of the sexes.[28] As argued, reduced judicial discretion diminishes the possibilities for subjective assessment and the individualization of sentencing, a tendency exacerbated by over-prescriptive guidelines.

More recently, the retributive paradigm has been crudely manipulated as part of a more deliberate policy agenda to accommodate the ever increasing (and therefore politically significant) demands for restorative solutions. The UK government's call for the integration of restorative justice approaches provides a useful illustration of this trend (Ministry of Justice 2010: paras 79–81[29]). Unfortunately, this policy initiative did not indicate how to integrate the ideals or ethics of restorative justice into penal ideology, nor did it suggest how, or on what basis, restorative values might be integrated into the existing deserts-based framework. Although some progress has been made in allowing courts to defer sentence, thereby facilitating restorative justice where both victim and offender are willing to participate (Legal Aid, Sentencing and Punishment of Offenders Act 2012 (LASPO)),

[28] Note the argument for gender neutrality in sentencing.

[29] For an overview of current Ministry of Justice restorative justice initiatives, including Actions Plans see https://www.gov.uk/government/collections/restorative-justice-action-plan.

the penal values and institutional arrangements within which such restorative objectives operate remain those of the prevailing neo-liberal, retributive paradigm. The aims and values of this paradigm are effectively realized through the adversarial process which shapes trial relationships, controls evidence, and manages outcomes.

Trial-based restorative opportunities sit uneasily with the adversarial paradigm's blinkered focus on establishing individual guilt, thus hampering the fulfilment of restorative objectives, both in purpose and practice. Hence, policy-makers have been unable to exploit the sensibilities, emotional, and relational differences between men and women by routinely facilitating restorative interventions, or suggesting new structural arrangements for their greater incorporation at sentencing.

The structuring of the trial and the evidential requirements of the adversarial paradigm facilitate and reinforce a disproportionate reliance on stereotypical and outmoded notions of gender relations and family responsibilities when sentencing. Current sentencing policy tends to exacerbate this problem by defining women as either offenders or victims, when the social experiences of women traverse this artificial divide. Regrettably, few specific mechanisms exist within the sentencing framework for identifying the individual or social needs of women, other than issues coming to light through the normal processes of giving trial evidence, or as part of mitigation in sentencing.

Arguably, in practice, a gradual reduction in socially relevant information in Pre-Sentence Reports (PSRs) has also worked against women's interests. This trend accelerated in 2014 with the privatization of rehabilitation under the UK government's 'Transforming Rehabilitation' agenda mentioned earlier, relevant information being condensed into a target-driven, risk-based, 'tick box' exercise.[30] Certainly, the introduction of equality impact assessments (EIAs) as an integral part of the consultation and policy development process appears to have done little to ameliorate gendered patterns of sentencing, detailed

[30] See Gomm (2013) for further analysis of the adverse impact of these proposals, and Gilbert (2013), who argues that focusing intervention and supervision on high risk offenders would be detrimental to women since the majority of perpetrators of domestic abuse are likely to be assessed as posing a medium risk of offending.

analysis of social impact information being minimal. Thus, policy remains the same; judges and magistrates lack the normative flexibility to engage more directly with social justice issues relevant to women (see Birkett and Castell 2013).

Larsen (2012) makes a number of significant points in this connection. She favours the 'gendering' of sentencing decisions through the informed exercise of judicial discretion where cases involve dependent children because this is more likely to afford the deliberative space to reflect upon and accord respect for the ethics of caring. However, the wider implications of Larsen's comments are especially prescient. In particular, they direct policy-makers to think more carefully about the kinds of social and personal circumstances that should mitigate desert and deterrent constraints in individual cases, and, more broadly, how to balance utilitarian concerns for the greater good against those of an offender's dependent child or children.

Although Larsen (2012) comments on the Australian position, she raises questions of general import; more particularly, how to identify contextual factors which might count as relevant mitigation in women's sentencing for reasons of the common good—in this case, the goods of maintaining stable and caring family relationships whilst also ensuring consistent and proportionate sentencing. Australian sentencing law provides for 'exceptional circumstances', allowing judges to exercise their discretion in admitting contextual evidence as to what constitutes 'hardship' to dependent children, and in determining whether such hardship is extreme in cases where the offender is the only person capable of relieving that hardship. Arguably, such factors should carry significant weight in sentencing, rather than being filtered through a narrow legal interpretation of 'exceptional circumstances'.[31]

The prevailing sentencing paradigm in England and Wales mirrors the constraints prescribed by criminal offence definitions[32] and the limited extent to which social factors are permitted to

[31] Although social disadvantage may be recognized as a mitigating factor in some jurisdictions, such as Australia, the problem remains of how this should be taken into account by judges and magistrates when determining the appropriate sentence (Warner 2011: 136).

[32] Certain offences may be racially or religiously aggravated; see Anti-terrorism, Crime and Security Act 2001 s 39.

intrude upon the evidence required to establish any necessary mental intention (Duff 2007). The focus on establishing individual legal responsibility, or 'guilt', precludes wider consideration of factors such as religion or culture in shaping beliefs, values, attitudes, or motives for action, matters that remain at best tangential to the determination of conventional liberal understandings of intent.[33] However, such factors are of vital importance in understanding some forms of criminality within ethnic minority and faith communities (Nyakudya 2013).

The criminalization of migrant women and its social consequences

It has been argued that Garland's (2001) social control thesis deals inadequately with the social reality of women's victimization, especially the cultural contexts which inform its nature and extent (Gelsthorpe 2005). Furthermore, research by the Fawcett Society (2010) suggests that variations exist in the way different groups of ethnic minority women experience and perceive violence. Thus, the nature of their interactions with the criminal justice system are heavily dependent upon cultural factors, such as language, community and family structures, and are to that extent unique to particular communities and cultures.

The impact that the sentencing of women has on social cohesion is complex. To begin with, ethnic minority and foreign national women are disproportionately represented in the prison population (Fawcett Society 2010; Easton and Piper 2012). Particular concerns are that such women are more likely to feel isolated in custody, less likely to seek help, and face additional language and cultural barriers. Foreign national women as a group make up nearly one in five of the female prison population and may be particularly isolated from children and family. In addition, a

[33] For an example of the complexities of this debate in the indigenous context (see Australian Law Reform Commission 1986: ch 18). The addition of more serious offences where motivated by religious or racial hatred, or the reflection of these factors as aggravating factors in sentencing, does not change the fact that related evidence remains constrained by the adversarial and retributive justice paradigm.

disturbingly high rate of mental illness exists among female prisoners generally (Ashworth (2010: 247).

Hales and Gelsthorpe's (2012) research on the criminalization and punishment of migrant women in England and Wales provides disturbing evidence of the adverse social consequences for such women of the current sentencing paradigm. Evidently, the 'public interest' is ill-served by a system that penalizes women who may have felt compelled through poverty or duress to participate in criminal activity. Moreover, extracting early guilty pleas in such cases is unlikely to have any deterrent value and, arguably, contravenes fundamental human rights (Ashworth 2015: 179). Such practices diminish due process and extol the virtues of retribution and social exclusion, when far more could be achieved by employing restorative interventions to address the social causes and consequences of crime for migrant women.

Responding to penal neo-liberalism

When allied to neo-liberal values, the distinctly retributive and adversarial focus of the contemporary criminal trial is ill-suited to engaging with the social realities of poverty, social exclusion and multiple victimization that characterize the lives of many women, especially those appearing before the courts. Thus, the morality of a political economy that systematically reinforces socially disadvantageous and repressive patterns of control over women is highly questionable.

Despite this knowledge, women's life experiences continue to receive scant attention in sentencing. As Player (2012: 266) confirms, the principle of equality of impact for women in sentencing remains constrained by the proportionality requirements of just deserts. The required scale of any deviation would appear unacceptable despite the desirability of the ulterior purpose (von Hirsch and Ashworth 2005: 162). Consequently, the impact of significant socio-cultural variables, such as 'women's histories of abuse, their caring responsibilities within the family, and the effect of sentences on innocent third parties', continue to be left to the vagaries of judicial discretion (Player 2013). The impact of the sentence on the family life of the offender may have some mitigating effect in the case of less serious crimes but, for more serious offences, perceived victim and public demands for 'just deserts', together with attendant pressures for consistency and proportionality, are far more likely to predominate.[34]

A consensus has evolved that parsimony in the use of imprisonment for women should become the prevailing norm, since women commit less crime, their offences are less serious, and they are less likely to be reconvicted than men (Gelsthorpe 2010). In particular, difference and diversity should be recognized in the *form*, rather than in the amount or level of punishment, thus maintaining the important principles of proportionality and desert (Gelsthorpe and Sharpe 2015: 130).[35] Notwithstanding, reducing imprisonment for both sexes is desirable to enhance social justice and promote the legitimacy of the criminal justice system (Paternoster and others 1997).[36]

However, I have argued that any reform of sentencing policy should go much further than this. A focus away from retributive notions of individual responsibility towards more relational forms of justice that address the social identities, interests, intersecting relationships, and responsibilities of women more directly is crucial for sustaining relationships of community and promoting social cohesion.[37] Socially responsive forms of sentencing are more likely to counter the adverse impacts of victimization and discrimination. Thus, ideology and practice needs to change so that criminal justice interventions can respond more effectively to women's distinctive needs and pay greater attention to those of their dependent children, especially where both parents are imprisoned.[38] A profounder engagement with the social reality of women's lives is therefore vital to enhance social justice

[34] See eg *R v Petherick (Rosie Lee)* [2012] EWCA 2214 and commentary at [2013] *Criminal Law Review* 80.

[35] The suggestion by Roberts (2015b) that additional sentencing guidelines might include 'disposal-specific' rather than 'offence-specific' guidelines might usefully focus on sentencing women offenders. See Malloch, McIvor, and Burgess (2014) on developments in Scotland.

[36] Community justice centres such as that established in North Liverpool were favoured by Corston (2007: 54) because they offer a more holistic and therapeutic solution to the kinds of problems afflicting many women offenders.

[37] Gender essentialism and neglect of differences attributed to race, ethnicity, and class are possible risks should specialist women's courts be adopted (Gelsthorpe and Sharpe 2015: 132).

[38] Arguably, this should also extend to the wider family responsibilities that generally fall to women, such as caring for elderly and often severely incapacitated parents or siblings.

for women in sentencing. Gendered patterns of sentencing will remain where neo-liberal economic values continue to prioritize retributive and deterrent aims that marginalize social factors relevant to victimization, criminalization, and penalty.

Economic and political forces are predominant in shaping the values that inform criminal justice policy and in defining the value-related dimensions of institutional activities such as sentencing. This relationship also influences the emergence of economic values and the power relationships that sustain them over time; in particular, the distributional choices that prioritize aims and shape impacts in sentencing. Thus, understanding how the political economy interacts with social values is crucial in explaining why late modern penal practices continue to institutionalize gendered patterns of sentencing. Moreover, as Lacey (2012) points out, since the political climate and electoral arrangements are key determinants of penal ideology and practice, there is an urgent need to engage in a systematic analysis of how political institutions shape penality.[39] The expansion of this endeavour to explain the relationship of economic forces to political change is crucial in suggesting why particular social values predominate at certain moments in time, or in particular contexts, and may also signal ways of developing political arrangements to support future changes in penal praxis. This understanding also extends to factors that cause socially complex and diverse communities to favour certain economic values over others and the social and political consequences, including the deployment of penal rationales and practices to defend such values. Values such as those identified in the BA Report (2014) must be shared by civil society before they can hope to secure political legitimacy. The political challenge is then to provide the strategic and institutional infrastructure for realizing those values. Until this occurs policy will continue its struggle to find a socially valued rationale for the criminalization and punishment of women.

[39] Lacey argues that the 'neoliberal penality thesis' is inadequate in this respect.

6

Establishing New Foundations and Structures for Governance

Introduction

The argument developed in this book, that sentencing should reflect shared social values, relies on a fundamental change in penal ideology. However, it is not suggested that this alone will provide the necessary impetus for change. Rather, changing penal ideology so that particular social values are prioritized in sentencing is regarded as a vital first step towards validating a complete reconceptualization and restructuring of the sentencing process.

This chapter begins by arguing the case for recasting the moral foundations of sentencing and discusses the policy implications of such a fundamental change of approach. It draws on work by Findlay and Henham (2005, 2010) and develops later work by the author (Henham 2012, 2014) in proposing new foundational principles, and explores how such a moral transition might be reflected through structural reforms to domestic sentencing. The discussion then highlights the difficulties of recasting the values and structures of sentencing as a mechanism for engaging with social justice issues.

Specific areas of policy change within England and Wales are examined, and the problems of moving from theory to practice considered through the analysis of recent government reforms. The discussion explains how a restated moral mission, together with significant structural changes, could enhance the perceived legitimacy of sentencing in a morally pluralistic world. The issue of legitimacy is explored further in considering the implications of reduced judicial discretion in sentencing, the prioritizing of procedural justice over substantive justice as exemplified by the disproportionate emphasis given to guilty plea sentence discounts, and the renewed policy focus on 'swift and sure' justice with its thinly disguised cost-cutting agenda.

In sum, the chapter explains the rationale for the proposed change in theoretical focus and elaborates the implications for restructuring sentencing and beyond. Fundamentally, it emphasizes how such changes might help the state fulfil its moral obligation to promote shared social values through sentencing policy. What this chapter makes clear is that, as in so many areas of public policy, fragmented, politically-motivated, and short-term market driven 'solutions' are unlikely to redress penal or social injustice. Rather, I argue that nothing less than a fundamental re-evaluation of the values underpinning sentencing policy and the trial's capacity to reflect punishment's social value at sentencing is needed to ensure its continued legitimacy.

Recasting the Moral Values that Inform Penal Ideology

The discussion begins by explaining exactly why a reflection of shared values in penal ideology is considered crucial to ensure the legitimacy of sentencing. Such a sharing of values is, as discussed earlier, conceived as something that is characterized by the notion of 'community', in the sense that certain values are commonly held within particular social contexts. This implies, first, that there needs to be some identifiable consensus about the purposes for which those values are held, although the moral value attached to those purposes and the means prescribed for their realization will always be a matter of conjecture (Hudson 2003). Secondly, such values are seen as conferring legitimacy because they signify a commonly held belief in the capacity of sentencing to deliver outcomes that have social value. In other words, values should have an explicitly beneficial social role in the theory and practice of sentencing.

A brief resume of the framework for conceptualizing the legitimacy of sentencing in these terms is provided below before discussing the kind of moral framework envisaged by a reconstituted penal ideology (Henham 2012: ch 2). The following elements are regarded as key to the proposed reconceptualization of sentencing:

1. Values must be grounded in some kind of identifiable social reality if they are to be effectively transmitted through policy

to the structures and practices of sentencing. Value pluralism and the transient and fragmented nature of community in late modern society make this imperative increasingly relevant. Hence, the degree to which such values are shared has important implications for social cohesion and the role of penal policy in sustaining the legitimacy of the state.

2. Accordingly, the morality underpinning penal ideology should be shared. There should be greater congruence between the values underpinning policy choices and the reality of those values on the ground. Shared values are seen as providing the moral authority for sentencing policy, whilst penal ideology is validated through sentencing's recursive practice.
3. Once accepted, this new ideology would have profound ethical and normative consequences. Hence, reconceived ethics would shape the norms and structures of sentencing, empowering decision-makers to deliver outcomes that have social value.
4. Beyond that, sentencing practices that are grounded in shared values are more likely to influence social morality and future behaviour, including desistance from crime. Sentencing is more likely to be perceived as fair and non-discriminatory where it resonates with shared values. Thus, social reintegration and cohesion would become stated policy objectives.
5. The recursive component of this conceptual framework is the notion that sentencing practice consistently reinforces the shared values that inform penal ideology, and so influences sentencing policy. The nature of this recursive interaction between value and ideology varies according to structure, time, and space (cf Giddens 1984). Thus, the social reality of sentencing is viewed as recursively constituted.

To summarize, the above conceptualization is based on the assumption that an important link exists between the social values underlying sentencing policy and the extent to which such values are positively reinforced through the decision-making process. However, which social values are affirmed by the penal process as a result of policy decisions is determined politically. Evidently, the criminal process, and sentencing in particular, is not an inherently positive force for good. Rather, its structures and norms may be deployed as instruments of domination by the political elite. Therefore, whilst stricter regulation of judicial discretion and rights protection may characterize the nature of penal governance within the neo-liberal retributive paradigm, it does not necessarily confer legitimacy on sentencing praxis.

Theories that focus disproportionately on systems and spaces[1] tend to decouple ideas of human value from social reality,[2] failing to grasp the fundamental point that fact and value are essentially intertwined (Tamanaha 1997). The exercise of discretionary decision-making power in sentencing publicly expresses this connection. For this reason, sentencing should be conceived as something more than simply facilitative, as serving the ends of retributive justice or other ends or justifications (Roberts 2006). Failure to recognize this suggests that notions of trust and legitimacy are more likely to be conceived in purely instrumental or mechanical terms, devoid of context. That being so it is imperative that the measurement, assessment, and evaluation of 'facts' about sentencing that precede policy-making should possess contextual and 'subjective' authenticity.

The aim of realizing shared values through sentencing may be for the common good if it tends to promote social justice. This implies that any structure dedicated to conflict resolution such as the criminal process should concern itself with restoring social harmony by paying closer attention to the impact of punishment on relationships of community such as mutual awareness and responsibility for the welfare of others, or at the very least enabling that potential to be realized. Hence, state punishment should consider how criminal justice can engage with humanity as 'victim' in a broader social sense. From this perspective sentencing can help to restore and strengthen social bonds by being more inclusive, rather than merely symbolic or declaratory.

The Implications for Sentencing Research

The realization of such a transformed sentencing paradigm requires profound contextual research and analysis as a precursor

[1] Interfaces, communicative structures, and networks all have contextual meaning.

[2] A salient example is the ongoing crisis in the provision of mental health services in England, the responsibility for which has consistently been blamed on 'system flaws' and 'financial levers' failing to respond, as if these systems and structures had an agency of their own, one that is impervious to human agency in the shape of an effective government policy (interview with then Care Minister, Norman Lamb, *BBC Radio 4* 'Today' Programme, 5 May 2014).

to policy-making. The theory and method for contextual analysis developed here was first outlined by Henham (1990) and later elaborated by Findlay and Henham (2005) as part of a broader reconceptualization of the purposes and form of international trial justice.[3] Following Giddens (1979; 1984), structuration theory is suggested as a powerful heuristic tool for deconstructing sentencing because it recognizes structure, organization and interaction as interconnected aspects of the same social practice, offering three levels of understanding depending on context. Its organizing or interpretative constructs allow researchers to identify elements and processes concerned in the recursive nature of the application of rules and resources by social actors. The theory makes it possible to understand the way in which different structures of trial process exist and are recursively created and patterned over time, whilst also appreciating the ways in which they are realized by human agency through institutional practice. For example, the patterning of sentencing principles and their existence as formal rules can be conceived as a structural context in which the situational reality of sentence decision-making takes place.

Developing this theoretical approach, the contextual modelling that precedes research design is multi-layered, combining qualitative and quantitative approaches. Contextual modelling has a dual focus in that it seeks to account for sentencing as an interactive process, revealing how decision-makers subjectively reach their decisions (evaluation in context), whilst at the same time explaining how those decisions and the influences brought to bear upon decision-makers flow from differing contextual environments (evaluation of context). Thus, the subjective aspects of the sentencing model are concerned with perception, interpretation, and meaning (the phenomenology of sentencing), whereas the contextual components deal with external factors that shape shared understandings, such as social morality (the social construction of sentencing).

In short, the most important point to emphasize is that contextual modelling seeks to conceptualize the nature and direction of the relationship between action and value in sentencing

[3] Only a brief outline is possible here. See Findlay and Henham (2005) for a detailed account of the theory and methodology of comparative contextual analysis.

as a recursive and reflexive process. By combining inductive and deductive strategies, its methodology aims to deconstruct the social reality of sentencing, the focus being on deepening our understanding of how contextual factors influence the value attached to sentencing according to time and place.

The Impact on Criminal Justice Governance

The proposed normative changes demand new moral foundations for penal ideology that reflect shared values. Crucially, 'sharing' must be 'real'. In other words, it must exist empirically, with the contextual implications understood and interpreted correctly before findings can be factored into policy-making. Accordingly, the development of contextual analysis as a methodology to inform policy-making is predicated on accepting this fundamental proposition. This approach therefore differs from that which seeks to promote legitimacy through policies based on detailed empirical observations regarding the perceived utility of deserts-based sentencing (cf Robinson 2013).

The notion that the state has a moral obligation to promote the common good gives *apparent* legitimacy to penal ideology and so invests policy with a degree of moral authority—a crucial duality. This duality presumes a sharing of responsibility between citizens, and between citizens and the state, for the punishment of crime—in other words, it has both horizontal and vertical dimensions. Thus, the state's obligation may be described as one of responding to this shared morality by giving social meaning[4] to the values that inform penal ideology at the point of sentencing. Moreover, I suggest that the state's moral obligation should go far beyond that of merely recognizing and realizing shared values, it should actively *promote* shared values through the principled development of sentencing policy. Hence, the notion that sentencing involves a sharing of responsibility for crime and punishment between citizen and state is one that should be positively advanced through policy and practice. In sum, state policy should be more concerned with developing notions of collective responsibility and suggesting appropriate forms of local accountability.

[4] Contextual knowledge explains how value attaches to the everyday social reality of sentencing and is crucial in understanding the meaning of penal legitimacy and governance.

Criminal justice policy should take greater account of changing social values, especially in conceptualizing the relationship between citizen and state. Ashworth and Zedner (2007) draw particular attention to how changing conceptions of the state as regulatory, preventive, or authoritarian can alter the governance framework. An example is the move towards greater self-governance and responsibility through contractual governance (Crawford 2003). Such perspectives may expose critical points of tension between the state and citizens within the existing penal framework, particularly practices that induce or otherwise pressurize participants at important decision-making sites within the system, such as the practice of discounting sentences in return for guilty pleas (discussed below and see Dawes and others 2011).

Promoting social values that support mutual awareness and social responsibility are central to effective penal governance, and key to loosening the narrow punitive straightjacket of neo-liberal crime control and prevention strategies (Ashworth and Zedner 2014; Carvalho 2015).[5] Adopting relational and communitarian notions of responsibility which acknowledge the collective dimensions of criminality should lead to more socially inclusive and morally acceptable sentencing practices—practices based upon, and evaluated against, a shared vision of the responsibilities of the individual citizen *within* the community. Sited within penal policy development more generally, this ethos should then permeate other structures and institutions of governance.

Problems of Moving from Theory to Practice

This section details the practical changes that would follow the ideological and normative transformation described above. Subject to this, prosecutors, defence lawyers, judges, and relevant social agencies would collaborate through pre-trial deliberation to produce a 'trial programme' aimed at addressing the identifiable justice needs of the offender, victims, and the community where the offence was committed (cf Findlay and Henham 2010). As argued, the focus for reconciling 'needs' should be that of social value.

[5] The nature and scope of criminalization has important implications in this respect (see Tadros 2011; Duff and others 2014).

Chapter 1 explained that sentencing should be concerned with realizing the values that inform penal ideology. This means that, if adopted, 'core' social values such as those advocated by the BA Report (2014) would need to be realized in some concrete way for each individual who is convicted and sentenced. However, to achieve this objective would necessarily involve victims and the communities where crimes have been committed, particularly to maximize the potential for desistance and reintegration. Thus, as envisaged, state values would guide the ordering of priorities and the nature of the sentence decision-making process as it sits within the framework of the trial as a whole. Correspondingly, the same rationale would inform pre-trial deliberations and the design of the trial programme.

The aim of the trial programme would be to set objectives and suggest an agenda for the trial and sentencing phases of the criminal process. The trial's purpose would be to achieve a principled outcome through a process which aims so far as possible to identify, accommodate, and reconcile competing justice claims within the new framework. Such claims might reflect retributive and restorative justice considerations, in addition to other consequentialist aspirations. Sentence enforcement would focus on promoting the original objectives of the trial programme in the light of the subsequent sentencing decision in order to arrive at a holistic and integrated programme of penal intervention.

The most appropriate way of visualizing this process, following Morris and Tonry's (1990) suggested dichotomy between the purposes *of* sentencing and the purposes *at* sentencing, is to say that the proposed change in penal ideology is concerned with changing the moral focus of conventional aims such as retribution, deterrence, and rehabilitation to that of promoting certain 'core' social values. Realizing this aspiration in any specific case would thus become the purpose at sentencing.

Moving on, the verdict and sentence phases of the trial would remain identifiable stages, but have different symbolic and operational significance within a merged process. A mediated outcome would become possible at any point, either before or after the start of the trial proper, and the trial programme would be designed to facilitate this. Further, the concept of 'probative value' would take on a broader significance in the context of the transformed trial, so that the criteria for admissibility would reflect the social value of such evidence. Therefore, the introduction of victim impact testimony (for example) before the verdict would not automatically be regarded as 'prejudicial' to a 'fair' trial, as is currently the case within the context of a purely adversarial process. Indeed, the introduction of evidence that could lead to 'truth-finding' and reconciliation where the judge directed a mediated process would be welcomed, especially reconciliation between the offender and the immediate victim(s) within the context of broader communitarian purposes such as desistance and reintegration.

Deciding whether or not to merge the verdict and sentencing phases of the trial is fundamental in re-evaluating the criminal process's capacity to deliver more socially meaningful forms of sentencing. Most importantly, the decision is crucial in identifying the appropriate epistemic context for realizing the potential of judicial discretion to advance the integration of restorative themes in trial decision-making (cf Jackson 2009). Adversarial 'justice' delivers a particularized form of 'truth' that is conventionally validated by the test of whether or not 'facts' have 'value' within the trial context. So it is a 'truth' conceived and manufactured to establish individual guilt or innocence within that distinctive normative framework. Such norms present procedural obstacles to the inclusion of socially relevant evidence on behalf of victims and communities which pertain throughout the criminal trial process; constraints that otherwise facilitate retributive and deterrent sentencing solutions.[6]

Neither the merger nor the separation of the verdict and sentencing stages would fundamentally change this negative assessment of the evidentiary rules as they currently exist, because neither would deal with the present system's failure to deliver a more inclusive and communitarian form of justice based on recognizable social values. Accordingly, I argue that such impediments to justice could be effectively resolved if the structures and processes of sentencing were informed by a new ethical and normative framework based upon core social values.

However, it is important to emphasize that marking out the public deliberation and pronouncement of the sentence as something distinct from the verdict has an enormously powerful

[6] The 'facts' needed to determine guilt are narrowly circumscribed by offence definitions and normally exclude information relevant to sentence (see King 2012).

symbolic effect in drawing attention to, and dramatizing, the infliction of punishment, as well as promoting psychological and emotional feelings such as forgiveness, atonement, and closure (Doak 2011). Arguably, a unified verdict and sentencing process would obfuscate the public justification of sentences and diminish the deliberative space for decision-makers to explore more communitarian forms of penal intervention.

A two-stage verdict and sentencing model also serves to emphasize the qualitative distinction between the pre and post-conviction phases of the trial by signifying that different substantive and procedural norms apply. In England and Wales, the sentencing phase of the trial is frequently heard separately, allowing time for medical and social background reports to be prepared. However, the basic principle is that the sentence should follow the verdict wherever possible. Thus, the systematic analysis of relevant aggravating and mitigating evidence is associated with, and developed within, this legal and procedural culture. Arguably, this tendency is suppressed within a unified process, particularly one dominated by a predominantly retributive ideology that does not encourage greater transparency, or a more extended and constructive analysis of evidence at sentencing (cf Henham and Mannozzi 2003).

The proposed pre-trial deliberation would address a number of core considerations. Fundamentally, the perceived social value of any likely penal intervention within the community where the alleged offence took place would be evaluated. Consideration of such information would be mandatory when developing the trial programme, so helping to ensure (as far as possible) that penal interventions resonate with local concerns and are sufficiently engaged with perceptions of what is fair and just within the local community. This differs from the notion of 'community impact' in that the focus is on understanding the social impact of sentencing policy in terms of its underlying values, the aim at sentencing being to give precise normative effect to this mandate.[7] Hence, the introduction and assessment of such information during the sentencing phase would provoke a discursive space during which the adversarial contest is supplanted by a concerted search for common ground—where the social value of the individual

[7] The role of the Sentencing Council in providing this kind of contextual information is considered in the next chapter.

penalty is considered within the context of sentencing policy's broader engagement with shared social values and social justice.

The proposed trial programme would therefore facilitate an outcome that promotes social value in a 'real' sense on the basis of empirical evidence, whilst also encouraging the exercise of judicial discretionary power to take advantage of opportunities for alternative forms of intervention, mediation, or resolution during the trial and sentencing phases. Subject to this, the trial programme would recommend particular forms of diversionary process, the necessity or otherwise of expert evidence, and the extent to which particular parties, including legal professionals, might participate in the decision-making process. Decision-making would remain the sole prerogative of the judge.

In short, the procedural changes envisaged are wide-ranging, and, in addition to the trial programme, include changes to verdict delivery and sentencing practice, changed rules for the admissibility of evidence, reconceptualized notions of responsibility, changes to the burden of proof, possibilities for judicial intervention and diversion through enhanced discretionary power, the development of new forms of sentencing guidance, modified rules for victim and community representation, changed roles and ethical codes for legal professionals within the process, and reconceptualized procedural roles for plea and sentence bargaining (see further Findlay and Henham 2010).[8]

The Role of Judicial Discretion

A key factor in reconceptualizing the trial and sentencing phases of the criminal process concerns the issue of 'trust' and the perception that judges and magistrates are capable of exercising their discretionary powers for the common good.[9] The enhanced discretion and more flexible normative regime proposed would

[8] The introduction of pre-sentence restorative justice interventions in the crown courts of England and Wales signalled an important step in the right direction, but this kind of approach still fails to deal with the inherent ideological drawbacks of the current penal regime (Kirby 2014; see also Sherman and Strang 2012: 216).

[9] Lack of space precludes discussion of the possible effects of demographic variables such as social background or political affiliation on sentence decision-making (see Henham 1990, 2012, and the earlier discussion in ch 4).

allow sentencers to divert the process from one justice paradigm to another, whether before the commencement of the trial proper, during the trial itself, or during the so-called enforcement phase. Thus, judges would determine how 'facts' consistent with the purposes set for the trial are produced; whether penal purposes should include retributive or restorative considerations or a combination of these and other objectives; and how such purposes might be achieved in practice. Moreover, judges would be given enhanced discretion to ensure access and participation for all relevant participants in the process, both lay and professional, as consistent with the agreed objectives.

Enhanced judicial discretion in sentencing would require new guidance for balancing and prioritizing the interests of victims and communities, especially principles ensuring effective rights of participation and decision-making, as appropriate, within the sentencing process. Such guidance would be developed within an overarching framework designed to monitor and respond to concerns about consistency and proportionality. This guidance would include detailed practice directions allowing judges to reduce the formalism of proceedings where necessary, and facilitate the contributions of lay participants. As explained below, new guidance would also be needed to expand the scope of the judicial role beyond adjudication to include the supervision and enforcement of sentencing decisions. The overall emphasis would be on exercising judicial discretion to invoke procedural norms, such as those governing plea and sentence discounts, on the basis of their capacity to contribute to the achievement of the broader social objectives set for the trial and sentencing phases discussed above, rather than for reasons of expediency, or purely systemic concerns.

This section concludes by examining the implications for social justice of enhancing judicial discretionary power to include the supervision and enforcement of sentences in England and Wales within the context of the changes proposed.

Beyond sentencing

The supervision and enforcement of sentences in England and Wales is currently an executive function. The rationale for greater judicial involvement in this area is that it would enhance the social value of individual sentences and therefore assist in promoting the 'core' social values underpinning policy.

Such an augmentation of judicial power would extend far beyond the sentencing parameters conventionally associated with adversarial forms of criminal trial. Supervisory functions in England and Wales are by convention exercised by administrative authority under executive control.[10] Indeed, it may be argued that the judicial function should not extend beyond giving particular effect to the declared purposes for punishment following conviction and sentence. Under the current regime, where imprisonment is deemed appropriate, the sentencing function normally consists of determining a proportionate prison sentence according to just deserts principles, although conditions attaching to subsidiary objectives such as rehabilitation may be applicable (see section 142 of the Criminal Justice Act 2003). Beyond having the power to specify minimum terms of imprisonment in the case of life sentences, English judges, unlike some of their continental counterparts, have until recently[11] remained relatively unconcerned with administrative contingencies such as early release or the appropriateness of particular rehabilitative regimes, or with any appeals relating to their operation. Such differences of approach between adversarial and inquisitorial forms of criminal trial are firmly rooted in social, political, and cultural history (Radzinowicz 1966: ch 1).

In the common law world, recent debate has focused on the wider structural significance of what has become known as 'back-end' or 'back door' sentencing, and how to rationalize it (Travis 2007; Padfield 2014). The conventional objections to change reflect inherent system conflicts between the sentencing and parole authorities; namely, that the courts perceive parole as usurping their rightful control over the length and objectives of sentences of imprisonment. This is also a particularly significant factor in public misconceptions about the purposes of parole and who has responsibility for the actual terms served, factors readily subject to political and media manipulation. Thus, the objectives of parole are easily obfuscated and conceptually detached from those of the sentencing courts, varying according to time and place (Barnard 1976; Herzog-Evans 2015).

[10] See Herzog-Evans (2015) for comprehensive comparative analysis.

[11] Note the obligations of the Sentencing Council in this respect when framing sentencing guidelines (see s 131 of the Coroners and Justice Act 2009).

The logic of combining the process of adjudicating over violations with the imposition of the sentence has been extensively scrutinized (Travis 2007). The contemporary consensus among sentencing scholars is that regimes which diminish the liberty of convicted offenders through back-door measures are essentially penal in character. Travis (2007: 637) advocates an empirically informed rights-based approach to combat this tendency, arguing that the only way to ensure consistent and principled decisions about the deprivation of liberty in this context is by basing policy and principle upon sound empirical research (cf Robinson 2013).

Unfortunately, empirically informed decision-making is no guarantor of liberty. Travis (2007) argues that, without the development of such principles, back door sentencing, just like its front door counterpart, is more likely to continue to serve the interests of state power, in effect, a further extension of state control over 'deviant' minorities (Feeley and Simon 1992; Simon 2007). Nevertheless, a counter argument is that, whilst such measures may well reduce abuse, the system itself and more importantly its foundational ideology remains unchanged, and therefore, so does the fundamental problem of the potential abuse of state power. Parole is such an effective control mechanism that it is always likely to be abused, either for political, or more narrow systemic administrative or bureaucratic reasons, such partiality becoming further entrenched in law and legal rationality (Weber 1958).

Notwithstanding, applying just deserts principles to back door sentencing is also problematic due to a lack of transparency and public confidence (Roberts and Hough 2005: ch 5). Therefore, if specific sentencing guidelines for parole decision-making were to be introduced in a bid to ensure more equal treatment for prisoners in England and Wales, it is important to consider how this might affect the balance of power between the executive and the judiciary in terms of controlling the exercise of that discretion. Whilst there has been much greater control of judicial discretion in front door sentencing this has not occurred further along the process, the executive's entitlement to take early release decisions having been consistently confirmed by the superior courts (Padfield 2009). However, the Parole Board may have little control over the factors upon which the decision is based, such as the degree of risk posed and the extent to which the prisoner has been prepared for release. In addition, the relative role of key players such as probation and prison staff may be unclear. Beyond that, giving the executive too great a role opens the way for undue political interference in the process.

Travis (2007: 641) rightly suggests that back door sentencing should be viewed as a transitional mechanism for returning those subject to incarceration to a state of liberty by encouraging desistance, reintegration, and reconnection with family, peer networks and communities supportive of such values. Again, more empirical research is suggested to justify what should be rare occurrences, when deprivation of liberty is necessary to promote compliance with welfare goals of public safety and prisoner reintegration. However, one might argue that the entire process of sentencing is transitional for the offender, the victim, and the wider community. Viewed constructively, it should be the first step in helping the offender to come to terms with what has happened, so the penalty should become part of a positive process of reintegration (Duff 2007). Thus, greater involvement by the offender in sentence planning is likely to place much greater emphasis on multi-agency responsibility and community involvement (Padfield 2014).[12]

Padfield (2014) concludes that 're-thinking the way sentences are designed or more accurately simply "happen" could reinvigorate the debate on aims', so that we might perhaps develop more 'ambitious aims'. This is an important point. As things stand, sentencing policy often appears to have no other coherent moral or social justification beyond the achievement of short-term, politically desired, but predominantly economic goals. Certainly, there is little sense in which policy helps to mediate between competing social demands on the basis of a shared vision between citizen and state about the social value of punishment.[13]

Whilst the social value attached to rehabilitation may be shared, there is little appreciation of how the interactions and

[12] However, practices such as arrest on the basis of a fresh allegation of breach of condition, rather than a requirement that only a fresh conviction should justify recall, may be regarded as counterproductive to reintegration.

[13] In terms of public perception, several cases involving the early release of serious and violent offenders by the Parole Board of England and Wales can be cited in support of the 'obfuscation thesis'. Two recent examples are the release of Philip Lawrence's murderer, Learco Chindamo, and the escape of Michael Wheatley from an open prison while being considered for early release (see *BBC News* 2014b, 2014c).

understandings of the various actors involved produce discretionary decisions about offender risk (cf Hutton 2014), and a great deal of media-fuelled public suspicion regarding the competency of decision-makers. Arguably, such a lack of trust may be reduced through greater public accountability and transparency within the decision-making process (Ashworth and Zedner 2014). However, I suggest that, without fundamental changes to the values underlying punishment and consequential modifications to the system, merging the sentencing and enforcement phases of the criminal process in England and Wales is likely to further public mistrust of the judiciary and intensify demands for stricter controls on the exercise of discretion. Whilst transparency and accountability are always paramount considerations, reforms are only likely to succeed if explanations and justifications for action can be judged against values that have widespread public support.

Implications for change

Building coherence and a shared purpose for sentencing and its aftermath remains an elusive goal. The kind of shared vision advocated herein goes far beyond the idea of building community cohesion through constructive citizenship. It argues for a radically different penal ideology from that which currently pertains, one which shapes the norms and structures of every aspect of sentencing, including front and back door sentencing, and beyond, to engage with wider communitarian interests and values.

Such a move would have important implications for the rule of law and penal governance. Sentencing has a socially instrumental function that extends far beyond the consequences of merging different phases of decision-making within the criminal process. Hence, incremental changes to the structures and functions of the penal estate are unlikely to prevent demands for greater moral credibility if repeated policy failures impact disproportionately on levels of criminality and recidivism. However, egalitarianism demands effective rights protection. A socially disconnected and overregulated penal system encourages unfair treatment and discrimination and may conceal broader cultural and social concerns. Penal agents should therefore focus more on interventions that secure social reintegration as a long-term goal for *all* interested parties.

The notion of a penal ideology that sustains norms, processes, and practices which resonate with contextualized notions of social value is a challenging one for policy-makers. Sentencing, like law itself, is part of a constantly changing penal landscape in which the state strives to keep pace with citizens' perceived demands. To achieve this, penal measures need to be interventionist and socially responsive rather than reactive and detached from broader social concerns. Whilst changing penal ideology along the lines suggested should make sentencing more effective in terms of promoting social justice, further political and social change would be necessary to remedy perceived failures of democratic accountability.[14]

Prioritizing Substantive Justice

I have argued that sentencing policy should be more constructive in promoting social justice within the domestic setting. However, penal legitimacy in a morally pluralistic world demands a more meaningful engagement with citizens' values. State values and purposes should resonate with offenders, victims, communities, and civil society so far as possible for 'justice' to be realized in a substantive or 'real' sense. Empathy or emotional engagement with procedure does not validate the morality that underpins sentencing policy or the substantive law of sentencing. Regrettably, procedural justice has progressively become the measure of substantive justice in the late modern era, despite the fact that its disproportionate focus on system demands ignores the cultural and socio-political contexts that shape sentencing policy and its delivery. This tendency undermines the potential efficacy of substantive norms and so weakens penal governance.

The ongoing controversy regarding guilty plea sentence discounts provides a salutary example. Few penal practices have provoked such intense and prolonged scholarly debate (McConville and Marsh 2014) and their moral and social value remain contentious questions. Utilitarians, for example, might regard the expanded use of such discounts on economic grounds as morally acceptable on the basis that system efficiencies and economic

[14] As public trust in the ideologies and institutional practices of the state diminishes, so correspondingly calls for direct action tend to increase.

thrift are for the common good. Alternatively, one might argue that such mechanisms are morally acceptable only if they help to realize democratically expressed demands. According to this view the encouragement of guilty plea discounts is perfectly justifiable provided they sustain the rule of law, whatever its moral status. Unfortunately, both positions ignore the possible immorality of law, and the fact that penal policy is often socially oppressive and may discriminate unjustifiably against minority or socially disadvantaged populations (Tonry 2011).

Accounting for the social value attributed to such processes is essentially an empirical exercise, with findings likely to reflect diverse perceptions about justification and purpose. Explanations might for example, be sought to establish whether guilty plea discounts are regarded as fundamental to the smooth functioning of the criminal justice process on the basis that policy-makers ought to know whether citizens find them morally acceptable, and, if so, their reasons for doing so. However, guilty plea discounts may be theorized from competing perspectives that distort subsequent evaluations of value because they emphasize particular concerns. For example, functionalists might focus on the operational efficiency of criminal justice processes, whilst systems theorists stress communication structures and the normative control of human interaction. Alternatively, conflict and critical theorists might explore the hegemony of penal ideology (Vogel 1999), highlighting the notion that control mechanisms such as guilty plea discounts exist to provide an illusion of justice, whereas in reality they suppress 'truth' and diminish rights. Accordingly, policy facilitates political dominion; it symbolizes the partial and repressive penal state (Foucault 1977; Hall and others 1978; Mathiesen 1990).

The position adopted here is necessarily partial in the sense that I am arguing against the continued hegemony of neo-liberal values in sentencing. Thus, I suggest that deserts-based neo-liberal values tend to produce distorted accounts of victim and community harm, and so prevent sentencers from engaging fully with questions of value and accountability in their social context. Accordingly, the notion of social harm is easily displaced by that of negotiated justice on the grounds of administrative and bureaucratic expediency. In essence, the meaning of 'harm' itself is negotiated. This tendency may also have a disproportionate impact on racial minorities (Hood 1992; Bowling and Philips

2002),[15] signifying the penal state's wider failure to address discriminatory practices over a range of legal and non-legal factors. Policy-makers in England and Wales have resolutely avoided confronting this issue. Thus, the debate continues as to whether procedural mechansims such as guilty plea discounts actually disadvantage certain minority offenders, victims, and communities (see Shute, Hood, and Seemungal 2005).

Notwithstanding, I suggest that such control mechanisms could be reconceived within the framework of a penal ideology based upon core social values, as suggested by the British Academy Report (2014). Robinson (2013: 174) argues that enhancing the legitimacy of procedural justice may undermine the moral credibility of penal law by calling into question the balance between fairness and justice. Based on detailed research data, Robinson (2013) concludes that changes in a system's moral credibility produce changes in the willingness of citizens to defer to its judgments and values. In addition, the moral credibility of the system depends upon subjective reflection drawn from personal experience. Hence, it is important for policy-makers to note that the moral credibility attached to guilty plea discounts and similar procedural mechanisms reflects the social value attached to particular outcomes by offenders, victims, and communities.

Whereas particular social values may play a significant role in shaping the perceptions and norms of citizens and communities, it is difficult to generalize about the way systems, processes, and outcomes influence subjective experience. This largely depends upon how individuals perceive their social world and the value they ascribe to information, events, and interactions concerning criminal justice—specifically how individuals value 'facts' about sentencing. Hence, one might argue that common understandings of 'facts', what they signify and the value attached to them, result from shared experiences. This complexity demands sophisticated theory and modelling as a precursor to developing methodologies that are capable of deconstructing understandings of value, both shared and individual, in different social contexts (see Findlay and Henham 2007).

As with substantive justice, the extent to which social values currently underpin procedural justice is limited by the hegemony

[15] This is likely to increase given the projected population demographics for England and Wales (Coleman 2010).

of retributive ideology and the adversarial trial. A fundamental dichotomy exists between citizens' interests and the crime control agenda of encouraging and rewarding guilty pleas, suggesting the need for entrenched rights of consultation and participation for 'victims' in plea agreements and the discount decision-making process. The justice, rights-based, and decision-making models developed by sentencing scholars over many years lack sufficient dimension to explain the role of social values in shaping perceptions of institutionalized processes and outcomes. However, I have explained elsewhere how guilty plea discounts could be reconceptualized within the context of a changed penal ideology (see Henham 2012: ch 5).

Countering the Secularization of Justice Delivery

Arguably, the greatest threat to promoting social justice through sentencing is the singular pursuit of economic goals, particularly when the social consequences of value pluralism and the increasing secularization of society are consistently ignored.[16] Failure to consider sufficiently the impact of moral diversity and cultural differentiation on crime and punishment effectively leaves a policy vacuum wherein economic worth can more easily emerge as the sole or primary measure of social value. Once entrenched, economic values begin to shape the meaning and practical significance of punishment within different communities.[17] More particularly, assessing the preventative value of sentencing in purely economic terms ignores human sensitivities and the emotional dimensions of punishment, especially the need to provide some measure of closure for victims. In addition, economically driven policies may lead to the abandonment of initiatives and alternatives to conventional forms of penalty that are more sensitive to contextual factors.

Sensitivity to social values and the social and cultural forces that sustain them has been distinctly lacking in recent criminal justice policy initiatives pursued in England and Wales.

[16] By this I do not mean secularization in a religious sense, but rather the absence of shared values.

[17] As Ashworth and Zedner (2007) point out, economic opportunity cost analysis influences the 'real' choices that defendants have to make, such as the decision whether or not to plead guilty.

The 2012 White Paper 'Swift and Sure Justice' provides a useful illustration.[18] The White Paper's focus on the notion of justice as 'sure' was essentially aimed at low-level offending and anti-social behaviour. It proposed a 'Justice Test', a 'non-bureaucratic framework' aimed at extending local police discretion to filter cases thought to be most suitable for out-of-court disposal. Arguably, as with the proposed abandonment of formal cautions (see *BBC News* 2014d), the 'Justice Test' was criticized on the basis that it favoured a loosely regulated extension of police discretionary power at the expense of the closely regulated sentencing sytem, encouraging well-known attendant dangers such as net-widening (Cohen 1985) and the prioritization of system goals (Cicourel 1968).

In addition, the invocation of 'sure justice' heralded an expanded use of restorative interventions in the form of neighbourhood justice panels, involving partnerships between local agencies, the police, local authorities, and local communities. Whilst a welcome extension to community justice, their evaluation proved problematic, with delivery models ranging from formalistic and punitive to casual and voluntary, and variable follow-up (Turley and others 2014). Promoting 'sure justice' was thus firmly aligned to the 'democratisation' agenda; increasing public confidence and the need for greater involvement by the magistracy in localized justice delivery, particularly the extension of their remit to regulatory offences to offset their diminishing trial role. Swiftness and greater transparency were linked directly to increased public confidence, prompting further proposals for court closures and the dispensing of 'on the spot' magistrates' justice from inside police stations, and the development of 'justice hubs' (Policy Exchange 2014).

Subsequently, the UK government's criminal justice efficiency drive has continued to target delays, unnecessary duplication, and improved compliance and case administration within the court system (Ministry of Justice 2013c). The emphasis has remained on streamlining case management and information provision through digitalization, video links, and 'live' conferencing (Leveson 2015; Ward 2015). Social interaction is gradually being reduced to a bare minimum and replaced by a swifter and more

[18] See Ward (2015) for an assessment of the impact of this policy on procedural justice in the lower courts of England and Wales.

impersonal form of 'virtual' justice. Moreover, in reviewing the criminal justice 'landscape' following publication of the White Paper 'Transforming the Criminal Justice System' in 2014, the National Audit Office (2014) made constant reference to changing systems and working cultures, in addition to linking 'problems' and 'problem-solving' directly to the amount and quality of efficiency data. Systemic failure was thus conceived in terms apparently devoid of human value. Again, Weber's portent of a self-perpetuating bureaucracy looms large.

Fortunately, there is some cause for optimism. The importance attached to corporate social responsibility and the social return on investment (SROI) movement has accelerated in recent years, largely thanks to the activities of certain non-governmental organizations (NGOs) (see, for example, Arts Alliance 2011). In particular, the New Economics Foundation (NEF) and Centre for Justice Innovation have been at the forefront of linking criminal justice policy on court innovation and alternatives to prison for women offenders to measures of human value; for example, through stress on improving the victim experience and enhancing court support and advice services. However, whilst the emphasis is on strengthening inter-professional and court management links within local justice settings, the focus remains firmly tied to ways of introducing measures of social value into the existing penal framework. For example, the authority for effective court innovation is linked to 'credible proportionate sentences' and a greater role for the courts in enforcing them (NEF 2013). In its report 'Unlocking Value' (2008) the NEF used SROI analysis to justify greater use of locally administered support-focused community penalties for women offenders, taking into account the broader economic and social costs involved. The report emphasized that the definition of value by relevant stakeholders should form part of a long-term measurement strategy for public policymakers, so that the Treasury, for example, is kept fully informed of the broader social effects and consequences of sentencing outcomes. Of particular relevance was the suggestion that the sentencing authorities should be kept abreast of social cost factors.

However, I would argue that these suggested reforms, although welcome, do not go far enough. Whilst speed and efficiency are balanced against principles of fairness and authority linked to communitarian values, the prospects for promoting social justice through sentencing continue to be constrained by existing penal values. Improvements to procedural justice, communication systems, and greater local involvement in decision-making are therefore evaluated against the conventional governance framework for justice delivery. In particular, following SROI analysis, engagement with broader measures of social value through enhanced judicial discretion would still be linked to an unchanged penal ideology and normative structure. Without a fundamental change in penal ideology the moral foundation for promoting particular social values through sentencing policy is likely to remain fragmented and self-serving, rather than a shared vision for justice delivery forged between citizen and state. Thus, politically pragmatic penal solutions driven by economic values are more likely to predominate, perhaps tempered by vaguely articulated allusions to the virtues of social responsibility and social return. Consequently, identifying and prioritizing social values for the common good is likely to remain an awkward and unresolved policy issue for sentencing in England and Wales.

In terms of penal governance, the state's obligation to identify and respond to changing social values should always be viewed as a crucial aspect of policy-making, particularly since the need for coherence and moral credibility increases as moral boundaries shift. Hence, the way values are perceived and understood within different social contexts should be constantly monitored, reflected, and acted upon if oppressive and discriminatory policies are to be avoided (Borch 2015). Arguably, penal neo-liberalism is undergoing a slow governance 'transition' from the dominant retributive paradigm to that of a more multi-layered, flexible model of penal intervention, including various forms of restorative justice. But such transitions are unlikely to promote social justice consistently as a coherent imperative for policy unless accompanied by a fundamental change in penal ideology. 'Transition' thus suggests a fundamental change from one value system to another, or a process whereby shared values are recognized and adopted, so providing the moral authority for the ideological and practical changes necessary to underpin penal governance—the position adopted here.

Fundamental challenges to the status quo of power relations may act as a positive force for change, and in the penal realm, present the state with opportunities for forging more egalitarian forms of justice intervention. Whereas penal governance is presently characterized by economically motivated policies that extol the virtues of de-centralization, 'responsibilisation', and localism, the consequences of failing to engage with shared values at the local level may be to further alienate already marginalized populations (Crawford 1997; Garland 2001). Social justice can only be achieved where social values are linked to commonly understood notions of fairness and equality, and where this vision is consistently reinforced through penal policy and practice.

Behaviours labelled as crime and punished within 'democratic' settings often stem from what are perceived to be oppressive policies and social injustices perpetrated by the state and its criminal justice agencies over many years. Arguably, this tendency has increased during the late modern era, with excessively punitive neo-liberal retributive justice policies closely allied to value economics. Such penal oppression may exacerbate the plight of already disadvantaged communities and do little to address the social causes of crime. I have argued that this likelihood increases where policies fail to promote a coherent penal vision based upon shared values. This failure not only means that judges and magistrates lack the capacity to take proper account of punishment's social value at sentencing, it also diminishes the prospects for achieving social justice.

7

Some Practical Implications for Policy and Practice

Introduction

This penultimate chapter explains the practical consequences of what has been proposed. It begins by evaluating current models and suggested approaches for incorporating public opinion into sentencing, before seeking to explain how the changes proposed in this book would differ. It then sets out some practical reforms to sentencing in England and Wales based on the arguments developed earlier, including greater coordination between the national regulation of sentencing discretion through the Sentencing Council[1] and regional or community-based sentencing practices. Regional branches of the Sentencing Council are also advocated in addition to new principles and practice directions to ensure that sentencing discretion is exercised within a nationally coordinated, but locally relevant, policy framework. Further guidance from the Sentencing Council is proposed to integrate the rules governing out-of-court disposals with existing principles of proportionality and consistency relevant to sentencing. The overall aim is to explain how the approach taken in this book would promote penal interventions informed by a publicly justifiable framework of penal objectives based on shared values.

Further practical reforms are proposed, including merging the sentencing and enforcement phases of the trial within a reconceptualized and broadened normative framework that prioritizes social impact, the monitoring and evaluation of sentencing's social impact by multi-agency, community-based panels, and the establishment of new objectives and principles to ensure

[1] See Ashworth and Roberts (2013) on the history and function of the current sentencing guidelines system in England and Wales.

that social impact evidence relevant to sentence is given greater consideration during the trial phase. An interdisciplinary policy working group of the Sentencing Council is also advocated to monitor the degree of congruence within and between different regions, and to inform the framing of sentencing guidelines and any preceding impact assessment. Further suggested changes include a greater role for the Sentencing Council in the ethical surveillance of sentencing, the development of new procedural rules, and enhanced training for judges and magistrates. Finally, a closer working relationship between the Sentencing Council, the Courts, the CPS, defence lawyers, and the Probation Service is advocated to develop guidance clarifying their role within the new sentencing framework.

Strategies for Achieving Practical Reform

This section considers the relative merits of various approaches aimed at giving citizens a greater voice in sentencing. Given limitations of space, this can only be a brief overview of what is now an enormous and burgeoning literature (Feilzer 2015). Unfortunately, the notion of 'giving citizens a greater voice' is a wide-ranging and contentious one, ranging from limited rights of access and participation for 'direct' victims of crime, to that of allowing the wider public to participate in the actual process of sentence decision-making, be it as individuals, or in the form of a group of citizens representing the views of the local community (Tomaino 1997).

As befits the late modern state's preoccupation with measuring, evaluating, and 'satisfying' perceived 'public opinion', its reflection in sentencing has become a major focus of policy debate. Accordingly, the promotion of public confidence in sentencing is a factor that the Sentencing Council must take into account when formulating its sentencing guidelines (section 120(11)(d) of the Coroners and Justice Act 2009). However, academic opinion differs widely as to how the question of reflecting public opinion should be conceptualized, and which approach should be adopted to achieve this objective.

From a theoretical perspective, as Ryberg and Roberts (2014: 4) suggest, it may be convenient to classify existing models for reflecting public opinion in sentencing as either inclusive or exclusory; in other words, for or against the idea of giving the public (howsoever defined) a greater say in sentencing. A third position is that of compromise, namely acknowledging the validity of greater participation in principle, but restricting the degree of such participation for reasons associated with retributive or consequentialist aspirations.

Each model has its shortcomings. For example, the idea of equating community values with public opinion immediately raises problems of definition, such as the meaning of 'community', 'value', 'public', or 'opinion', in addition to significant methodological questions, as discussed earlier. The principle of 'qualified public input' is, however, the favoured approach. From a consequentialist perspective, the need to accommodate public opinion arises from its impact on the effectiveness and legitimacy of penal measures, whereas, for retributivists, the question of how to accommodate public opinion might arise, if at all, in the shaping of principles to ensure proportionality.[2]

From a functionalist perspective, the need for sentencing in England and Wales to reflect public opinion in some form has long been recognized (Roberts and Hough 2002, 2005; Freiberg and Gelb 2008). Indemaur (2008: 51) emphasizes the need for contextual measures of public opinion at the preparation and consultation stages of formulating sentencing policy, suggesting that public input should inform the overarching principles of sentencing and the principles that govern the choices between competing aims. Significantly, Indemaur (2008: 54, 56) also acknowledges that sentencing is concerned with 'collective morality' and establishing 'convincing pictures' of accountability, something that populist penal policies often fail to do where they effectively disenfranchise the very citizens they pretend to protect (Hall and others 1978). However, like Tonry and Rex (2002), Indemaur (2008: 62) is not confident that mechanisms imbued with a judicial and legalistic culture are able to deliver on these goals and therefore advocates an alternative structure to factor in public opinion, potentially involving a mixture of institutional partners (Allen and Hough 2008, Hutton 2008).

More recently, the normative significance of public opinion in sentencing has attracted greater attention (Ryberg and Roberts

[2] Bagaric (2014), on the other hand, believes that community experiences of crime should be factored into the assessment of seriousness when considering retributive proportionality.

2014; Roberts and de Keijser 2014). Brooks (2014a), for example, advocates the notion of 'stakeholder sentencing' whereby 'those who have a stake in penal outcomes should determine how they are decided'. Brooks describes the limitations of restorative justice in terms of identifying the community members to be restored and establishing conference membership with its limited applicability, suggesting that these problems can be overcome through the accurate identification and involvement of relevant stakeholders in sentencing. Brooks extends the restorative model further by developing the concept of 'punitive restoration', the notion that restorative justice need not necessarily exclude imprisonment, thus expanding the therapeutic reach of restorative justice (cf Doak 2011). Brooks (2012) contends that stakeholder sentencing has the potential for improving the quality of restorative justice by increasing public confidence, reducing reoffending, and being more cost-effective, as part of a unified theory of punishment.

Stakeholder sentencing is based on the idea that the protection and maintenance of rights embodied in the criminal law through punishment should engage with individual rights in such a way that sentencing and its outcomes have a common source of justification (Brooks 2014a: 202). However, as argued, the social reality of rights merely reflects the social contexts in which the individuals or communities holding those rights are presently situated. Consequently, unless state penal ideology is imbued with a different or new morality advocating social justice as an imperative for sentencing policy on the basis of identifiable shared values, the moral purchase of rights will not materially change or alter the impact of punishment on the quality of people's lives in disadvantaged and poorer areas.

The potential source of such contextually significant citizen input remains a matter of some conjecture (Roberts 2014, Roberts and de Keijser 2014). Dzur (2012, 2014) sees constructive citizen involvement as the key to assuming responsibility for public problems. In Dzur's opinion, providing lay citizens with a voice through jury sentencing presents an important opportunity to influence penal outcomes through actual participation. It heightens public awareness of the emotional consequences of crime by focusing on questions of responsibility and respect as 'real' issues tied to citizens' everyday experiences of crime (Dzur 2012: 14). Undoubtedly, fostering collective awareness of the manifest failings of the social order is a laudable enterprise, but, as Dzur (2012: 157) himself points out, there is a limited normative consensus as to what should be the guiding values. In other words, although one may well agree with the principle that communitarian solutions effected through collective action such as jury sentencing are more likely to engage with community values, this does not answer the question of how to construct a society based on 'democratic' or other socially desired values, let alone how such a society might actually translate such values into practical and effective penal solutions. Hence, there is no guarantee that 'reconstructing the jury as a communicative forum' will ultimately foster the moral development of citizens and so deliver a greater 'sense of justice' that has 'real' normative impact.

In principle, one might agree with Dzur that increased lay participation would reduce the social distance between the trial and the ordinary citizen, or Mill's assertion that greater public participation hinders the hegemony of the political elite, or Duff's contention that greater legitimacy depends upon reversing the trial's 'normative exclusion', signifying a reappropriation of the 'conflict' by the civis. However, few scholars have addressed the normative aspects of these questions convincingly (Ryberg and Roberts 2014). Robinson (2013, 2014) has gone some way towards injecting the 'how' debate with some important practical suggestions, employing detailed empirical data as a basis for evaluating community judgments of desert within the extant normative framework. Robinson (2013: 174) argues that changes in the system's moral credibility produce changes in citizens' willingness to defer to the system's judgments, and, more particularly, its underlying values, effectively increasing the likelihood that such values will be internalized. Moreover, he highlights the importance of tracking community views (2013: 188), especially in pointing out areas where the apparent legitimacy attached to procedural justice enhancement actually conceals or undermines diminishing moral credibility in the system as a whole. Robinson (2013: 196) confirms the general consensus that guidelines, not individual judges, are preferable in determining how societal interests are to be balanced against what is necessary to ensure effective crime control, a consensus that is challenged here.

Robinson's prodigious analysis contains many useful insights. For example, he stresses the importance of taking extra-legal factors into account in building moral credibility with the community, something that Green (1961) identified as crucial in explaining variability in judicial sentence decision-making over fifty years ago. Robinson (2013: 403) is also careful to link notions of liability and accountability in suggesting that community views as to culpability, alternative offence formulations, offence grading, and justifications for action should all be empirically monitored. Robinson (2013: 494–5) explicitly recognizes the problem of reconciling relativities in relation to extra-legal punishment factors and the need for explicit guidance in ensuring this while retaining moral credibility with the community when relying on such factors (2013: 531). Countering the distorting effect of the media is therefore paramount. Hence the need for more detailed empirical research to discover the true nature of shared intuitions as to the meaning of 'justice' (Roberts and de Keijser 2014).

Dzur (2014: 214) is surely correct in suggesting that the solution to the credibility problem lies beyond the normative reach of retributive or deterrent approaches to dealing with crime. However, the implication that what is needed is to somehow reinvigorate 'such a diffuse and quasi-autonomous system' through greater lay involvement in sentencing appears unsatisfactory. Rather, as argued, a fundamental change in penal ideology is required, suggesting that the problem, and its solution, is more deeply rooted. A key priority is absent from the justificatory language used by states to underpin sentencing policy and practice—the reflection of shared values for the common good.

None of the scholars cited argues for a fundamental shift in penal ideology. Dzur (2012: 72), citing Mill and others, suggests that open and transparent government fostered through greater civic engagement enhances political legitimacy. But, lack of moral credibility remains a major issue for political legitimacy, a situation that has not improved despite an enormous increase in the regulatory measures introduced by successive governments to ensure transparency. Leaving aside conjecture about excessive regulation, a moral credibility gap exists where citizens place little or no credence in the state's capacity to deliver penal accountability. A clear example is continued misunderstanding concerning the relationship between the sentence imposed and early release.[3] If

[3] See eg the case of Michael Wheatley and its aftermath (Telegraph View 2014).

citizens do not empathize with such fundamental aspects of state policy, there is little chance that they will do so at the community level, where the real personal and social ramifications of policy are felt. Hence, I would argue that more civic engagement does not necessarily deliver greater social justice. Rather, an enhancement in the moral credibility of sentencing policy and practice is a necessary precursor.

Roberts (2014: 232) distinguishes the notion of increasing public input to bolster legal compliance from that of increasing public input to bolster public confidence. As to the former, he sees little evidence that empirically based adjustments are likely to foster greater moral realignment with the law, or indeed that greater moral realignment or perceived legitimacy might promote compliance or cooperation. Roberts (2014: 233) is equally dismissive of the second notion, suggesting that, whilst perceived legitimacy may increase as a result of measures designed to bolster public confidence, 'there are insufficient justifications for *determining* punishments with this objective in mind' (emphasis in original). In sentencing, Roberts (2014: 236) favours an approach that is sensitive to, and takes account of, community views about offence and offender characteristics as they relate to decisions about harm and culpability within a proportionality based system. As far as implementation is concerned, and on the assumption that the case for limited public input is made, Roberts (2014: 237) is sanguine about direct public input into sentencing, preferring instead an approach which sensitizes 'the community to the punishments being inflicted in their name'.[4]

Roberts and de Keijser (2014) criticize the work of Bibas (2012), Dzur (2012) and Robinson (2013)[5] on incorporating community views or values into sentencing, concluding that this notion poses a consummate threat to 'principle', as exemplified by proportionality, consistency, and parsimony. However, the kind of 'principle' Roberts and de Keijser are talking about, and which they are defending, is precisely that which has been critiqued in this

[4] Roberts (2014: 243) also decries proposals for jury sentencing as lacking evidence that it would reflect community values more effectively, even with appropriate training. Rather, he invokes de Keijser's (2014) observation that, whilst intuitive public judgments are often unprincipled, informed public opinion may well be unrepresentative of the general public.

[5] See Robinson and others (2014) for a detailed response.

book, namely 'principle' that does little to address the negative social implications of neo-liberal penal ideology. Roberts and de Keijser appear to characterize all potential threats to 'principle' as dangerous forms of populism. Arguably, the proposal that 'Sentencing guidelines authorities should continuously monitor the nature of public opinion with a view to identifying discrepancies between judicial practice and community views' (2014: 494), whilst a sound practical suggestion, misses the vital point (consistently emphasized herein) that system changes designed to accommodate public opinion, however well intentioned, are likely to prove meaningless and ineffective unless the normative and institutional infrastructure charged with delivering the desired outcome is informed and infused with the appropriate ideology. In other words, there is a fundamental need for policy to engage with the underlying values that inform 'public opinion', but, crucially, values that are shared on the basis that they are perceived as common good values. This does not entail a modified version of neo-liberalism, with its partial vision of social justice, but an ideology predicated on values that prioritize social justice as a necessary and achievable moral goal.[6]

My argument therefore takes a different approach from Roberts and de Keijser. I have suggested here and elsewhere (Henham 2012) that sentencing ideology, policy, and practice as presently constituted is at a critical juncture. As with many other institutions of state governance, sentencing increasingly suffers from a lack of moral credibility in the eyes of citizens, a situation exacerbated in communities characterized by value pluralism, poverty, and low social cohesion. In addition, it may be argued that the state's hegemony over the socially disadvantaged further victimizes citizens living in such communities. For these reasons, I do not believe that merely sensitizing penal policy to perceived changes in 'public opinion' is an adequate response. Rather, I suggest that the only way sentencing policy can restore its moral credibility is by recognizing the fundamental nature of the link between the value attached to punishment and its perceived legitimacy. So whilst penal ideology should reflect shared social values, sentencing policy and practice should be concerned with realizing such values on the ground, taking into account

[6] The practical implications are addressed later in this chapter and in ch 6.

factors connecting poverty, discrimination, and victimization to crime and desistance. Hence, I do not advocate a greater role for social impact at sentencing in order to bolster legal compliance, co-operation, or public confidence in the precise sense suggested by Roberts and others.

Reflecting Social Value

As argued, taking account of social value is not the same thing as taking account of public opinion in sentencing. Notions of social value are inextricably linked to individual subjective experiences of community and the moral attachments these invoke (Bagaric 2014). Measures of public opinion, on the other hand, shared or otherwise, invariably fail to take this contextualized subjective experience into account. In addition, as discussed in Chapter 4, the moral credibility of penal policy must be based upon a deeper understanding of the relationship between individual and shared experience, especially in shaping notions of mutual awareness and responsibility. Developing our knowledge of how such values are socially constructed is therefore crucial in developing a practicable definition of the common good. Conventional measures of public opinion do not probe this level of understanding.

At this point it may be useful to summarize what a more contextualized understanding of punishment's social value might reveal:

- A deeper appreciation of commonalities and intersecting relationships of community, so that penal policy is informed by a coherent vision of why competing values exist and how they may be reconciled.
- A more profound understanding of how values of respect for human dignity and the welfare of the individual are socially constructed.
- Deeper knowledge of how individual conceptions of civic identity are socially constructed.
- Greater understanding of how relationships between the emotions and attitudes and perceptions influence notions of social value within different social settings.
- An appreciation of why and how belief in the social value of punishment is shared, and the nature of such shared beliefs, in different social settings.

- Whether or not judicial discretionary power in sentencing is regarded as a potential threat to social justice, or as a force for the preservation of human rights within different social settings.

As suggested earlier, a plurality of disparate values inform the thoughts and actions of most citizens. Such values are shaped by complex social, cultural, and spiritual experiences, many of which may not be shared by others, or reflect the values implicit in penal ideology. The difficulty for sociological interpretations is how best to explain the social construction of shared value systems and the meanings attached to such values by individual citizens. Rather than modelling different accounts of 'public opinion' in sentencing, the primary task for policy-makers should be to develop methods for identifying and monitoring the social value attached to punishment within different social settings.

A Publicly Justifiable Framework of Penal Objectives

Theoretical considerations

The previous chapter explored the growing tendency to link investment with some kind of measurable social return as a way of addressing the social value deficit in sentencing. Defining relevant stakeholders and responding to their concerns was seen as forming part of a long-term strategy for public policy-makers of engaging with the broader social consequences of sentencing decisions. Particularly important was the suggestion that the sentencing authorities should be kept abreast of social cost factors.

However, I also argued that this narrow approach would tend to diminish substantive justice, since community justice resolutions and alternative forms of penal intervention would still be evaluated against extant neo-liberal justice criteria. In particular, possible engagement with broader measures of social value through enhanced judicial discretion would remain constrained by an unchanged penal ideology. Thus, the desirability of promoting social value as a major governance objective for penal policy-makers was mooted, a value that would remain under constant surveillance.

Fundamentally, the difference between this and other approaches lies in the notion that decisions about social value, howsoever gauged and evaluated, cannot be effective if values are simply incorporated into the existing penal framework. Therefore, change is needed, not only in the social values that underpin sentencing policy, but, more profoundly, in the way such values are realized in a normative sense at sentencing. In distributive terms, this suggests that the ethics and practice of sentencing should be empowered to promote social justice as a common good, thereby linking moral principle and social reality.

I suggest that this approach is not reducible to an argument about the nature of democratic accountability, nor a philosophical debate about how best to configure the justice relationship between citizen and state. Rather, it is in an essentially sociological contribution with significant practical implications for penal governance. My focus is the normativity of penal law. In suggesting that the moral value of criminal accountability should be reflected in a penal ideology that engages with social value my argument inextricably links the moral to the social question. I suggest that an appreciation of this argument is fundamental to effective reform.[7]

Practical constraints

The conventional approach for dealing with aggravating and mitigating factors in English sentencing has been shaped by the exigencies of the adversarial trial paradigm and a predominantly just deserts sentencing philosophy (Roberts 2011b). Various scholars have criticized this methodology for its failure to take into account the impact of social deprivation and poverty on criminality, or the nature and extent of the victimization social factors engender (Hudson 1998, Piper 2007, Manson 2011). Principled grounds for rejecting change are generally based on a belief that the existing framework of liberal values and rights protection is best placed to balance the interests of citizen and state in penal matters (Ashworth 2011).

Von Hirsch and Ashworth (2005) propose extending impact mitigation where it can be justified on principle, a point of

[7] See Lee (2015) for further analysis of the issues.

particular contemporary significance given the relentless increase in the prison population. However, Piper (2007: 154) argues that this would require the further structuring of sentencing discretion to counter the threat to consistency and proportionality under the deserts regime. Calls for increased guidance on aggravation and mitigation have been met with resistance on the ground that the introduction of detailed contextual information carries with it the potential for producing more variability in sentencing (Ashworth 2011). Realistically, it is far too prescriptive to try and pull together all the factors that might constitute aggravation or mitigation for all types of case and attach relative weights to them.[8] Furthermore, the approach to aggravation and mitigation tends to vary as between different courts. The inherent subjectivity of decisions regarding age and victim vulnerability, for example, already points to possible difficulty in articulating guidance that can be effectively regulated.

The fact that the punishment itself has an impact on offenders, victims, and the wider community that may go far beyond the imposition of the sentence presents a fundamental dilemma for the retributive model. For example, whilst von Hirsch and Ashworth (2005: 63) are prepared to countenance the possibility of reduced culpability as a principled response to some aspects of social disadvantage, a finding which may make the difference between a custodial and a non-custodial sentence (Wasik 2004), they go no further, suggesting instead the use of compassion where appropriate. However, there is little consensus on where the line should be drawn, which factors should be reflected in the penalty, and which factors should remain outside the purview of criminal justice policy altogether.

Scholars who defend retributivism as the main justification for punishment argue that sentencing should not concern itself with social policy questions such as social deprivation (von Hirsch 1993). The political conditions necessary to secure justice through punishment are unlikely to be achieved in the short term. The harm caused to crime victims is not lessened by the knowledge that social disadvantage may have contributed to the offender's criminality. Hence, improved social policies that deal adequately with social deprivation are needed to influence crime

[8] See Harris (2015) on the need for reform.

patterns. Sentencing should focus on delivering a principled and consistent response to behaviour that has been criminalized by the state.

Furthermore, allowing judges and magistrates greater discretion in deciding what weight to give to such factors in mitigation is a recipe for inconsistency and incoherent sentencing. Easton (2008), for example, argues that compensatory justice at the point of sentencing is a 'blunt instrument', incapable of resolving what are deep-seated social injustices and inequality. So the best way forward for sentencing is to endeavour to be as even-handed as possible, to avoid discrimination by adopting a rights-based approach, rather than widening the parameters for exercising judicial discretion.

However, I would argue that the more retributive justice is perceived as partial in reinforcing social disadvantage, particularly through disproportionately punitive responses, then the more difficult it becomes to challenge offending behaviour within communities by promoting citizenship values or enhancing rights of access and participation. Promoting such values requires the input and collective commitment of citizens and communities. Retributive justice remains individualistic in focus and largely detached from the fact that the harm caused by crime has social repercussions that go far beyond the immediate victims. Although these effects may be difficult to predict and beyond the control of the courts, it is vital that the criminal process, and so sentencing policy, becomes more proactive in engaging with social reality by promoting the moral credibility of punishment within society. Ultimately, retributive justice may be justified within more inclusive restorative or reintegrative ideologies where the overriding priority is the promotion of social harmony rather than a narrow focus on individual culpability and harm.

Easton suggests that formal proportionality in retributivism is necessary to preserve what citizens generally regard as the 'correct' relationship or balance between the gravity of a crime and the appropriate punishment. But I have questioned whether any of the reforms to the existing regime currently proposed are capable of achieving this goal. Questions of harm and culpability need to be addressed by a penal response that is more in tune with shared values and the link between the moral and social contexts of crime. In my view, a socially responsive ideology is more likely to be effective in promoting core social values at the community level than one which attempts to regulate injustices through rights whose moral credibility is suspect because they lack social meaning.

Retributive precepts are based on the assumption that retaining the existing paradigm, with certain modifications, is preferable to exposing citizens to the uncertain destabilizing effects of greater social impact mitigation. My argument is far broader in scope. I suggest that maintaining the present distance between sentencing policy and social policy is untenable because the moral credibility of sentencing is intimately connected to wider social policy concerns. As Garland (1990) suggests, punishment is socially embedded. Accordingly, sentencing's role in promoting social justice is more likely to be realized where its ideology, structures, and outcomes reflect values that are shared by the majority of citizens. However, this should form part of a coherent policy commitment to social justice. Since the existence of such a commitment cannot be assumed, the state should consistently seek to monitor social values and consider the implications in formulating sentencing policy. This is not an individual compensatory approach of the kind criticized by Easton; rather, I argue that the ideology informing the principles of distributive justice is itself untenable. As presently conceived, the current regime is far more likely to produce sentencing outcomes that ignore questions of social value, and so contribute to, rather than ameliorate or prevent, unfair and discriminatory practices by working against the common good. Furthermore, rights protection is only effective in so far as rights are contextualized and reflective of social value, which is currently not the case. So the 'balance' between values and rights must be grounded contextually.

Hence, what is proposed is not the abandonment of deserts theory in favour of unbridled consequentialism. Linking penal ideology more directly to social values is intended to provide a changed normative and ethical paradigm for sentencing wherein the relevance of social impact evidence can be maximized, without sacrificing core principles of proportionality and consistency. By extending the inclusivity of the process, value is shifted from individual guilt to allow a principled engagement with collective notions of liability. Since punishment's primary aim would be to promote social justice based on shared values, harm and culpability would be addressed within a more communitarian context of accountability—one sensitized to the need for sentencing, and penal policy more generally, to engage with the social and moral significance of crime and punishment at the grass roots level.

The Crown Court Sentencing Survey

Despite its limitations,[9] the now discontinued Crown Court Sentencing Survey (CCSS) commissioned by the Sentencing Council provides some important new data on the use of aggravating and mitigating factors by crown court judges.[10] The data on previous convictions and guilty pleas reductions[11] are especially pertinent to the issue of social justice in sentencing, providing an important indicator of the extent to which judges are presently hindered in promoting sentences having 'real' social value, given the restrictions placed upon their discretion by existing legislative constraints and the current guidelines regime.[12]

[9] The non-response rate was roughly 35 per cent, although this did not, of course, change outcomes. In addition, the form itself was only able to mirror the small amount of discretion made available to judges by the guidelines. It is also worth noting that the CCSS did not record regional variations in sentencing practice, nor was there a similar exercise covering sentencing in the magistrates' courts, despite the fact that they deal with the overwhelming majority of guilty plea cases. Neither did the CCSS take account of gender, race, or social class (see Roberts and Pina-Sanchez 2015 for further discussion).

[10] Data collection ceased on the 31 March 2015 with the results for 2014 being published on 25 June 2015. Thereafter, the Sentencing Council decided to adopt a new research approach focusing on specific offences and guideline subject areas in both the crown court and the magistrates' court, making the CCSS's extensive data base available more generally to academic researchers as well as other interested parties (see further https://www.sentencingcouncil.org.uk/blog/post/sentencing-council-analysis-and-research-to-take-new-approach-in-2015/).

[11] Guilty plea discounts have steadily increased in importance since the Sentencing Guidelines Council (SGC) first formulated a definitive guideline on the subject. According to the 2014 CCSS (Sentencing Council 2015a), 90 per cent of offenders sentenced in the crown court pleaded guilty. The 2014 survey also included analyses of proportionality at the individual offence level, as well as the level of sentence discount where offenders had pleaded guilty at the first reasonable opportunity. Of the 90 cent pleading guilty, 81 per cent did so before or at the plea and case management hearing (PCMH). Eighty-nine per cent of those pleading guilty at the first reasonable opportunity received the maximum permissible discount.

[12] Forcing courts to take previous convictions into account generally increases sentence lengths and hinders prospects for rehabilitation, whilst guilty pleas curtail evidence, including victim and community input.

As Roberts and Hough (2015) point out,[13] the CCSS data differ markedly from that produced by the Ministry of Justice as it records how judges actually[14] applied the information contained on the court file in their sentencing decisions. Interestingly, CCSS data confirm that judges generally adopt the progressive loss of mitigation test when dealing with previous convictions, whilst the expected reductions in sentence length following a guilty plea are roughly in line with Sentencing Council recommendations. However, controlling for the timing of the plea, reductions exceed Sentencing Council guidelines where multiple mitigating factors are present.[15] Yet, neither previous convictions nor guilty plea reductions are relevant to Step 1—the determination of the offence category by reference to varying degrees of culpability and harm. Previous convictions are only relevant to Step 2, along with a host of other possible aggravating and mitigating factors, including remorse, while guilty plea reductions are dealt with at Step 4.[16]

As regards mitigating factors, the focus is numerical rather than contextual. The 2013 CCSS (Sentencing Council 2014c) concluded that those offenders with many mitigating factors were

[13] See Wasik (2012a), Pina-Sanchez and Linacre (2013), and Roberts (2013) for further comment and analysis.

[14] The reliability and validity of this exercise was questionable since, without any further analysis of the sentencing remarks in each case, it was not possible to determine why and how a judge reached a particular decision. The CCSS form merely recorded what the judges recalled.

[15] The role of judicial perception may have been crucial here, yet this information was unavailable.

[16] CCSS data show that the key factor in deciding the level of discount is the timing of the plea rather than the type of offence, consistent with the approach laid down by the Sentencing Council guidelines and s 144 of the Criminal Justice Act 2003.

More recently, a change of approach by the Sentencing Council in the priorities that determine seriousness within the existing framework is evident with, for example, the Robbery Guideline Consultation of October 2014 suggesting that too much emphasis on the value of the goods stolen as an indicator of the level of harm would be likely to distort sentences (Sentencing Council 2014d: 15). Instead, after detailed analysis of a sample of sentencing transcripts, the consultation suggested that greater emphasis should be placed on the harm caused to the victim. However, while rightly prioritizing victim harm, the constraints of the existing paradigm preclude any consideration of wider social demographic and contextual factors.

less likely to receive a custodial sentence, yet there was little variability in the time spent in prison when compared to offenders with fewer mitigating factors. The presence of fewer than three mitigating factors had little bearing on the time spent in prison. Interestingly, the report suggested that 'aggravating factors have a stronger influence on the sentence length than mitigating factors' (Sentencing Council 2014c: 26).[17]

Commentators have criticized the guidelines taxonomy for drawing artificial distinctions and adversely restricting personal mitigation so that it counts for less in the overall determination of sentence (Cooper 2013). Whilst the guidelines may be useful in limiting the impact of previous convictions[18] or guilty plea discounts within the extant system of offence based proportionality, it is difficult to discern the actual role and potential limits of the mitigation plea when so many claims may be made against it. For example, the CCSS highlights remorse as a very powerful factor across all offence categories, yet its exact influence is particularly hard to gauge. It is worth noting that remorse was formerly considered crucial to the determination of the guilty plea discount (Thomas 1979), yet guilty pleas discounts are now associated with cost saving and increased bureaucratization in criminal justice (cf Blumberg 1967).[19] Unfortunately, the CCSS did not reveal how judges distinguish the two.

Further knowledge about the way discretion operates is crucial since, in the case of remorse for example, it may be associated with an increased willingness to engage in more restorative forms of resolution.[20] Whilst it may be logical to exclude remorse from the offence category decision on the grounds that the offence is no less serious—harm and culpability remain the same—its confinement as a poorly articulated mitigating factor operating within narrowly-framed deserts-based guidelines limits the capacity of judges to exploit its potential social value, albeit within

[17] This trend was confirmed in the 2014 CCSS (Sentencing Council 2015a).

[18] There seems little scope for taking account of broader contextual influences such as the impact of social deprivation on recidivism within the current retributive paradigm for weighing previous convictions (Roberts 2008).

[19] It is also worth noting that the nature of the defendant's plea changes the context for personal mitigation (Jacobson and Hough 2011: 160).

[20] Dhami (2013) suggests that greater attention needs to be paid to developing a psychological understanding of human judgment and decision-making in sentencing.

an already highly constrained discretionary regime.[21] With social impact evidence already strictly circumscribed, it seems reasonable to argue that the Sentencing Council's numerical emphasis on aggravating factors, coupled with diminishing sentencing discretion, is far more likely to encourage longer sentences than promote restorative or similar reintegrative interventions.[22]

Accommodating factors relevant to social value

Nevertheless, the fundamental question of how broader contextual influences on crime and criminality,[23] such as poverty or social deprivation, might be brought into the penal equation without undermining the existing norms and values that underpin sentencing in England and Wales remains unanswered. Several alternatives may be mooted.

Given the fact that section 142 of the Criminal Justice Act 2003 provides no overriding rationale or means for prioritizing or reconciling the different purposes for sentencing,[24] one might argue that the Sentencing Council's remit in section 120(d) of the Coroners and Justice Act 2009, which deals with the need to promote public confidence in the criminal justice system, should extend to that of promoting the moral credibility of its processes and practices, and therefore the legitimacy of the criminal justice system as a whole. If so, that might include repositioning the

[21] See Maslen (2015) for further discussion of the role of remorse in mitigation.

[22] Arguably, the analysis of judicial sentencing remarks in each case would have added immeasurably to the quality of the CCSS data set (see further Henham 1999).

[23] Shapland (2011: 73) and others have repeatedly argued that personal mitigation should reflect the connections between criminality and social context more effectively since they are crucial in understanding what leads to desistance. The present focus on the prospects for individual rehabilitation belies the complexity and interaction of other factors that are relevant to desistance, particularly the need for social support in building 'social capital' (Bottoms and Shapland 2011).

[24] Ashworth (2004: 528) stated that: 's.142 of the Criminal Justice Act 2003 sets out five different purposes of sentencing to which courts are expected to have regard. Far from being the great advance that the Government claims, it is both fatuous—since it is simply a list that provides no means of resolving the inevitable conflict between purposes, and establishes no order of priority ... The Government proclaims the importance of consistency, and yet s.142 is self-evidently a recipe for inconsistency of approach'.

ideological and policy-making framework within which these statutory provisions are situated, as I have argued.[25]

Another possibility concerns the Sentencing Council's wider role in relation to the effectiveness of sentencing under section 120(11)(e) of the Coroners and Justice Act 2009, which provides that the Sentencing Council must have regard to 'the cost of different sentences and their relative effectiveness in preventing re-offending' when exercising its functions (Cavadino 2013b). Whilst desistance may be relevant to sub-section 11(e), it also raises broader questions about sentencing's role in maintaining the 'appropriate' balance between offender and communitarian interests (McNeill 2013). Merging the sentencing and enforcement stages, and bringing these within judicial rather than administrative control, could be a way of ensuring that the sentence is better tailored to the needs of the offender and the community. However, as with victim participation, the impact of offender variables on the sentencing decision may need to be circumscribed to avoid destabilizing the system. Merging the sentencing and enforcement phases would also require a new normative framework, as discussed in the previous chapter. One suggestion is that the Sentencing Council should employ focus groups to measure public opinion and feed this information into the decision-making process when framing new guidelines (see Roberts and Hough 2015: 4).[26] However, the administration of such a process would need to be consistent and representative. Furthermore, there is no guarantee that it would engage with questions of social value.

Section 120 also raises broader questions about the role of victims and communities in the sentence decision-making process. Edwards (2012) has explored the possible import of section 120(11)(c) of the Coroners and Justice Act 2009, which deals with the Sentencing Council's duty to have regard to the impact

[25] Referring to s 142 of the Criminal Justice Act 2003, the SGC's Overarching Principles merely state that: 'The Act does not indicate that any one purpose should be more important than any other and in practice they may all be relevant to a greater or lesser degree in any individual case—the sentencer has the task of determining the manner in which they apply' (Sentencing Guidelines Council 2004: A1.2).

[26] See Kirby and Jacobson (2014) in connection with the framing of the new guideline on drug offences in which the authors highlight the need for greater attention to be paid to public concerns regarding harm.

of sentencing decisions on offence victims, suggesting that such 'impact' might extend beyond the immediate victim to the community in which the offence took place; even society as a whole may be regarded as a victim. Edwards (2012) rightly urges the Sentencing Council to take greater account of victim impact in formulating guidelines as part of a wider remit of public policy reform, the emergence of the victim as a major driver of policy being mobilized as a weapon against discrimination. However, victims rarely feature in the aims and objectives of enabling legislation in terms likely to bridge the democratic deficit. This, Edwards argues, surely increases the need for the Sentencing Council to play a more active role in identifying the aims and interests of victims.[27]

Alternative ways of involving victims more directly through victim allocution, or by developing the idea through jury sentencing are often mooted (see generally Bottoms and Roberts 2010). Again, there would need to be safeguards against inconsistent and disproportionate sentencing. More particularly, the emotional influence of victims on other decision-makers and on the whole tenor and delivery of the sentence is difficult to control, especially within a deserts framework. Victim input would need to be calibrated or weighed in some way, or other mechanisms devised to limit its influence. The problem remains that of objectifying what is essentially a subjective response—attaching meaningful procedural significance to victim input whilst not destabilizing the present system. Ultimately, one might argue that it is the responsibility of sentencers to ensure consistency and proportionality through the 'principled' exercise of discretion. But the nature and potential impact of discretionary power

[27] Although an increasing focus on victims has characterized recent guidelines issued by the Sentencing Council on fraud and burglary, the fact remains that the scope and meaning attached to 'community impact' is constrained by the normative straightjacket of just deserts. Thus, 'community impact' is conceived narrowly within the sliding scale of penalties that characterizes the assessment of seriousness and determines how specific aggravating and mitigating factors might be taken into account. Whilst, for example, the burglary guideline included the context of general public disorder as a factor indicating greater harm, the Sentencing Council took no account of wider contextual factors such as the impact of social deprivation on crime when formulating the guidelines.

is a function of sentencing's underlying values and objectives—currently those of the neo-liberal retributive paradigm, howsoever modified. Hence, this paradigm shapes the meaning and practical consequences of 'being principled', or of 'exercising discretion in a principled manner'.

One may therefore question whether the Sentencing Council, as presently constituted, can either identify or protect the kinds of interests that victims, and victim communities more generally, require to be protected. Although the social impact of the offence is taken into account by the Sentencing Council in formulating guidance, the constraints imposed by the current paradigm's values and objectives preclude the routine consideration of broader social impact information concerning offenders, victims, communities, or society in general. Arguably, the Sentencing Council should have a far broader remit in preventing reoffending and victimization, particularly in terms of encouraging alternative forms of intervention and resolution such as restorative justice, yet this area remains largely underdeveloped. Noting that judges can already depart from guidelines in the 'interests of justice', Edwards (2012) argues that the Sentencing Council needs to be flexible enough to access victims' interests and to take account of their preferences, where appropriate. His suggestion that the Sentencing Council is well placed to promote values of care and inclusion is one worthy of consideration. However, in so doing, I would argue in favour of a much broader reconceptualization of its remit and some major consequential restructuring within the context of the system reappraisal advocated.

As with desistance, constant speculation and system adjustments of the kind outlined above highlight a broader failure of sentencing's present ideological and ethical framework to engage with the contextual dimensions of social value. Difficulties in identifying a way forward for the Sentencing Council when framing appropriate guidance and the narrowness of its remit are simply a reflection of this fundamental problem. Hence, debates about how to reform the present normative structure so that judges and magistrates can engage more effectively with questions of social value tend to become circular and unproductive, inviting regression to the politically safer territory of the status quo.

Some possible alternatives

As suggested,[28] the project of incorporating a workable concept of social value into the *existing* ideological and penal framework for England and Wales is fraught with difficulty. Considerations of value in sentencing remain constrained by neo-liberal political agendas and the reactive and punitive focus of retributive and populist policies.

However, accepting the proposition that law and social morality are interconnected, and that penal ideology should emphasize this connection, raises some difficult practical questions, not least of which is whether it is possible to devise workable legal tools for assessing, weighing, and incorporating social value as a factor in sentencing.[29] The idea of operationalizing abstract measures of social value as distributive principles for achieving 'justice' in individual cases is a familiar one. However, such an unregulated approach, whilst perhaps more appropriate to the 1970s, would today be politically unacceptable. Faced with this situation, a possible role for the Sentencing Council would be to develop and elaborate guidance for judges and magistrates based on some form of legal test.

Various options drawn from both criminal and civil law, or combinations thereof, could signal a way forward. Within the context of a changed penal ideology, the normative test for determining social value might, for example, be conceived along the lines of the 'welfare test' employed in family disputes over the custody of children. This test treats the child's welfare as paramount, taking account of such factors as: ascertainable wishes and feelings; physical, emotional, and educational needs; effect of a change of circumstances; age, sex, and background; harm suffered or risked. There is a presumption of non-intervention unless in the child's best interests, as well as a presumption of

[28] I have argued that any normative change should be preceded by a new penal ideology based upon the core values identified in the BA Report (2014). The implications of this approach for developing a test of social value are considered in the next section, whilst the substantive merits of the Report's proposals are discussed in ch 1.

[29] An important preliminary issue to be decided by the Sentencing Council within the current regime is whether broader social impact factors are to be given weight in determining the offence category (Step 1), or the seriousness of the offence within the offence category (Step 2).

involvement by each parent. The Children and Families Act 2013 presumes that any such involvement will further the child's welfare, with mediation the primary and preferred option.

Whilst at first sight a 'welfare test' approach might, by analogy, appear to provide for a balanced consideration of an offender's emotional and practical needs, both individual and social, a problem may lie in establishing exactly what rights a community has[30] in law that a court would be forced to balance against such needs.[31] Ultimately, therefore, whilst a more caring and social welfare orientated approach is needed for the reasons indicated, it may be impractical to develop an overarching legal test similar to the 'welfare test'. In practice, within existing constraints, judges would continue to exercise their discretion on an individual basis, without guidance on determining the penalty's likely social value, or in attaching any particular weight to it. Although a sliding scale attributing weight to social value in specific cases might be developed and adapted to the existing guidelines model, this would not address the underlying weaknesses of the present system; namely, its failure to reflect 'core' or shared values and so provide a credible practical basis for reconciling competing values.[32]

[30] A possible objection to this kind of approach is that the offender has committed an offence against the community whereas a child clearly has not. Therefore, there is a fundamental difference in the nature of the communitarian interest, the rights requiring protection, and so the purpose of the test. However, the aim here is not to propose parity, merely to suggest that there may be some merit in developing a test that is ethically similar to the 'welfare test', the promotion of 'welfare' through sentencing being conceived as something of benefit to both the offender and the community and so consistent with the aim of social justice.

[31] However, I have argued that, where criminality results from poverty, social disadvantage or victimization attributable to failures of policy, this constitutes a moral failure on the part of the state meriting a deeper, more individualized, engagement with the vulnerabilities, needs, and contextual concerns of offenders. As a normative injunction for sentencing, a 'welfare approach' benefiting both individual and communitarian interests could be developed for sentencing by exploring the 'ethics of care' approach (Coverdale 2014).

[32] The expansion of Family, Drug and Alcohol Courts in England, combining a therapeutic care-centred approach with multi-agency involvement, represents an important step forward; helping courts in care proceedings to engage directly with families and communities in coming to terms with the problems of drug and alcohol addiction, thereby preventing more children from being taken into the care of the Local Authority (see Nuffield Foundation 2014; *BBC News* 2015a). Such an approach might usefully be linked to crime and desistance.

Alternatively, instead of its current marginalization, social value might be determined by subjecting the facts of each case to an evidential and public interest test similar to that utilized by the Crown Prosecution Service (CPS) in England and Wales in deciding whether or not to prosecute. The test consists of two stages; the evidential stage—whether sufficient evidence exists to provide a realistic prospect of a conviction, and, the public interest stage—whether a prosecution is in the public interest, given that there is sufficient evidence to justify it. The evidential burden is discharged on the balance of probabilities, weaker than the prosecution has to discharge at a trial proper, and upon which a criminal conviction depends. Admissibility, reliability, and overall importance are the criteria for assessing the evidence. The public interest stage addresses such factors as offence seriousness, culpability, victim harm, age, community impact, and proportionality of the response. As to 'community', the CPS Code suggests that prosecutors should 'have regard to how community is an inclusive term and is not restricted to communities defined by location' (clause 5).

Whilst recognizing the significance of 'community' the factors currently taken into account in the decision to prosecute are circumscribed. The CPS has no remit to consider the broader social ramifications of its function, particularly the possibility that trials and sentencing have a normative reach and social purpose extending far beyond the courtroom—one concerned with social justice and promoting social cohesion. Nothing in the CPS Code suggests what the social goals of the trial might be, nor the communitarian values and rights that a public interest test might be expected to prioritize and protect, or at the very least, consider.[33]

Such criticisms may, of course, be countered. Prosecutors should be chiefly concerned with narrow evidential questions related to specific charges, rather than interpreting ill-defined 'public interest' criteria for measuring social value. Yet, despite their current narrow remit, some commentators have advocated a far greater role in sentencing for prosecutors (Rogers 2006). The ethical and practical implications of this injunction might indicate a need for the CPS Code to develop a broader social dimension. The Code's current engagement with notions of social

[33] The views of victims and their families form only part of the wider 'public interest' so far as the CPS is concerned (Ashworth 2014b).

justice and rights appears weak when set against broader societal concerns. Although the Code effectively objectifies the evidential criteria justifying prosecution within the existing paradigm, it could, I suggest, derive greater moral credibility from an empirical evaluation of the 'public interest' that factors in considerations of social value. However, such a link between prosecutorial goals and the broader social agenda beyond the trial has yet to be articulated.

Developing a Workable Test of Social Value

It is frequently argued that the impact of mitigating (and aggravating) factors should be firmly tied to the established purposes for sentencing in order to ensure consistency of approach (Roberts 2011b). Ashworth (2015: ch 5), however, accepts that additional factors might be recognized, although their identification and weight remain problematic. However, I have argued that the parameters for such a debate would alter dramatically if the existing penal framework was reconceptualized so that social justice became a primary consideration for sentencing policy. Yet developing a workable test for reflecting social value in individual cases is challenging. Attaching weight to factors that might be related to criminality, such as poverty or social disadvantage, is a hugely complex exercise. This complexity is magnified if related concerns of race, ethnicity, religion, or cultural practice are also factored in. Nevertheless, such precision is crucial within a narrowly circumscribed guidelines system. I suggest that the task is both necessary and manageable with appropriate education and training, and within a framework of changed values and norms to validate the rationale and discretionary parameters required by sentencers.

Accordingly, determining social value at sentencing would differ fundamentally from the practice of weighing social impact as part of the mitigation process under the current sentencing regime. Instead, social value determinations at sentencing would routinely take account of local interests and perceptions—more precisely, how factors related to offender criminality, social harm, and the likely social impact of any proposed penalty are perceived by victims and the 'victim' community where the offence(s) took place. Social value in specific cases would therefore be evaluated against the purposes set for the trial, following pre-trial deliberation and settling the trial programme.

As proposed, sentencing would be underpinned by core social values—more specifically, those favoured by the BA Report (2014) (see Chapter 1). The 'penalty'[34] determined at sentencing would therefore provide an indication of the extent to which state values are realized in practice. Whilst the long-term individual or social impact of any penalty cannot be predicted at sentencing, factoring in empirical evaluations of social value at this stage should contextualize the outcome and so assist in promoting social justice at the local level. Accordingly, where guidelines indicate a particular penalty or range, some adjustment could be made to take account of social value, if deemed appropriate. This process would be facilitated through the enhanced discretion available to sentencers within the framework of the trial programme, allowing them to be proactive in pursuing interventions that enable the reconciliation of competing values and interests, and so engage with the social consequences of the penalties they impose. Guidelines would therefore suggest how to weigh social value alongside other factors, as consistent with the objectives set for the trial. The overriding aim is to validate a deliberative context within which decision-makers have both the moral authority and the necessary flexibility to exploit more reintegrative and restorative solutions at all stages of the trial process, alongside more conventional measures.

With this in mind, the following elements are considered fundamental for policy-makers in developing an effective normative framework for promoting social value at the sentencing stage:

1. the precondition of a changed[35] penal ideology making social value a key priority at sentencing
2. the development of criteria for identifying and measuring social value
3. the effective communication of this information to policy-makers and the courts
4. the development of relevant guidance for judges and magistrates.

Points 2 and 4 above are of particular concern in this section.

[34] The word 'penalty' as used here refers to any form of intervention that may be deemed appropriate by the sentencing court.

[35] This means an ideology based on the core social values identified in the BA Report (2014).

Regarding the development of appropriate criteria, the focus on social accountability advocated by the SROI principles (NEF 2013) (discussed in Chapter 6) provides a useful starting point. Adopting this approach would entail:

1. involving stakeholders[36]—understanding the values and aspirations for justice of relevant stakeholders
2. establishing the justice priorities of stakeholders and those who are excluded or feel alienated from the process
3. determining which penal values are shared and why
4. prioritizing only those penal objectives and aspirations that are commonly shared because they are perceived as being for the common good of the community as a whole, and society in general
5. understanding the role of competing values and negative perceptions
6. making decisions about what to prioritize on the basis of thorough ongoing contextual analysis and empirical evidence as described in Chapter 6
7. developing benchmarking criteria for measuring sentence performance and impact against shared values and aspirations
8. developing equivalent research tools for comparative analysis of regional performance
9. ensuring transparency and accountability through independent verification
10. ensuring policy-makers justify what they have done and explain how priorities were chosen
11. providing effective rights protection.

These imperatives are primarily concerned with understanding why and how social values are shared in reality, and devising ways of monitoring this. As argued in Chapter 1, these matters are crucial because policy is concerned with devising strategies for realizing the core values that underpin penal ideology.

[36] Brooks (2014a) argues that 'those who have a stake in penal outcomes should determine how they are decided'. My argument is that *all* citizens have a stake in penal outcomes in the sense that all actions taken by the state against citizens attract value. However, to justify punishment as social justice implies a sharing of values. I argue that the state is complicit in perpetuating social *injustice* where it fails to prevent discriminatory practices in sentencing. Thus, the state's moral authority is weakened if it does not take a lead in identifying and reflecting such concerns when formulating sentencing policy.

Engaging with social value as a policy imperative does not ensure that judges and magistrates are sufficiently equipped to take it into account in individual cases. The latter is harder to achieve, particularly since a significant enhancement in discretionary power at sentencing is contemplated. Moreover, which social factors should actually count in sentencing and what weight should be attached to them in individual cases remain difficult normative questions. However, I suggest that important insights may be gained by examining how indigenous mitigation has developed, the problems encountered, and the compromises made. Hence, the discussion begins by exploring post-colonial approaches to sentencing indigenous populations in Australia and Canada (Warner 2011).

In Australia, a more socially sensitive approach to sentencing Aboriginal people based on their distinct cultural heritage has been evident for many years, particularly in cases of alcohol and drug abuse and domestic and sexual violence (Charles 2010). Research by Jeffries and Bond (2010) in South Australia examined a large range of questions covering factors 'unique' to the indigenous experience including community dislocation, community dysfunction, and societal marginalization. Community and cultural (re) connection was perceived as a risk reduction mechanism in terms of its mitigating effect. Significantly, indigenous crime was viewed as an inevitable consequence of the high level of community dysfunction, echoing positivist explanations of modernity. Hence, the South Australian judiciary has adopted the notion of indigenous mitigation in an attempt to counter the incremental marginalization of the Aboriginal population.

In her review of the research evidence, Warner (2011: 141) suggests some limits on the effective operation of indigenous mitigation:

1. difficulties in establishing a causal connection between the particular factor and offending
2. less weight being given to indigenous factors in serious and violent cases
3. problems of specifying the weight to be given to indigenous factors once they are accepted as relevant—as with discounts for guilty pleas, transparency is essential for building trust in the sentencing process, particularly for victims, offenders, and the wider public.

Acknowledging that the role of sentencing is not to correct past or present social injustices, Warner (2011: 142) suggests that: '[s]entencing should at least strive not to exacerbate inequalities or contribute to the problems of over-representation of disadvantaged groups such as indigenous minorities'. With Ashworth (2015), Warner's concern is that factors relating to social and economic disadvantage are applied in such a way that they do not contravene the core principles of fairness, proportionality, and equality before the law. However, she strikes a more positive note in suggesting that the debate at least opens up a 'deliberative space' for greater community engagement.

Anthony (2013) has also explored the origins and significance of the legal and social factors that influence the sentencing of indigenous peoples in Australia.[37] Her work draws particular attention to the important issue of why and how penal ideology is realized through sentencing, and the extent to which sentencing practices engage with the hegemony of penal law. Although technical difficulties are inevitable in identifying and weighing social and economic disadvantage as a mitigating factor in the case of indigenous peoples, it may be argued that these arise largely because of the narrow penal lens through which their accommodation is perceived—that of a predominantly retributive and deterrent based post-colonial penal ideology. Therefore, although restorative and other more socially engaged forms of communitarian justice resolution such as circle sentencing may be prevalent, or indeed encouraged, this remains constrained by the fact that state penal ideology itself does not prioritize social value so that it is infused throughout the criminal process and beyond.

As to the practical consequences, the next step would require the development of appropriate sentencing guidance for judges and magistrates. Adopting a new penal ideology and ethical approach to sentencing that prioritizes social value does not diminish the need for principles to ensure procedural justice. Furthermore, as the Australian experience demonstrates, it is important not to expect too much of sentencing policy as

[37] The limitations of existing paradigms of community justice for engaging with the sensitivities of indigenous peoples are explored by Clamp (2014).

presently configured.[38] A public policy approach that relies solely on the development of appropriate sentencing guidance alongside common law principles is likely to prove inadequate in reducing rates of minority overrepresentation in prisons. Amending legislation, as in Canada, either in combination with existing or modified common law principles, seems unlikely to change this (Roberts and Stenning 2001). Specialized courts or programmes that depend upon interdepartmental co-operation between corrective services, juvenile justice, health, education, employment, and community services, are more likely to be successful in decreasing prison overrepresentation (Manuell 2009).

However, as argued, prioritizing social value at sentencing requires a policy stance that envisions judicial discretion as a positive and creative force, and provides guidance on factoring in the impact of social factors such as poverty, inequality and discrimination on criminality as mitigation. Ongoing and effective dialogue, and the monitoring and evaluation of social demographic change, is a fundamental perquisite in promoting this approach (cf Anthony 2013). The changes in sentencing policy argued for here, namely, greater social engagement through reconceived ideals, ethics, and practices, recognize the limited contribution sentencing as currently conceived is able to make in promoting social justice, particularly in terms of maximizing prospects for desistance and reintegration. The constraints of the existing penal regime suggest that little may be expected in terms of legislation, policy, or sentencing guidance that impacts recidivism rates in poorer or socially disadvantaged areas. Yet, sentencing's engagement with social justice need not be so limited. A changed penal ideology based on core social values should[39] provoke a greater moral acceptance of sentencing and its outcomes, more particularly in promoting commonly accepted notions of moral and social responsibility at the local level. This approach should bolster the perceived legitimacy of sentencing in conjunction with similar changes in other areas of social policy.

That said, the development of workable legal principles to ensure equality of treatment within this novel environment is fundamental.

[38] Manuell (2009) concludes that, despite the formulation of the *Fernando* principles in 1992, the proportion of indigenous prisoners and detainees in NSW has since increased dramatically.

[39] Provided such values are shared and capable of being realized in individual sentencing decisions.

One avenue might be to adapt core principles such as those developed in the Australian cases of *Neal* and *Fernando*.[40] Accordingly, the following principles could provide the basis for a changed praxis:

- Sentencing principles should be applied generally without social or cultural differentiation. However, those factors contributing to social disadvantage that arise by virtue of such social or cultural differentiation are legitimate considerations for sentence determination.
- Sentencing should prioritize commonly accepted social goals for sentencing as identified by ongoing and detailed contextual research (see Chapter 6). Whilst the social value placed upon the punishment of a particular offence is not of itself a mitigating factor, it must be taken into account in responding to the offender's criminality. In so doing, the court must take account of how social and cultural differences define the social value of punishment within victim communities and the reasons for this.
- The objective seriousness of the crime and the particular subjective circumstances of the offender should be assessed in the context of the social setting. However, these considerations should be balanced against prospects for desistance that engage with social and cultural definitions of social value.
- The resolution of contradictory policy considerations arising in sentencing should take account of differentiated social and cultural definitions of social value. Desired penal impacts should engage with how individuals perceive themselves, and are perceived, within particular communities in terms of moral accountability, not simply legal accountability.[41]

Developing an Integrated Sentencing Framework

The need for an integrated approach

It has been argued that the state should take a moral and strategic lead in developing a new penal ideology that places greater

[40] *Neal* (1982) 149 CLR 305; *Fernando* (1992) 76 A Crim R 58 (see Warner 2011 for further critical analysis).

[41] As Harris (2011) explains, emotions influence self-perception and identity, and so values and adherence to social norms. Correspondingly, changing the collective perception of punishment may help to promote social harmony and so transform social relations.

emphasis on the social value of penal intervention. This overarching framework would inform the establishment of regional branches of the Sentencing Council to monitor and produce contextually sensitive guidelines. At present, court closures and the rapid urbanization and digitalization of the criminal justice estate suggests a further distancing of trials and sentencing from local communities and their values and interests. The continuing development and refinement of sentencing guidelines within this context is likely to reinforce the distancing of 'justice' and a consequential polarization of values.

Changes in the social value attached to crime and punishment should therefore be reflected through localized adaptations of sentencing guidance, focusing on indigenous and broader multi-agency justifications for penal intervention. Regional sentencing objectives sensitive to local social policy concerns would be formulated to fulfil this overarching imperative, as would implementation strategies and evaluation criteria. Demographic variables and ongoing contextual research would inform the determination of regional boundaries for this purpose. However, such boundaries would always be regarded as tentative, recognizing that moral values are transient, interconnected, and shaped by social and cultural factors that vary significantly even within relatively small areas. Since poverty and social disadvantage often go hand in hand with repeat victimization and criminality, appreciating the nature and distribution of this morality is seen as a crucial precursor to developing socially meaningful sentencing policies at the local level.

To date, the focus of academic debate has been on the functioning of the present system and how best to reform the guidelines system to produce more consistent and proportionate sentencing (Ashworth and Roberts 2013; Frase 2013). However, policy-makers seem to have lost sight of the fact that increasing consistency and proportionality in sentencing does not automatically increase its perceived 'fairness' (Hutton 2013: 90; Padfield 2013: 50). As Cooper (2013: 159) suggests, the potentially debilitating reductionism[42] characteristic of guideline systems, far from

[42] This refers to the inherent tendency of restrictions on the exercise of judicial discretion to reduce our understanding of the complexities of human experience and their relationship to criminality and desistance.

encouraging a greater sensitivity to community values, actually militates against the introduction of such possibly 'disruptive variables'. This lack of flexibility, coupled with a failure to mandate explanations for category departures or provide proper feedback to the judiciary on the effectiveness of sentences (Reitz 2013: 197), has hampered the ability of the English judiciary to engage in a publicly transparent and effective way with issues of social justice, particularly in terms of taking account of social value at sentencing.

For many years the Magistrates' Association's sentencing guidelines have been modified in order to reflect local perceptions of crime seriousness and the utility of applying particular levels of penalty to crime committed locally.[43] Such modifications take particular notice of regional variations whilst also safeguarding consistency and proportionality at the national level. Alternatively, one might argue, as many have done in supporting jury trial over the years, that greater lay involvement increases the community's stake in sentencing and so enhances the social value of sentencing decisions (cf Dzur 2012). There are also, of course, other arguments related to closing the democratic deficit and increasing local accountability (Young and King 2011: 209). More generally, it may be argued that the need to engage with citizens and their concerns at the local level increases where the moral and social networks that bind communities together become fragmented, primarily because local justice is more likely to have greater legitimacy in identifying and reconciling conflicting interests. Hence, one might question the wisdom of closing so many magistrates' courts in England and Wales.

Whilst crown court judges deal with far less, although more serious crime, I would suggest that regionalized sentencing guidance is a more credible way of bridging the 'legitimacy gap' than centrally formulated and delivered Sentencing Council guidelines (Mason and others 2007). Increasing legitimacy does not simply imply greater community input prior to guidelines formulation, or giving additional weight to social impact. Rather, it is concerned with ensuring that the social value of punishment can be

[43] The Local Crime, Community Sentence (LCCS) is an important initiative that involves co-operation between magistrates, probation officers, and local communities aimed at improving public confidence in sentencing and raising awareness of the effectiveness of community penalties. See LCCS 2010.

taken into account in discretionary decision-making by providing the necessary deliberative space at the local level.[44]

Regional branches of the Sentencing Council are therefore advocated to facilitate the local implementation of the changes in ideology and policy outlined above.[45] This would allow policy to be operationalized effectively at the local level, developing guidance aimed at ensuring that sentencing judges have the discretion and knowledge necessary to engage with social value. In my opinion the remit of the Sentencing Guidelines Authority proposed by Roberts (2014: 246), reflected in the suggestion that such an authority 'might want to consider whether the benefits in terms of increased public acceptance of sentencing might justify deviations from a purely retributive model of sentencing', does not go far enough. Centralized adjustment at the level of principle when courts and communities are 'judged' to disagree suggests an inadequate mechanism for any meaningful judicial engagement with social value at the local level. Such a reactive approach to guideline development, where the guidelines authority and different communities somehow edge towards compromise when disagreements erupt publicly, is likely to have a negative impact on penal governance. Rather than enhancing the perception that the state intends to promote social justice for *all* citizens, it may induce the opposite effect.

Regional branches for the Sentencing Council would require new principles and practice directions to assist judges in integrating alternative penal interventions with mainstream sentencing disposals within the new policy framework. The kind of integrated model envisaged would therefore be informed by regionally modified sentencing guidance where account is taken of local context through ongoing research programmes. By modelling sentencing guideline implementation over time, it may also be possible to predict how changes in social value, or changes in related demographics, might need to be accommodated.

Research programmes could be either state or community funded through national or local taxation, or a combination of

[44] Hutton (2013) suggests extending the role of Judicial Information Systems (JIS) beyond helping to provide consistency in the case of individualized sentencing to performing a wider role in relating social impact factors to sentencing.

[45] These would work closely with local courts, judges and magistrates, legal advisers, the CPS, defence lawyers, and other relevant agencies.

both, signifying a more democratically accountable penal policy agenda. Rather than establishing new, centrally controlled structures and bureaucracies, existing university criminal justice infrastructure could be mobilized to deliver the necessary research locally. Reporting to, but acting entirely independently from the institutions of local and state penal governance,[46] such research would effectively capitalize on local knowledge and 'independent' research expertise, whilst enhancing the practical contribution of the academy to the delivery of local justice. Research programmes would regularly monitor the social value of sentencing decisions and the extent to which penal outcomes are consistent with local perceptions of social justice. Multi-agency, community-based panels would initiate such programmes and evaluate the results.[47] New objectives and principles would also be required to evaluate the impact of social factors on sentencing.[48]

In short, the taxpayer would fund the proposed research; settling research remits would fall to local multi-agency panels; delivering research programmes would be the responsibility of local universities; findings would be reported back to the local multi-agency panels who would also be responsible for ensuring their effective integration into local justice delivery.[49] A three-year rolling programme of research is proposed.

Extending the remit of the Sentencing Council

Finally, an interdisciplinary policy working group of the Sentencing Council is also advocated to monitor regional variations in practice,

[46] Such research would fall outside the remit of Higher Education Funding Council for England's (HEFCE) research funding decision-making powers, thereby preserving academic integrity and independence, appropriate allowance being made in the HEFCE exercise. Thus, neither system nor wider political interests would compromise the research. Rather, impartiality would be guaranteed by the kind of social accountability only a hypothecated tax can provide; in this case, a tax levied for the common good whose moral virtue derives from shared values.

[47] Membership would consist of regional Sentencing Councils, the local judiciary, court and relevant social agencies, the police, the CPS, and the legal profession, as well as victim and community representatives.

[48] See Henham (2014: ch 5) for further analysis of the problems of establishing criteria for evaluating the impact of sentencing.

[49] This would include responsibility for liaising with local branches of HM Courts and Tribunals Service to ensure the consistent and accurate communication of essential research data.

reporting to the Sentencing Council on an annual basis. The resulting data would inform the framing of sentencing guidelines set centrally as well as any preceding social impact assessment. Further practical changes include a greater role for the Sentencing Council in the ethical surveillance of sentencing, the development of new procedural rules, and enhanced training for judges and magistrates. This would ensure that the purposes and scope of access and rights norms are clarified in new sentencing guidance. For example, the extent to which victim or community rights of access and participation might be constructively advanced together with those of other trial participants and the wider community would need to be explained. In addition to the training required for trial professionals operating the new sentencing regime, a closer working relationship between the Sentencing Council, local courts, the CPS, defence lawyers, and the National Probation Service is advocated to assist in the development of guidance, and to clarify their respective roles within the new sentencing framework.

A collaborative and coherent approach to criminal justice reform is important, not just for the future development of trial justice, but also because penal solutions now increasingly involve the participation of a wide range of other discretionary actors who interact with each other as well as with the judiciary (Tata 2014).[50] The growth of 'quasi-judicial' forms of sentencing raises important questions about the future of penal governance, not least of which is the likely future of court-centred judicial sentencing.[51] Hence, it is important that the values underpinning the proposed new penal ideology inform the ethics and practice of all

[50] A useful example is Kirby's (2014) research looking at inter-agency collaboration in the operation of pre-sentence restorative justice in the crown court. The following inter-agency issues are identified as important: data sharing, access, location, risk assessment, capacity, funding, timescales, and conflicting priorities.

[51] A particularly salient point raised by Tata (2014) is the question of how conflicting professional ideologies might be managed by the state. In conceptualizing this, Hutton's (2014) use of actor network theory is instructive because it focuses on one of the most impenetrable issues in understanding professional justifications for action, namely, the invisible socio-psychological forces that influence choice (see Jamieson 2014). The impact such influences have on shaping the meanings actors attribute to both structure and action cannot be overstated (Rogers and Erez 1999).

penal interventions, not just sentencing, thus providing rationale and coherence.

If adopted, the new normative framework outlined above should, with appropriate training, infuse the sentencing process with a greater sense of common purpose, one that is reflected in the ethics and codes of practice that govern professional interaction. At present, professional knowledge and conduct norms are imbued with the ideology and values of adversarial justice and just deserts, thereby perpetuating the trial's narrow focus on individual liability and sentencing's overriding concerns of consistency and proportionality.[52] Further professional integration along the lines suggested may also counter the negative impact of what Dzur (2012: 161) describes as the 'epistemic and moral authority' professionals currently exercise in the courtroom. Rather, it should encourage a shared sense of civic responsibility among professionals and citizens alike; a responsibility rooted in a penal ideology committed to promoting shared values and delivering accountability at the local level.

[52] The notion of judicial discretionary power being exercised within the context of a wider community of professional actors is not new, the difference now being that the significance of judicially controlled court-centred power has diminished considerably.

8

Conclusion

The Case for Change

This book has argued that the promotion of social justice should become a primary objective of sentencing policy. The proposition that current forms of justice delivery can engage adequately with the social realities of social exclusion, discrimination, and poverty and their impact on criminality and victimization is therefore rejected. Rather, a deeper understanding of the moral values that underpin state punishment is advocated as a necessary prerequisite for future policy, one that resonates more convincingly with the justice needs and expectations of citizens and communities. The latter entails a fundamental change in penal ideology and practice, one that combines a novel theoretical focus with practical suggestions for reform. This new approach calls for a profound reappraisal and change of emphasis, so that shared values underpin penal ideology and are reflected in sentencing policy. Such a strategy acknowledges the state's responsibility to ensure that sentencing policy reflects shared values and that such values are effectively realized through practice, as far as possible. Appropriate research tools for monitoring and evaluating contextualized understandings of social value would provide the basis for operationalizing the state's penal ideology.

I have cautioned against a clear distinction being drawn between sentencing policy and social policy. This is a significant departure from the conventional neo-liberal retributive paradigm, yet I regard this as fundamental if sentencing policy is to play a more prominent role in promoting social justice (Hudson 1993). Hence, sentencing policy should move away from its present narrow focus on retributive forms of justice, or modifications or variants thereof. The notion that sentencing should only concern itself with norm enforcement, reflecting the 'real' harm done to victims by offenders whilst marginalizing the impact on

Sentencing Policy and Social Justice. First Edition. Ralph Henham. Published 2018 by Oxford University Press.

criminality of social deprivation, discrimination, and victimization, is regarded as flawed. Such an individualistic ideology is likely to perpetuate rather than ease social tensions. Similarly, the idea that modified paradigms of retributive justice can respond adequately to the impact of social inequality and deprivation on crime and punishment is rejected. Rather, there are important social advantages to be gained over existing arrangements by merging certain key aspects of sentencing and social policy. These advantages may be summarized as follows:

- greater reflection of the impact on criminality of social disadvantage, vulnerability and incapacity in sentencing decisions
- promoting more therapeutic sentencing outcomes for victims and communities
- acknowledging the links between individual and collective responsibility by broadening concepts of culpability and harm
- broadening notions of collective accountability by working with social agencies within the community in fulfilling sentencing objectives
- recognizing moral diversity and countering prejudice by explicitly promoting shared values to underpin the rule of law within communities and society at large
- providing meaningful participatory rights for all participants in the sentencing process
- maximizing scarce resources by integrating community interventions and sentencing.

Policy engagement with social value is crucial for realizing the above objectives and in providing the necessary moral authority for the proposed extension of judicial discretionary power into areas such as supervision and desistance.

From a theoretical perspective, I suggest that far greater attention needs to be paid to the connections between the social and normative realities of people's lives. More particularly, policymakers need to know why and how links between subjective experience and perceptions of social value are formed and sustained over time, and the implications for fulfilling the state's penal governance obligations. Any meaningful sociological discussion of social justice for present purposes should therefore be based upon the assumption that the criminal process, and trial and sentencing in particular, can be described in 'objectively' verifiable terms—in other words, that there are commonly identifiable processes, participants, and outcomes. This perspective informs the book's main thesis that the values underpinning penal ideology should not only be shared by citizens, but that the normative practice of sentencing should engage with such values in a real sense—in other words, the policy and decision-making framework should facilitate a principled engagement with social value at the local level. Significant aspects of social value may concern:

- The perceived appropriateness of criminalization—whether certain acts or omissions should be criminalized.
- The perceived culpability of offenders and common perceptions of the harm caused.
- The perceived appropriateness of sentences—for example, perceived leniency; perceived injustice of parole.
- Doubts about the effectiveness of sentences—for example, perceived failure to protect communities from particular types of offender, or insufficient engagement with interventions relevant to desistance.
- Feelings of alienation, stigmatization, discrimination, or exclusion linked to sentencing—where citizens and communities feel victimized by the state's public policy failures.
- Perceived failures of procedural justice—for example, failure to satisfy victims' needs; perceived limits on access and participation; lack of adequate witness protection or other process failures.

However, securing more egalitarian forms of sentencing requires effective rights protection. Thus, I have argued that social distance and over-regulation encourages (or conceals) unfair treatment and discrimination and therefore fails to reflect broader cultural and social concerns. Rather, the efforts of penal agents should be more focused on securing social reintegration as a long-term goal for *all* interested parties on the basis of realizing shared values for the common good. The state's moral obligation to engage with different conceptions of social value implicitly recognizes that rights relating to punishment have both individual and collective dimensions. Thus, citizens hold rights individually—the right to expect that penal policy will protect and promote their intellectual and physical integrity, and, collectively—in that the communities to which they belong should enjoy corresponding rights of protection by the state. The latter includes the right to a fair, transparent, and coherent sentencing system that protects their interests because it is underpinned by shared values.

Whereas punishment is directed at the individual, the state collectively exercises the right to punish offenders on behalf of citizens generally as long as they are guaranteed equal treatment before the law. However, equal treatment before the law is no guarantor of non-discrimination in areas of public policy that impact on collective social welfare. Since law is socially embedded, it seems plausible to suggest that it should reflect social values. Yet, in reality, a democratic deficit persists for the disadvantaged poor and socially excluded, so rights accorded in law may have little value, social or otherwise. Penal policy-makers should therefore recognize that individual and social rights are essentially intertwined. The moral legitimacy attributed to individual rights is shaped by social experience. However, rights in sentencing remain largley detached from social factors associated with criminality and victimization such as poverty and social neglect. Thus, policy-makers should acknowledge that rights are similarly embedded in social networks and relationships of community and that their social value may be equally diminished.

The book's theoretical approach stresses the recursivity of sentencing's processes and structures over time. This activity establishes patterns of behaviour and sustains the values used by the state to justify punishment. Accordingly, state values are embedded in penal ideology and realized recursively through the day-to-day operations and decision-making practices of the sentencing process. The proposed new paradigm is designed to strengthen the moral justification for punishment and counter the continued hegemony of penal neo-liberalism, effectively linking the values that justify punishment to values as commonly understood, experienced, and shared by citizens. This fundamental normative connection informs my emphasis on the need to reflect social value in the everyday practice of sentencing.

The case studies suggest significant deficiencies in the existing sentencing paradigm and a pressing need for reform. Chapter 1 concluded that the present paradigm's underlying neo-liberal values encourage sentencing outcomes that exacerbate the social exclusion, marginalization, and victimization of irregular migrants. Rather than strengthening the social value of sentencing decisions, the moral justification for state punishment is weakened by a continuing failure to engage with the economic and social impact of increased irregular migration on criminality, as well as the adverse consequences of existing sentencing practice on offenders, victims, and communities. Similarly, Chapter 2 suggested that the state's decontextualized sentencing response to the 2011 English riots failed to engage with the complex value-related dimensions of offending behaviour. This undermined the social value of the penalties imposed and perceptions of equality and fairness, both substantive and procedural. Chapter 3 argued that, whilst sentencing for financial crime has recently begun to recognize the appropriate moral terrain for punishment, the current paradigm lacks the capacity to exploit the social value of alternative forms of penal intervention by, for example, suggesting means for integrating individual and corporate forms of penal accountability or helping to effect changes in corporate culture. Finally, Chapter 5 explored the impact of the neo-liberal paradigm's persistent failure to engage sufficiently with social factors related to female offending behaviour, particularly cultural influences, the nature and complexity of relationships and family responsibilties, and situational factors relevant to victimization. Again, the differential impact of sentences and a failure to effectively engage with the impact of sentencing policy on social cohesion were identified as significant policy issues.

The book's main conclusions and their broader implications for the future development of sentencing policy may be summarized as follows:

1. The state has a moral obligation to ensure that sentencing policy promotes social justice. Correspondingly, individuals and communities have obligations of mutual welfare and social responsibility. However, social reality does not mirror this idealistic vision. Consequently, sentencing policy must reach a satisfactory compromise or accommodation between competing social values.
2. The social change and value pluralism of late modernity threatens the fundamental nexus between penal ideology and sentencing policy. Common agreement about the moral and social value of punishment and sentencing is often lacking. The state has responded to this dilemma with a narrow interpretation of community interests and the increasing politicization of penal policy, thereby reinforcing existing social arrangements and further obfuscating the social value of penal intervention.

3. Sentencing policy and practice has a significant governance role to play in redressing and stabilizing social relations, particularly where the moral and social cohesion of communities is threatened or no longer exists. In so doing, improving rights of access and participation for citizens and communities is meaningless unless such rights are socially grounded. Rights do not replace the need for sentencing to reflect shared social values.
4. Transitional justice concepts offer important insights into how one might think about sentencing policy's potential contribution to social justice, particularly where the state lacks a coherent moral mandate for criminalizing and punishing offenders. Fundamental challenges to the status quo of power relations may therefore precipitate a greater understanding of how to achieve more egalitarian forms of justice intervention.
5. Consideration of the 'public interest' in sentencing policy needs to move away from its present narrow individualistic focus towards a greater recognition of collective forms of accountability. Penal ideology should also acknowledge that states and citizens share responsibility for the effectiveness of criminal justice interventions. Decisions about social value, however gauged and evaluated, cannot be effective if they are simply incorporated into the existing penal framework. Change is needed, not only in the way social value is accommodated in penal policy, but, more profoundly, how the state's relationship with citizens is conceived in terms of justifying punishment.
6. The ability of sentencing policy and practice to engage with 'justice' in a socially meaningful way necessitates a recasting of penal ideology. Tensions between neo-liberal retributive ideology and utilitarian values continue to define the narrow approach taken by the courts when deciding sentence. This prevents judges and magistrates from taking account of factors related to social or cultural differentiation that contribute to criminality; factors that help to define the social value of punishment within victim communities. Punitive neo-liberal justice policies have consistently ignored the adverse social consequences of punishment, thereby pre-empting further crime problems and a fragmentation of penal policy responses on the part of the state. Understanding the relationship between social fragmentation or instability and the social value of punishment is therefore vital in shaping sentencing policy.

7. For social justice to become a realistic goal for sentencing, policy-makers must be able to draw upon common understandings of penal aims, how principles of distributive justice are perceived, and the social value attached to the practices and outcomes of sentencing within particular social contexts. Sophisticated methodological tools are required to access contextualized understandings of social value, and provide the means for translating this information into practical principles within an overarching strategy.
8. A change in penal ideology cannot be simply engineered or imposed by the state, but must be achieved through the reconciliation of competing values. The declaratory nature of sentencing as a public platform expressing social values, particularly those likely to promote social cohesion, is therefore invaluable in promoting such reconciliation. However, for these values to be realized in the policy and practice of sentencing, there has to be some agreement as to what the underlying or 'core' values of sentencing should be. Accordingly, I have argued that the core values identified by the BA Report (2014) should be adopted as the foundational values of a new penal ideology (see Chapter 1). Such values would then provide the moral foundations justifying punishment by the state. The crucial question for policy-makers is whether they accord with the values held by citizens and communities, and the extent to which these perceptions are shared.
9. Further developments in social theory and methodology are needed to help policy-makers understand how social values are shaped in different social contexts. Furthermore, the state should create structures and facilitate empirical research that is capable of explaining their nature, origins, and social significance. Social theory and methods are therefore envisaged as playing a major role in explaining what makes it socially acceptable and morally desirable for certain values to flourish in different social settings.
10. A publicly justifiable framework of penal objectives should inform all penal interventions. Over-regulation, neo-liberal values, and the constraints of the adversarial trial currently diminish the capacity of sentencers to engage with issues of value and social justice in individual cases. New foundational principles would provide judges and magistrates with the deliberative space required to engage more effectively with

issues of social justice. The principled exercise of discretion within this new framework is seen as crucial to enhancing the moral credibility of sentencing.

Thus, the book's suggestions for policy change are premised on the notion that promoting social justice is a necessary and realistically achievable purpose for sentencing. However, these suggestions depend upon enhancing the discretionary power of sentencers, not restricting it. Ultimately, therefore, the success of the book's proposals for a more communitarian and regionally focused sentencing system will depend upon the strategies policy-makers adopt to restore public confidence and trust in discretionary justice, especially its ability to engage with social justice issues. The book ends by exploring what this might entail.

The Implications for Sentencing Policy

As explained in Chapter 1, whether something has social value is an empirical fact. The social values that inform sentencing policy are best seen as moral prescriptions that do not exist in the 'real world'—they shape the purposes of sentencing. The task of sentencing policy is to provide mechanisms for realizing such values at sentencing in a tangible and meaningful sense. Thus, the crucial test of sentencing's moral credibility is the extent to which state values are effectively translated into practical outcomes that citizens value. The extent to which such perceptions are shared is regarded as fundamental to effective penal governance.

Hence, within the proposed new sentencing framework, notions of consistency and proportionality would have a different reference point from that of just deserts. As stated, the extent to which state values are socially embedded and shared is fundamental to the moral credibility of policy and practice. Consequently, policy should provide a suitable normative context for realizing the state's core values, including the principles that regulate proportionality and consistency. Ideally, therefore, individual sentencing decisions should not only possess social value, but also reflect the extent to which the state's core values are *actually* shared by citizens—in short, whether the values justifying punishment by the state produce outcomes that have social value. Thus, shared values should be paramount in determining the relative seriousness of criminalized behaviour (cardinal proportionality) and the relative severity of penal measures (ordinal proportionality). Regrettably, this has not proved to be the case hitherto.

Deserts credibility in England and Wales has diminished incrementally in recent years as a consequence of a number of external factors, particularly the steady increase in custody levels for offences throughout the range following the introduction of the Criminal Justice Act of 2003.[1] Arguably, a serious consequence of this tendency is that it has become far more difficult to sustain the moral credibility of the offence categorizations that underpin cardinal proportionality in terms of their social value.[2] As with the 2011 riots, penalties may reinforce negative values among those members of ethnic and other minority communities who regard themselves as disproportionately targeted by inappropriate criminalization, oppressive policing strategies and greater sentencing severity. Social unrest and the diminishing moral credibility of penal policy may pose instrumental challenges to the rule of law of which sentencing forms an integral part. Raising or lowering custodial thresholds, providing alternative non-custodial options, or including additional factors relevant to culpability and harm or mitigation will not address the problem of justifying determinations of cardinal proportionality. The latter are inextricably linked to the morality that underpins the rule of law.

Moreover, there is little social value in penalizing repeat offenders where poverty, social deprivation, and duress are the primary motivators.[3] Such factors are marginalized where neoliberal values determine the ordering of penal priorities, particularly since prevalence may justify harsher penalties, (see, for example, Sentencing Council 2016: 16 in the case of theft from a shop). So, for example, despite the fact that mitigating circumstances in shoplifting cases may include being the sole or primary carer for dependent relatives or 'exceptional' financial hardship, or the potential availability of diversionary or community orders, the paradigm validating the operational parameters of all such factors remains unchanged. Thus, 'core' values of liberty, autonomy, solidarity, dignity, inclusion, and security are unlikely to be

[1] See Ministry of Justice (2013d) for a useful overview.

[2] The issue gains in significance where prison numbers are escalating (see Howard League http://www.howardleague.org/overcrowding/).

[3] See von Hirsch and Ashworth (2005: ch 5) and Hudson (1998) for competing arguments.

realized in specific cases unless they are first embedded as ideology. The task of policy is then to design a system capable of realizing such values for *all citizens* so the ethos of social justice imbues the entire sentencing process.

Accordingly, a more flexible system justifying local or regional variations in determinations of cardinal and ordinal proportionality to reflect social value should become the norm. Such principles would operate within a new normative framework, with greater attention paid to the social dimensions of criminality and its significance for determining seriousness and setting penalties at the local level. As Hudson (2006: 272) suggests, the links between law, criminal justice, and the concept of community are important for understanding how crime categories and punishments are perceived. The relationship between law and community is not only reflective of values, it is also 'mutually constitutive' in suggesting how common experiences and approaches to solving conflicts evolve as the source of moral and social obligations. Rather than sustaining social tensions, I have argued that such 'bonds of community' should be recognized and form the basis for institutionalizing social value and local accountability in sentencing.

Central government would retain overall responsibility for monitoring consistency and proportionality and for regulating decisions taken locally. Again, practical oversight would fall to the Sentencing Council.[4] The proposed ideological changes are therefore designed to provide a normative framework that facilitates the exercise of localized discretionary power within parameters set centrally and elaborated as guidance in the form of overarching principles, to maintain overall coherence and stability.

Retaining the status quo of penal ideology and its normative consequences is not a viable governance option in the longer term because it marginalizes public opinion at a time when it is increasingly important for the state to take a moral lead. Thus, in order to rebuild trust and legitimacy, penal policy, and sentencing policy in particular, should be justified on the basis of shared values, reflecting the wider imperative of building social capital through public policy initiatives (BA Report 2014). An essential

[4] The complexities involved in identifying and reflecting social value would seem to militate against the viability of trying to sustain cross-border or multi-state (federal) standards by which to fix cardinal proportionality (cf Roberts 2013).

aspect of this concerns citizens' perceptions of 'seriousness' and its social dimensions. Hence, notions of culpability, as well as harm, should be reconceived to include a significant social component, one that is consistent with identifiable measures of social value within victim communities.[5] Value could then be quantified for scaling purposes (Hudson 1998), thereby enabling judges and magistrates to take account of communitarian perceptions of offender culpability[6] and harm within a coherent framework.[7]

Hudson's (1998: 241) notion of 'categorical leniency', by which the seriousness of certain offences such as property and violent crimes would vary according to specific factors associated with social deprivation, was rejected by von Hirsch and Ashworth (2005: 72) in favour of principles based on the concept of a 'living standard' that focuses on the means and capabilities available for achieving a certain quality of life (2005: 186). The categorization of social value proposed herein differs from such approaches in three fundamental respects:

1. It depends upon a reformulation of penal ideology based upon the BA Report's (2014) 'core' social values as the justification for penal intervention.
2. The state's moral authority is contingent upon empirical evidence that the 'core' values actually exist and are shared by the majority of the population, albeit that the form in which they exist and the manner of their expression may differ according to social context. A crucial factor here is that the 'core' values are not only shared but that they are perceived to exist for the common good of civil society.
3. Realizing the state's moral mandate requires a reconstituted sentencing paradigm and norms operationalizing the social value criteria outlined in Chapter 7. Hence, the values

[5] I am not suggesting here that determinations of harm and culpability should be context-specific to be determined only within the confines of specific restorative processes (see Dignan 2003). Rather, 'core' social values would inform a process whereby findings of harm and culpability are directly linked to social value.

[6] This might also include the social value of criminalizing the behaviour in question.

[7] Reflecting social value also requires some acknowledgement of previous criminality. However, calibrating appropriate penal responses to recidivism has proved one of the most contentious areas of existing penal policy (see Roberts 2008).

justifying intervention and individualization are inclusive and non-discriminatory as is the policy setting out the ethical and normative framework for sentencing. Taking account of social value in individual cases therefore requires the exercise of empirically informed discretionary power.

Such a value-oriented and contextualized approach to sentencing should allow decision-makers to maximize both the individual and social potential for desistance and reintegration, particularly in the supervision and enforcement phases (McNeill 2016). Moreover, the late modern expansion of global and transnational crime, particularly that which is politically or religiously motivated, has challenged conventional notions of accountability and increased the necessity for conceptions of harm and culpability to be couched in more contextually sensitive terms. Hence, as O'Malley (2010) suggests, states should strive to develop penal policies that aim to engage more with the social and cultural origins of such crimes, rather than respond aggressively.

The reconceived penal ideology proposed should facilitate such a normative change. The notion of promoting shared social values signifies doing justice through various forms of penal intervention, so respecting the exigencies of individual rehabilitation and incapacitation where appropriate,[8] but also acknowledging the broader relational and communitarian dimensions of desistance and reintegration. This injunction should provide the ideological, ethical, and normative impetus for a more socially responsible kind of sentencing. As argued, social justice is more likely to be achieved where the state effectively externalizes public understandings of the common good and its supporting values through policy and practice; engaging with the social reality of citizens' lived experiences of crime and punishment within different social settings.

'Transforming Rehabilitation'—a salutary lesson

The recent history of the Probation Service in England and Wales in the aftermath of the 'Transforming Rehabilitation' agenda provides a graphic illustration of the adverse consequences that may

[8] This differs from Brooks' (2014a) idea of punitive restoration by extending the stakeholder argument.

result where neo-liberal penal values are allowed to drive penal policy with little or no reference to social values.[9] Worrall (2015) argues that two approaches could influence the development of the Probation Institute's Ethical Code: the 'what works' market driven approach, or the pursuit of traditional or 'core' probation values. Whilst the latter is likely to be more effective in promoting social justice, other factors such as working with other agencies in multi-agency partnerships have become increasingly important in testing and shaping boundaries. However, linkage to the courts (trial and sentencing) and the criminal process as a whole remains a crucially under-developed aspect of this enterprise.

A fundamental question that remains unanswered is the extent to which probation's 'core' values can engage with the value pluralism of wider society, with its competing interests, individualistic values, and neo-liberal approach to justice delivery. This in turn raises the wider question of whether 'transformed' criminal justice structures and processes such as probation, reconceived within the existing or modified neo-liberal paradigm, are able to insulate themselves from broader social policy concerns such as inequality, poverty, or the criminogenic impact of social and cultural differentiation. A possible response might be to argue that policies allowing practitioners to engage effectively with offenders, victims, and communities *on the ground* in individual cases are ethically acceptable. Acccording to this view, changes in government policy or strategy have limited individual or social impact since practitioners simply adapt by adopting an approach that is consistent with their pre-existing values, or at least they attempt to do so for as long as possible. Crucially, however, practitioner morale and consistent practice are likely to deteriorate over time.[10] Nevertheless, this argument suggests that, provided probation's 'core' values are effectively realized at the individual and community level, the moral virtue of state penal policy is largely immaterial. Consequently, pragmatism and economic determinism should determine policy, so there is no need for an overarching ideology, particularly one whose moral purpose is

[9] See *The Probation Journal* for June 2016 (entire issue) for detailed analysis.

[10] State control may be increased through greater regulation and a gradual reduction in discretionary decision-making powers, but this is more difficult where, as with probation work, the essence of 'success' lies in the building of personal relationships based on trust.

to promote ethics and practices that resonate with shared social values.

I suggest that the above argument is deeply flawed. It raises, but fails to address, significant questions about the state's role in criminal justice governance, particularly in terms of justifying policy by building trust between citizen and state; essentially moral questions with significant social dimensions. This book has argued that the state's obligations should extend to promoting values of mutual awareness, respect, caring, and social responsibility between citizens and communities, thereby building social capital for the benefit of the wider society. Such a socially inclusive and communitarian ideology obliges the state to consider how policy can realize core social values for *all* citizens—a moral injunction achievable only through the everyday ethical practice of criminal justice. The present approach contains no positive vision for social justice built upon shared values.

McNeill (2016) makes the important point that correctional processes should not simply aim at individual transformation, they should also concern themselves with 'moral' reparation (or restoration), judicial rehabilitation, and social reintegration, concerns which, for serious, and/or recidivist offenders, are almost always intertwined. I have argued that shared values should provide the unifying thread justifying all such processes, and that sentencing policy and practice have a central role to play in realizing this aspiration.

Enhancing the Moral Credibility of Sentencing

Chapter 2 considered how sentencing policy might help to stabilize social relations in communities where moral and social cohesion is weak or threatened. In particular, it concluded that greater attention should be devoted to realizing social values during what might be termed 'transitional phases' of moral and social reconstruction.[11] Such an approach would not only demand fundamental changes to penal ideology, but also a radical shift in the way judicial discretionary power is conceptualized and utilized within the sentencing process.

[11] Phases of social reconstruction might follow episodes of social breakdown and public disorder.

For penal policy-makers, the importance of thinking about social values as in a constant state of flux or transition cannot be overemphasized. However, the potential contribution of penal intervention during periods of social transition or reconstruction is not a phenomenon that applies exclusively to failed or war torn states (Henham 2012). Human societies are always in various states of flux or conflict, even to the point where conflict itself may be deemed the 'natural' social condition and primary determinant of social value. I have argued that a 'moral' state should be socially interventionist, so that it monitors and responds sensitively to changes in social values and the social conditions that shape them. This moral imperative has potential as a unifying force, since societies and communities may be at various stages of moral or social disintegration, often caused by deep fractures in the legitimacy attached to the activities of state institutions and the agencies of criminal justice such as the police and the courts.[12] Accordingly, sentencing policy can play a positive role in contributing to programmes of social reform and reconstruction in the aftermath of state neglect and oppressive penal policies.[13] The fact that sentencing is a predominantly legal institution does not imply that it should remain closed or insulated from wider socio-political imperatives. Rather, it could become an essential component in the dissemination of a new penal morality aimed at promoting greater social harmony (Findlay and Henham 2010).

As argued, sentencing should form part of a coherent penal strategy whose underlying values are shared by citizens, communities, and society at large, hence the legitimacy of any national sentencing policy is likely to be weakened considerably where interventions are not anchored to credible social values. So, for example, although domestic initiatives such as 'Justice Reinvestment' are often viewed as useful adjuncts to social reconstruction, difficulties of justification remain.[14] More particularly,

[12] Seminal examples are the Brixton and Broadwater Farm riots of 1985. See Van Dijk (1989) for analysis of the distorting role of the media in portraying these events.

[13] Notions of individual and community transition should be viewed holistically when developing programmes of social reconstruction aimed at desistance and reintegration.

[14] Initiatives such as 'Justice Reinvestment' are concerned with diverting low risk petty offenders from the courts to community-based, multi-agency offender

uncertainty persists as to whether the retribution exacted in any particular case is a consistent and accurate measure of the moral disapproval felt by the victim community, or of society in general.

The current absence of a coherent and principled framework for rationalizing penal interventions on the basis of shared values perpetuates the widely held belief that trial sentencing exists primarily to facilitate retributive and deterrent justice, whilst other interventions are otherwise justified and administered outside the courtroom by other agencies. The changes proposed for penal ideology and for extending the normative reach of sentencing envisage a socially interventionist role for the courts in conjunction with other relevant agencies; a role informed by values that connect in a meaningful sense with those of the communities in which we live (Henham 2012).

Promoting Social Justice as a Realistic Objective

The fact that the aims, norms, and structures of sentencing currently lack coherence is a significant obstacle to reforming the current paradigm. More specifically, it obfuscates the rationales and processes of decision-making and prioritizes system goals at the expense of broader social considerations that reflect shared objectives.[15] Hence, as argued, changes to the normative framework of sentencing must be supported by a coherent ideology based upon identifiable values; values perceived as common good values and shared by the majority of citizens.

Lack of ideological coherence may diminish the chances of effectively realizing the values that underpin state punishment and reduce the potential for taking account of social impact at sentencing. Sheirs (2014) highlights the relative autonomy of the aims of sentence implementation from those of sentence decision-making. More particularly, she argues that a better understanding is needed as to the meaning of 'reintegration', its objectives

management schemes, designed to maximize the prospects for desistance in a climate of severe financial cutbacks (see Fox, Albertson, and Wong 2013).

[15] As Rex (1998) suggests, the moral authority of rehabilitative ideology has been gradually undermined by the administrative imperatives of the late modern penal state.

and processes, concepts that do not necessarily have the same meaning in theory, policy, and practice (McNeill 2014).[16] These differences clearly have a significant impact on the objectives being sought, such as desistance, in addition to the building of social capital. 'Reintegration' when thought of as an aim of sentence implementation might include: enhancing 'the ability of offenders to return to and function normally in civil society after release'; different forms of treatment as a means of reducing the risk of recidivism; or ways of supporting offenders' rights to dignity by maximizing their opportunities to participate in all aspects of social life. Evidently, the meanings attributed to such objectives and practices and the factors that influence their chances of success are relative to culture, time, and place. Hence, to be effective notions such as 'rehabilitation', 'reintegration', or 'restoration' cannot simply be rights protected, they must be justified contextually, supported by common understandings and desired values.

Promoting public confidence and engaging with the public in an effort to enhance the moral credibility of penal measures is now regarded as essential for effective penal governance (Crawford and Hucklesby 2013). As for sentencing, although the Sentencing Council has made strenuous efforts to engage and communicate with the wider public,[17] as required by its remit, public mistrust and confusion persists regarding the way sentencing decisions are reached and their implications, particularly the impact of guilty plea discounts and early release provisions. Some of this mistrust may be attributable to a lack of information, or media distortion, but it is often compounded by the disconnect that exists between the political rhetoric employed to justify sentencing policy and the social consequences of individual decisions for victims and communities. Governments may extol the virtues of 'swift and sure' retributive or deterrent punishment, yet the public perception

[16] Sheirs (2014) points out that in Belgium the term 'rehabilitation' refers to the restoration of the offender's status as a full citizen, comparable to the French meaning: 'retablir dans ses droits', whereas it has different, more welfare-orientated connotations in Anglo-Saxon countries.

[17] Particularly through the development of its website, with interactive links such as 'You be the Judge' and its ongoing involvement with school citizenship programmes (see http://sentencingcouncil.judiciary.gov.uk/get-involved/you-be-the-judge.htm).

may be one of excessive leniency, the perceived inadequacy of the sentence being aggravated by the effect of incomprehensible, and largely misunderstood, early release provisions.

In addition, the apparent insularity of criminal justice agencies, with their disproportionate focus on pursuing system goals rather than shared penal objectives, has been exacerbated by ongoing funding reductions and the accelerated marketization of key penal functions, particularly prisons and probation. Thus, economic pragmatism and political expediency characterize penal policy-making, whilst obfuscation about the 'real' impact of rights, processes, and outcomes persists, so lessening moral credibility in the institutions and competencies of the penal state.

This incremental distancing of citizen and state, between rhetoric and reality, is seen as the root cause of the failure of successive UK governments to instigate sentencing policies that engage with social justice in a meaningful way, thereby reinforcing an unchanged penal ideology and normative landscape. Enhanced victim and community engagement with criminal justice is destined to remain a rhetorical political slogan unless policy-makers are committed to the ideological and practical implications of that engagement. Accordingly, the reforms proposed in Chapter 7 depend upon this ideological shift.

Strategies for Developing Judicial Discretionary Power

The relentless increase in the prison population of England and Wales over the last twenty years has been instrumental in prompting successive governments to seize greater control of the 'law and order' policy agenda. Although the judiciary has exercised a wide measure of discretion in fixing sentences and developing sentencing policy since the turn of the twentieth-century, its power to formulate sentencing policy is unsupported constitutionally (Radzinowicz and Hood 1979; Ashworth 1983: ch 2). Notwithstanding, the concept of judicial independence has remained the principal bulwark against executive attempts to persuade judges to reduce sentence lengths in recent years (Henham 1998). Hence, for politicians, the key question has become the pragmatic one of deciding how far the legislature should go in disturbing the balance between judicial independence, exemplified by the exercise of judicial discretion in individual cases, and executive power.[18]

The decline in the rehabilitative ideal, coupled with the drift towards empirically justifiable and resource driven policy-making, provided the perfect opportunity for the executive to increase the regulation of a potentially troublesome judiciary by curtailing its hitherto largely unfettered discretionary power (Thomas 1979). Since then, fuelled by a vociferous media and political rhetoric, the balance of power has gradually shifted towards greater state regulation of judicial discretion in sentencing. However, the values underpinning the exercise of executive power in penal matters have become increasingly detached from those of citizens and communities (Henham 2012). As a consequence, I argue that greater state regulation has reduced rather than increased the moral credibility of sentencing.

In addition, a number of unresolved tensions remain between the executive and the judiciary; more particularly, between the constraints imposed by the substantive law of sentencing and the difficulty of devising effective sentencing principles and guidance to operationalize such inflexible legal norms. For instance, the normative framework for preventative sentencing in the case of so-called 'dangerous offenders' still bears little relationship to the complex and onerous nature of the decision that a sentencing judge has to make and justify in individual cases. Wasik (2012a) points out that the essence of the judicial function is to determine whether the threshold for dangerousness has been crossed; judges are not concerned with risk assessment or prediction. Nevertheless, the social value of the decision depends upon the justificatory parameters set for both offender evaluation and the judicial function. As currently conceived, the neo-liberal values that underpin the sentencing of dangerous offenders marginalize the significance of social factors. This results in a distorted focus on offender metrics and produces judicial decisions regarding 'seriousness' that are largely devoid of communitarian considerations. The latter comprises values that define the relationship of the individual to the community, including shared perceptions concerning the appropriateness of different forms of

[18] The 'tipping point' came with the Criminal Justice Act of 1991 and the introduction of a statutory framework for just deserts sentencing.

penal accountability and the structures required for their effective realization.

This disjuncture is compounded by the fact that the different evidential requirements of the verdict and sentencing stages of the trial effectively marginalize the post-sentencing enforcement stage of the process, with its enormous significance for desistance and reintegration. Explanations as to the nature and risk of reoffending, motivation and prognosis for drug and alcohol related violence, and the definition and treatment of mental incapacity, rely increasingly on detailed and expensive expert evidence. Such evidence is admitted, interpreted, and applied judicially within the narrow framework of legal tests that lack a broader engagement with social values.

A lack of clarity persists as to the correct distinction between the control and regulation of judicial discretion in sentencing. Politically, unfettered judicial discretion is perceived as threatening because it can damage the credibility of the government's law and order agenda. However, control implies prescriptive guidelines that eliminate discretion. The nature and extent of regulated discretion is therefore the fundamental problem, since ineffective or insufficient regulation effectively allows the judiciary to make individual judgments about culpability and harm that may destabilize accepted hierarchical relationships of proportionality and undermine consistency. Greater constraint may induce policies that prioritize values of fiscal prudence and bureaucratic efficiency rather than shared values promoting the common good. The former tend to favour the standardization of penal decision-making, so reducing the scope for individualization.

Arguably, individualized sentencing introduces aspects of distributive justice that have no wider relevance in determining the moral limits of the criminal law.[19] Thus, the important distinction drawn by Hart (1968) between the concept of distributive justice and the moral limits set for the criminal law[20] might be regarded as obfuscating a crucial governance imperative, namely that penal law and practice should always engage with and constantly reflect changes in social morality. This imperative has

[19] A secondary issue is the extent to which individualized sentencing contributes to inconsistency and disparity.

[20] As enshrined in statute and interpreted in substantive law.

gained momentum since the demise of penal paternalism and the growth of the neo-liberal state in late modernity (Loader 2006).

However, there remain significant areas where both executive policy and judicial sentencing practice continue to ignore social values. The determination of 'undue leniency' under the Attorney General's reference procedure is a case in point (Wasik 2014: 292).[21] Arguably, the test for determining 'undue leniency' is restrictive and misleading, since public perceptions of justice cannot readily be equated with the need to prevent judicial errors of principle, which is the cornerstone of the Court of Appeal's approach (Henham 1994). An objective test for 'undue leniency', reflecting considerations of public perception, with due regard to sentencing convention, may be more appropriate. Certainly, one may argue that the sentencing process should be seen to respond more adequately to the fact that a crime is a social as well as an individual wrong, thereby reflecting the value attached to that wrong and its punishment by the wider community. This seems fundamental to the continued moral credibility of the reference procedure, particularly in the face of concerted media criticism and public misunderstanding.[22] In correcting unduly lenient sentences the existing test effectively precludes considerations of social justice and social accountability.[23] Consequently, judicial perceptions regarding the borderlines of public tolerance are likely to remain a constant source of tension, whereas legal tests such as that concerning the determination of 'undue leniency' should become more sensitive to questions of value.

The singular pursuit of system goals and the lack of a coherent penal strategy are equally destructive of the common good.

[21] See s 36 of the Criminal Justice Act 1988. Sentences were increased in 141 of the 180 cases referred to the Court of Appeal in 2016, a rise of 17 per cent over the previous year. This represents 16.8 per cent of the 837 cases received (see Attorney General 2017 for detailed analysis).

[22] As, for example, followed the sentencing of Rolf Harris and Dave Lee Travis (see *The Guardian* 2014a, 2014b).

[23] A suggested reform is to require the Chief Crown Prosecutor for the area to consider representations made by local MPs whenever the possibility of a reference is being considered. A statutory amendment could set out the test to be applied, obliging the Court of Appeal to give due consideration to the views of the local community and victims as represented to the CPS. Against this proposal is the argument that it would unjustifiably increase the politicization of sentencing.

Hence, any unjustifiable reduction in judicial discretion should be of profound concern to policy-makers seeking to ensure more effective penal governance, since a flexible, socially sensitive, and effective use of discretionary power is key to promoting social values in sentencing. Furthermore, the moral credibility of penal policies grounded in shared values also sustains their political legitimacy. Arguably, in the ideal world of a truly democratic state, the judiciary are more likely to be trusted as impartial mediators between citizen and state; enabling state values to be realized in individual cases, yet maintaining an 'appropriate' balance between individual and social rights. However, this remains a utopian vision.

Neo-liberal penal governance promises the promotion of system goals (Cicourel 1968) and legal rationality (Weber 1958) rather than the coherence of a changed penal ideology committed to reflecting shared values for the common good. Furthermore, over-regulation of sentencing discretion may facilitate its emergence elsewhere in the system, either through a proliferation of gatekeeping decisions, or in the shape of greater prosecutorial discretion, thus reflecting a more general trend in the common law world.[24] Discretion constrained in one place, such as the Sentencing Council guidelines, therefore tends to emerge at either the pre or post sentencing stage, or, more detrimentally, discretion may move out of the system entirely as a result of unnecessary and burdensome state regulation bordering on control. Thus, the coherence and underlying rationality of the system is considerably weakened.

It may be argued that the increasing influence of prosecutorial discretion on sentencing in England and Wales is likely to exacerbate the already high level of sentence severity more generally, although there is little research evidence regarding pre and post guideline practice. The role of the prosecutor in sentencing is explained comprehensively in the CPS Sentencing Overview,[25] which links the notion of representing the public interest to that of 'drawing the court's attention' to the impact of the offence on

[24] See Luna and Wade (2012) and Lippke (2014) for comparative analyses of the prosecutorial role.

[25] See http://www.cps.gov.uk/legal/s_to_u/sentencing_-_general_principles/, citing the Attorney General's Guidelines on the Acceptance of Pleas and the Prosecutor's Role in the Sentencing Exercise: Rule B:4.

the community, as well as the victim, howsoever defined. Yet one might argue that questions of value should precede any impact evaluation (Henham 2014). More specifically, it is important to define what is meant by 'impact' and to consider its value in terms of the sentencing process, and beyond.[26]

Clarifying which values should inform determinations of the 'public interest' is equally pertinent in deciding how aggravating and mitigating factors are likely to be perceived, particularly since the current retributive and adversarial trial paradigm favours individual rather than social dimensions of accountability. Similar objections might be raised about the prosecutor's role in advising judges as to their sentencing powers,[27] especially in relation to guilty plea discounts and the acceptability of pleas more generally. A difficult balance also exists between the court's duty to promote the efficient management of cases and its obligation not to pressurize prosecutors into accepting guilty pleas.[28] Such considerations tend to prioritize efficiency savings above questions of social value.[29]

Closing the gap between the judge and the offender by adopting the kind of seamless process advocated by Padfield (2014) is only part of the structural realignment needed to reposition judicial discretionary power within the framework of the proposed new penal ideology. Streamlining criminal justice through the Ministry of Justice's ongoing 'Transforming Criminal Justice' agenda (2013c) prioritizes factors likely to enhance the smooth functioning of the system at the expense of social considerations. Coupled with the increasing complexity and extent of CPS and defence obligations, both statutory and codified, such developments restrict the

[26] Thus, understanding the 'real' influence of victim impact statements in sentencing and parole decision-making requires clarification and a coherent approach.

[27] See *Attorney-General's Reference (No 24 of 2008) (R v Sanchez)* [2009] 2 Cr App R (S) 41 (CA).

[28] Prosecutors must not support a version of the facts that is detrimental to the victim's interests when accepting a plea.

[29] Note also the increasing importance of the plea and sentence document (PSD) prepared by the prosecutor to assist the court when sentencing, and its likely metamorphosis into a fully-fledged sentencing recommendation, as well as the increased relevance of the plea and case management hearing (PCMH) as a vehicle for moving directly to sentence following a guilty plea by the defendant.

potential reach of judicial discretion as well as making it more difficult to exercise (Hawkins 1995).

Thus, over-regulation is regarded as detrimental to the promotion of social values in sentencing. As argued in Chapter 2, sentencing policy cannot remain aloof and distance itself from contentious areas of social policy without undermining its moral credibility, a tendency that is exacerbated where the constructive potential of judicial discretion is diminished. Hence, the unjustified repression of sentencing discretion through various forms of regulation or 'guidance' may be regarded as contrary to the common good if it tends to standardize the production of 'justice' (Blumberg 1967). Notwithstanding, the judiciary and academics alike have generally lauded the refinement and expansion of Sentencing Council guidelines in England and Wales,[30] despite the argument that greater rigidity tends to downplay the role of mitigating factors and so reduces opportunities for factoring in considerations of social value.

Nevertheless, arguments for expanding discretionary power only hold good where the judiciary is perceived as impartial. Yet I would argue that a system which over-prioritizes retributive norms and regulates discretion unnecessarily is excessively partial. Reflecting shared values in penal policy is arguably a better way of exploiting the governance potential of discretionary power, since it alters the moral parameters for utilizing sentencing discretion for the common good. The constructive exercise of judicial discretion in individual cases is presently distorted by the normative injunctions of neo-liberal ideology, despite the advent of restorative and other forms of penal intervention.[31]

Reducing discretionary power and its over-regulation is counterproductive because it restricts the capacity of judges and magistrates to take account of social value at sentencing. Thus, narrowly conceived deserts-based neo-liberal values continue to shape the social dimensions of penal accountability. As argued, a sentencing policy committed to social justice should encourage

[30] It is hoped that the codification of sentencing law in England and Wales will simplify sentence decision-making, assist in the development of sentencing guidelines, improve consistency, reduce appeals, and increase public confidence in sentencing. See further, Law Commission (2017).

[31] It is important to note that these are not routinely available sentencing options.

rather than restrict the socially constructive deployment of judicial discretionary power. Increasing this capacity within the context of the proposed new paradigm should then ensure that the values underpinning sentencing policy are effectively realized for offenders, victims, and victim communities at the point of sentencing and beyond. This means opening up sentencing to a far greater dialogue with communities about social impact, particularly its wider potential for promoting desistance, reintegration, and social harmony.

Restoring Public Confidence and Trust in Discretionary Justice

Chapter 4 reflected on the need for sentencing policy to engage with the emotions and its implications in terms of building public confidence and trust by changing values (Ward 2014). Caution was advocated, since emotions and sentiments do not necessarily have any moral purchase in defining the common good (Murphy 2012). Deserts theorists who argue that the nature and extent of victim or other potential input must be strictly controlled within the framework of existing constraints and justifications also highlight such dangers. Alternatively, there is a strong case for arguing that, in distancing public emotion, the state is suppressing forces that may erupt later elsewhere with far more serious consequences for social cohesion. Thus, sentencing policy's failure to identify and engage meaningfully with shared values is likely to prove counterproductive, not only because it is profoundly undemocratic and a potential threat to social harmony, but more significantly, because it ignores the intimate connection between the emotional response to crime and the social value of punishment.

Consequently, it may be necessary to go far beyond the over-cautious approach of the penal status quo that treats meaningful victim input, let alone community input, with increasing suspicion because it threatens core principles of consistency and proportionality. Hence the objection that larger guilty plea discounts may undermine proportionate sentencing is only one reason for being cautious about allowing victim input into the discount decision. Such unresolved tensions are symptomatic of a much wider malaise—the absence of any significant conversation about the social value of victim or community input. Instead, penal policy remains socially distanced and reactive rather than driven by any principled imperative for 'real' social engagement at the local level.

With approximately 90 per cent of crown court cases now discounted following a guilty plea (Sentencing Council 2015a), there are clearly dangers in persisting with the current regime. Increasingly, there is little information as to why guilty pleas are put forward and a reluctance on the part of defence lawyers to explain the rationale for doing so, hence little transparency whilst pressure increases on defendants to plead guilty.[32] Yet no change is likely, as criminal justice moves incrementally towards the kind of 'bargain counter, assembly line' system foreshadowed long ago by Blumberg (1967). Thus, contentious issues of enormous moral and social significance, such as the possible discriminatory effects of guilty plea discounts, remain unresolved and marginalized. Nonetheless, justifications for the widespread use of guilty plea discounts and other procedural devices could be reconceived within the framework of the ideological and normative changes proposed (Henham 2012). As currently deployed such discounts ignore broader considerations of social harm or culpability. They remain essentially institutionalized economic expedients negotiated to fit the legal contingencies of each case. Far greater emphasis could be given to victim and community input in evaluating the plea's moral status and its broader social ramifications should notions of harm and culpability be expanded to encompass social value.[33]

Accordingly, as with bail considerations, wider public interest criteria inevitably come into play (Hucklesby 2007). Whilst bail restrictions aim to fulfil the state's obligation to protect citizens, they must also safeguard fundamental values of autonomy, liberty, security, and integrity, values prioritized by the BA Report (2014). On this basis, ideologies that recognize the social value of more egalitarian, transparent, and fairer contexts for the exercise of procedural justice should be justified (Tankebe and Leibling 2013). However, a wider acknowledgement that procedural

[32] The definitive guideline for those pleading guilty at the earliest opportunity may be regarded as further evidence of this trend (Sentencing Council 2017). But see comments by Treacy (2016: 490).

[33] Hales and Gelsthorpe's (2012) research on the guilty plea decisions of migrant women is surely a case in point.

justice operates within a commonly accepted and publicly justifiable ideological framework is also needed before this aspiration can be realized.

Public opinion research reveals a large measure of agreement as to what may be deemed 'fair' or 'unfair' so far as punishment and sentencing are concerned, particularly as to the kinds of penalties considered appropriate for cases of homicide, or serious violent and sexual offences. However, there are many other crimes where public consensus about the morality of criminalization and the justification for punishment remains elusive, more particularly, where the motivation for crime is profoundly influenced by social factors such as poverty, victimization, and discrimination, or by cultural factors, such as strict religious or other codes that advocate alternative moralities and penal justifications. In such circumstances continued repression by the penal state may further stigmatize and alienate already marginalized populations by diminishing their moral engagement with civil society and hampering prospects for desistance and reintegration.

The mobilization of social capital is required if the state is to effectively discharge its moral obligation of ensuring that offenders are not disadvantaged or unjustifiably excluded from the processes and outcomes of criminalization. Thus, there is an urgent need to develop conceptions of the 'public interest' that reflect shared values, then linking that ideological commitment through policy to sentencing practice. Countering weakening legitimacy requires a greater public appreciation of the rationale for sharing responsibility between citizen and state for criminal justice interventions. In achieving this, the state's commitment to increasing social capital through citizenship awareness programmes and similar public educational initiatives is vital.[34] Greater public understanding can help to embed the social values that underpin sentencing policy and so increase the social value attached to specific penal interventions.

In sum, working for policies that promote social inclusion is fundamental in closing the moral credibility gap between political rhetoric and penal practice. New foundational principles for penal ideology based on shared values have therefore been proposed to give sentencing policy greater moral credibility and

[34] Exemplified by Michael Sandel's repeated calls for public debate on moral questions (Sandel 2010, 2013).

social relevance. Developing judicial discretionary power within this new paradigm is seen as key to enhancing trust and the legitimacy of sentencing over time.

Concluding Comments

This book has proposed a series of practical measures aimed at repositioning judicial discretion within the framework of a reconceived ideology predicated on shared social values. The main objective of these reforms is to empower decision-makers by facilitating a principled engagement with social value at the point of sentencing.

However, the credibility of any sentencing policy ultimately depends upon the nature and source of the state's moral authority. A political mandate does not guarantee egalitarianism in sentencing. Hence, the rhetoric of greater victim and community engagement,[35] when set against the accelerated political impetus for localism and regional devolution in England and Wales,[36] poses a significant challenge for the future credibility of penal governance. A major problem is that any devolution of political power is unlikely to be accompanied by the provision of additional resources—probably the reverse. Consequently, policy decisions implemented or taken locally are far more likely to be driven by economic considerations (and powerful vested interests) than shared social values.

Without change, any further devolution of penal powers and functions is likely to diminish the state's ability to promote shared social values, thereby marginalizing questions of overall strategy, integration, and coherence. Devolving penal powers within an overarching governance framework of neo-liberal values committed to retributive and deterrent penalties is unlikely to increase social justice—it will merely transfer the problem of maintaining the moral credibility of sentencing to the local or regional level. Such a strategy would effectively obscure the state's responsibility

[35] See eg the replacement of cautions with more punitive sanctions in the form of community resolutions and suspended resolutions first piloted in November 2014 (see *The Guardian* 2014c). See McNeill and others (2009) for discussion of the 'governmentality gap' between penal policy rhetoric and practice.

[36] For a useful discussion of the complex relationship between devolved and state penal powers (see Mooney and others 2015).

for failure, since it would remain neither accountable for the exercise of those powers, nor for any adverse social consequences that may flow from them. Paradoxically, the state may even claim the moral high ground for having facilitated greater local accountability and democratized punishment. However, to achieve social justice, states and citizens must *share* responsibility for the justification and effectiveness of criminal justice interventions. Thus, sentencing policy should always be informed by an overarching and publicly justifiable set of penal objectives based upon identifiable social values.

The changes proposed herein are fundamental, but, I would argue, neither impossible to achieve, nor politically unrealistic. As currently conceived, sentencing often exacerbates social disharmony because decisions fail to equate with what citizens and communities perceive as social justice. Ultimately, this is a failure of both ideology and policy. A coherent link between sentencing and social values is lacking because neither ideology nor policy address the problem—such considerations are considered beyond the remit of sentencing as presently conceived, and criminal justice more generally. As a result, penal reform is often piecemeal, lacking in moral credibility, coherence or principle. New moral foundations and fundamental structural changes are urgently required to fully integrate restorative and other communitarian approaches for dealing with offenders into the mainstream sentencing system, thereby encouraging parsimony in the use of imprisonment and a move away from the profoundly damaging social consequences of neo-liberal retributive penality.

Contemporary sentencing policy should reflect shared goals and engage with social priorities for the common good, so restoring the essential link between penal ideology and the socially lived experience of crime and punishment. This book has suggested a new paradigm for operationalizing the requisite moral and normative changes; one that links the justification for penal intervention to shared values and offers a coherent practical agenda for their realization.

References

Albrecht H-J (2001) 'Post-adjudication dispositions in comparative perspective' in M Tonry and R Frase (eds) *Sentencing and Sanctions in Western Countries* Oxford: Oxford University Press

Allen R and Hough M (2008) 'Does it matter? Reflections on the effectiveness of institutionalised public participation in the development of sentencing policy' in A Freiberg and K Gelb (eds) *Penal Populism, Sentencing Councils and Sentencing Policy* Cullompton: Willan Publishing

Anthony T (2013) *Indigenous People, Crime and Punishment* Abingdon: Routledge

Arts Alliance (2011) *Unlocking Value: The Economic Value of the Arts in Criminal Justice*

Ashworth A (1983) *Sentencing and Penal Policy* London: Weidenfeld and Nicolson

Ashworth A (1990) 'Sentencing and the Constitution' *King's College Law Journal* 1: 29

Ashworth A (1994) *The Criminal Process: An Evaluative Study* Oxford: Oxford University Press, 1st edn

Ashworth A (2002) *Human Rights, Serious Crimes and Criminal Procedure* London: Sweet and Maxwell

Ashworth A (2004) 'Criminal Justice Act 2003 (2) Criminal Justice Reform: Principles, Human Rights and Public Protection' *Criminal Law Review* 516

Ashworth A (2008) 'English sentencing guidelines in their public and political context' in A Freiberg and K Gelb (eds) *Penal Populism, Sentencing Councils and Sentencing Policy* Cullompton: Willan Publishing

Ashworth A (2010) *Sentencing and Criminal Justice* Cambridge: Cambridge University Press, 5th edn

Ashworth A (2011) 'Re-evaluating the justifications for aggravation and mitigation at sentencing' in J V Roberts (ed) *Mitigation and Aggravation at Sentencing* Cambridge: Cambridge University Press

Ashworth A (2012) 'Departure from the Sentencing Guidelines' *Criminal Law Review* 81

Ashworth A (2013a) 'The struggle for supremacy in sentencing' in A Ashworth and J V Roberts (eds) *Sentencing Guidelines: Exploring the English Model* Oxford: Oxford University Press

Ashworth A (2013b) *What If Imprisonment Were Abolished for Property Offences?* London: Howard League for Penal Reform

Ashworth A (2014a) 'Prisons and Austerity' *Criminal Law Review* 91

Ashworth A (2014b) 'Victims' views and the public interest' *Criminal Law Review* 775

Ashworth A (2015) *Sentencing and Criminal Justice* Cambridge: Cambridge University Press, 6th edn

Ashworth A and Redmayne M (2010) *The Criminal Process* Oxford: Oxford University Press, 4th edn

Ashworth A and Roberts J V (eds) (2013) *Sentencing Guidelines: Exploring the English Model* Oxford: Oxford University Press

Ashworth A and Zedner L (2007) 'Defending the Criminal Law: Reflections on the Changing Character of Crime, Procedure, and Sanctions' *Criminal Law and Philosophy* 2/1: 59

Ashworth A and Zedner L (2014) *Preventative Justice* Oxford: Oxford University Press

Attorney General's Office (2017) 'Outcome of Unduly Lenient Sentence Referrals' https://www.gov.uk/government/organisations/attorney-generals-office

Australian Law Reform Commission (1986) *Recognition of Aboriginal Customary Laws* (ALRC Report 31)

Baker E (2013) 'Sentencing guidelines and European Union law' in Ashworth A and Roberts J V (eds) *Sentencing Guidelines: Exploring the English Model* Oxford: Oxford University Press

Bagaric M (2014) 'A Rational Theory of Mitigation and Aggravation in Sentencing: Why Less is More When it Comes to Punishing Criminals' *Buffalo Law Review* 62/5: 1159

Banking Standards Board (2016) *Annual Review 2015/2016* http://www.bankingstandardsboard.org.uk/wp-content/uploads/2016/03/BSB-Annual-Review-20152016.pdf

Barnard E (1976) 'Parole Decision-Making in Britain' *International Journal of Criminology and Penology* 4: 145

Bauman Z (2000) *Liquid Modernity* Cambridge: Cambridge University Press

Bauman Z (2011) 'The London Riots—On Consumerism Coming Home to Roost' *Social Europe Journal* http://www.socialeurope.eu/2011/08/the-london-riots-on-consumerism-coming-home-to-roost/

Bauman Z (2013) 'Europe Is Trapped between Power and Politics' *Social Europe Journal* http://www.socialeurope.eu/2013/05/europe-is-trapped-between-power-and-politics/

Bawdon F, Lewis P, and Newburn T (2012) 'Rapid riot prosecutions more important than long sentences, says Keir Starmer' *Guardian* 3 July https://www.theguardian.com/uk/2012/jul/03/riot-prosecutions-sentences-keir-starmer

BBC News (2011) 'Some English riot sentences "too severe"' 17 August http://www.bbc.co.uk/news/uk-14553330

BBC News (2013) 'Stoke-on-Trent food voucher project suspended' 11 August http://www.bbc.co.uk/news/uk-england-stoke-staffordshire-23654802

BBC News (2014a) 'Liverpool man with 45 points among 7,300 avoiding bans' 7 January http://www.bbc.co.uk/news/uk-england-25626147

BBC News (2014b) 'Head Teacher Philip Lawrence's killer to be released' 2 May http://www.bbc.co.uk/news/uk-england-london-27249769

BBC News (2014c) 'Skull Cracker' Michael Wheatley in court over robbery' 9 May http://www.bbc.co.uk/news/uk-england-27336796

BBC News (2014d) 'Police cautions to be "scrapped" in England and Wales' 1 November http://www.bbc.co.uk/news/uk-29859758

BBC News (2015a) 'Family Drug and Alcohol Courts to be extended in England' 18 February http://www.bbc.co.uk/news/uk-31512532

BBC News (2015b) 'Carney seeks tougher sentences for irresponsible traders' 10 June http://www.bbc.co.uk/news/business-33087604

BBC News (2015c) 'Trader jailed for 14 years over Libor rate-rigging' 3 August http://www.bbc.co.uk/news/business-33763628

BBC News (2015d) 'Banking culture inquiry shelved by regulator FCA' 31 December http://www.bbc.co.uk/news/uk-3520401

BBC News Magazine (2011) 'The competing arguments used to explain the riots' 14 August http://www.bbc.co.uk/news/magazine-14483149

Beetham D (1991) *The Legitimation of Power* London: Palgrave Macmillan

Bell B, Jaitman L, and Machin S (2014) 'Crime Deterrence: Evidence From the London 2011 Riots' *The Economic Journal* 124/576: 480

Bennett C (2013) 'Democratising criminal justice?' *ECAN bulletin* 21: 4

Bennett C (2014) 'Public opinion and democratic control of sentencing policy' in J Roberts and J Ryberg (eds) *Popular Punishment: On the Normative Significance of Public Opinion for Penal Theory* New York: Oxford University Press

Bibas S (2012) *The Machinery of Criminal Justice* New York: Oxford University Press

Bingham T (2011) *The Rule of Law* London: Penguin

Birkett G and Castell V (2013) 'Transforming Rehabilitation for Women? A View from the Courts' *British Journal of Community Justice* 11/2–3: 149

Bisgrove M and Weekes M (2014) 'Deferred Prosecution Agreements: A Practical Consideration' *Criminal Law Review* 416

Blau P M (1963) 'Critical Remarks on Weber's Theory of Authority' *The American Political Science Review* 57/2: 305

Blom-Cooper L and McConville S (2014) *The Case for a Royal Commission on the Penal System* Hook: Waterside Press

Blumberg A (1967) 'The Practice of Law as a Confidence Game: Organisational Co-optation of a Profession' *Law and Society Review* 1: 15

Bohman J (1998) 'Survey Article: The Coming of Age of Deliberative Democracy' *The Journal of Political Philosophy* 6/4: 400

Boone M (2012) 'Editorial: Rehabilitation perspectives for irregular migrants: Belgium, England & Wales, Greece and the Netherlands' *European Journal of Probation* 4/3: 1

Boone M and Kox M (2012) 'What works for irregular migrants in the Netherlands?' *European Journal of Probation* 4/3: 54

Booth L, Altoft A, Dubourg R, Goncalves M, and Mirrlees-Black C (2012) *North Liverpool Community Justice Centre: Analysis of Re-Offending Rates and Efficiency of Court Processes* Ministry of Justice Research Series 10/12, London: Ministry of Justice

Borch C (2015) *Foucault, Crime and Power: Problematisations of Crime in the Twentieth Century* Abingdon: Routledge

Boraine A (2004) 'Transitional Justice as an Emerging Field' Paper presented at the 'Repairing the Past: Reparations and Transitions to Democracy' symposium, Ottawa, Canada, 11 March

Bosworth M (2014) *Inside Immigration Detention: Foreigners in a Carceral Age* Oxford: Oxford University Press

Bottoms A (1995) 'The philosophy and politics of punishment and sentencing' in C Clarkson and R Morgan (eds) *The Politics of Sentencing Reform* Oxford: Oxford University Press

Bottoms A, Shapland J, Costello A, Holmes D, and Muir G (2004) 'Towards desistance: Theoretical underpinnings for an empirical study' *Howard Journal of Criminal Justice* 43/4: 368

Bottoms A and Roberts J V (eds) (2010) *Hearing the Victim: Adversarial Justice, Crime Victims and the State* Cullompton: Willan Publishing

Bottoms A E and Shapland J (2011) 'Steps towards desistance among male young adult recidivists' in S Farrall, R Sparks, S Maruna, and M Hough (eds) *Escape Routes: Contemporary Perspectives on Life after Punishment* London: Routledge

Bottoms A and Tankebe J (2012) 'Beyond Procedural Justice: A Dialogic Approach to Legitimacy in Criminal Justice' *The Journal of Criminal Law and Criminology* 102/1: 119

Boutellier H (2000) *Crime and Morality: The Significance of Criminal Justice in Post-Modern Culture* Dordrecht: Kluwer Academic Publishers

Boutellier H (2005) *The Safety Utopia: Contemporary Discontent and Desire as to Crime and Punishment* Dordrecht: Kluwer Academic Publishers

Bowcott O (2014) 'Police cautions replaced with punitive sanctions for three English forces' *Guardian*, 1 November http://www.theguardian.

com/law/2014/nov/01/police-cautions-abolished-staffordshire-west-yorkshire-leicestershire-forces-chris-grayling

Bowling B and Philips L (2002) *Racism, Crime and Justice* Harlow: Longman

Box S (1983) *Power, Crime and Mystification* London: Tavistock

Braithwaite J (1989) *Crime, Shame and Reintegration* Cambridge: Cambridge University Press

Braithwaite J (2002) *Restorative Justice and Responsive Regulation* Oxford: Oxford University Press

Braithwaite J (2009) 'Restorative Justice for Banks Through Negative Licensing' *British Journal of Criminology* 49: 439

Braithwaite J and Geis G (1982) 'On theory and action for corporate crime control' in G Geis (ed) *On White-Collar Crime* Lexington, MA: Lexington Books

Braithwaite J and Petit P (1990) *Not Just Deserts: A Republican Theory of Criminal Justice* Oxford: Oxford University Press

British Academy Report (2014) *A Presumption Against Imprisonment: Social Order and Social Values* London: The British Academy

British Journal of Community Justice (2013) 'Transforming Rehabilitation—Under the Microscope' 11: 2/3 Winter (whole issue)

Brooks O, Burman M, Lombard N, McIvor G, Stevenson-Hasgings L, and Kyle D (2014) 'Violence against women: effective interventions and practices with perpetrators: A literature review', SCCJR Research Report No 05/2014 http://www.sccjr.ac.uk/publications/violence-against-women-effective-interventions-and-practices-with-perpetrators/

Brooks T (2012) *Punishment* Abingdon: Routledge

Brooks T (2014a) 'Stakeholder sentencing' in J V Roberts and J Ryberg (eds) *Popular Punishment: On the Normative Significance of Public Opinion in Penal Theory* Oxford: Oxford University Press

Brooks T (2014b) 'Legal Positivism and Faith in Law' 77 *Modern Law Review* 139

Brownlee I D (2007) 'Conditional Cautions and Fair Trial Rights: Form versus Substance in the Diversionary Agenda' *Criminal Law Review* 129

Bullman J, Hegarty N, and Hill B (2012) *The Secret History of Our Streets: London* London: BBC Books

Burawoy M (2005) 'For Public Sociology' *British Journal of Sociology* 56/2: 259

Burke P (1992) *History and Social Theory* Cambridge: Polity Press

Canton R (2015) 'Crime, punishment and the moral emotions: Righteous minds and their attitudes towards punishment' *Punishment & Society* 17/1: 54.

Canton R and Hammond N (2012) 'Foreigners to Justice? Irregular migrants and foreign national offenders in England Wales' *European Journal of Probation* 4/3: 4

Carvalho H (2015) 'Review of Andrew Ashworth, Lucia Zedner, *Preventative Justice* Oxford: Oxford University Press, 2014' *Modern Law Review* 78/2: 394

Catholic Bishops' Conference of England and Wales (1996) The Common Good and the Catholic Church's Social Teaching

Cavadino M (2013a) 'King Canute, Economics, Politics and Penal Policy' *Prison Service Journal* 207: 3

Cavadino P (2013b) 'The Effectiveness of Sentencing' Oxford Sentencing Seminar, Centre for Criminology, University of Oxford, July

Cavadino M and Dignan J (2006) 'Penal policy and political economy' *Criminology and Criminal Justice* 6/4: 435

Chambliss W and Seidman R B (1971) *Law, Order, and Power* Reading, MA: Addison-Wesley Publishing

Chaplin J (2012) 'Person, Society and State in the Thought of Rowan Williams' http://www.vonhugel.org.uk/sites/default/files/Jonathan%20Chaplin_Paper%20on%20Rowan%20Williams_23Nov2012.pdf

Charles C (2010) 'The law of sentencing applied to aboriginal people in South Australia' http://www.aija.org.au/Ind%20Courts%20Conf%2013/Papers/Charles.pdf7/26

Cheliotis L K and Sozzo M (2016) 'Introduction: Democratisation and punishment' *Punishment and Society* 18/3: 263

Chibnall S (1977) *Law and Order News* London: Tavistock Publications

Christie N (1977) 'Conflicts as Property' *British Journal of Criminology* 17/1: 1

Cicourel A (1968) *The Social Organisation of Juvenile Justice* New York: John Wiley

Clamp K (2014) 'A "local" response to community problems?: a critique of community justice panels' *British Journal of Community Justice* 12/2: 21

Clamp K (ed) (2016) *Restorative Justice in Transitional Settings* Abingdon: Routledge

Clarke K (2011) 'Punish the feral rioters, but address our social deficit too' *The Guardian*, 5 September

Cohen S (1972) *Folk Devils and Moral Panics* London: MacGibbon and Kee

Cohen S (1985) *Visions of Social Control: Crime, Punishment and Classification* Cambridge: Polity Press

Coleman D A (2010) 'Projections of the ethnic minority populations of the United Kingdom 2006–2056' *Population and Development Review* 36: 3, 441

Cooper C (2012) 'Understanding the English "riots" of 2011: "mindless criminality" or youth "Mekin Histri" in austerity Britain?' *Youth & Policy* 109: 6

Cooper J (2013) 'Nothing personal: the impact of personal mitigation at sentencing since the creation of the Council' in A Ashworth and J V Roberts (eds) *Sentencing Guidelines: Exploring the English Model* Oxford: Oxford University Press

Cordella P (2006) 'Sanctuary as a refuge from state justice' in D Sullivan and L Tifft (eds) *Handbook of Restorative Justice: A Global Perspective* London: Routledge

Corston J (2007) *The Corston Report: A Report by Baroness Corston of a Review of Women with Particular Vulnerabilities in the Criminal Justice System* London: Home Office

Cotterrell R B M (1995) *Law's Community: Legal Theory in Sociological Perspective* Oxford: Clarendon Press, Oxford

Cotterrell R B M (1998) 'Why Must Legal Ideas be Interpreted Sociologically?' *Journal of Law and Society* 25: 171

Cotterrell R B M (1999) *Emile Durkheim: Law in a Moral Domain* Edinburgh: Edinburgh University Press

Cotterrell R B M (2002) 'Seeking similarity, appreciating difference: comparative law and communities' in A Harding and E Orucu (eds) *Comparative Law in the 21st Century* The Hague: Kluwer

Cotterrell R B M (2003) *The Politics of Jurisprudence: A Critical Introduction to Legal Philosophy* Oxford: Oxford University Press, 2nd edn

Cotterrell R B M (2006) *Law, Culture and Society* Aldershot: Ashgate

Cotterrell R B M (2008) *Living Law: Studies in Legal and Social Theory* Aldershot, Hampshire: Dartmouth

Cotterrell R B M (2011) 'Justice, Dignity, Torture, Headscarves: Can Durkheim's Sociology Clarify Legal Values?' *Social & Legal Studies* 20: 3

Cotterrell R B M (2012) 'The Concept of Crime and Transitional Communities: A Perspective from Socio-Legal Theory' Paper presented to the W G Hart Legal Workshop on Globalisation, Criminal Law and Criminal Justice, The Institute of Advanced Legal Studies, University of London, June

Cotterrell R B M (2013) 'Rethinking "Embeddedness": Law, Economy, Community' *Journal of Law and Society* 40/1: 49

Cotterrell R B M (2014) 'The concept of crime and transnational networks of community' in P Alldridge, L Cheliotis, and V Mitsilegas (eds) *Globalisation, Criminal Law and Criminal Justice: Theoretical, Comparative and Transnational Perspectives* Oxford: Hart Publishing

Coverdale H B (2014) 'Punishing with Care: Treating Offenders as Equal Persons in Criminal Punishment' Unpublished PhD thesis, London School of Economics

Crawford A (1997) *The Local Governance of Crime: Appeals to Community and Partnerships* Oxford: Clarendon Press

Crawford A (2002) 'Public Participation in Criminal Justice' *Criminal Justice Review 1999–2001* Centre for Criminal Justice Studies, University of Leeds

Crawford A (2003) 'Contractual governance of deviant behaviour' *Journal of Law and Society* 30/4: 479

Crawford A and Hucklesby A (eds) (2013) *Legitimacy and Compliance in Criminal Justice* Abingdon: Routledge

Croall H (2001) *Understanding White Collar Crime* Maidenhead: Open University Press, 2nd rev edn

Crown Prosecution Service (2013) *The Code for Crown Prosecutors* (7th edn) https://www.cps.gov.uk/publications/code_for_crown_prosecutors/

Dallo Z A (2015) 'Punishment, authority and political economy: Italian challenges to western punitiveness' *Punishment and Society* 17/5: 598

Dawes W, Harvey P, McIntosh B, Nunney F, and Phillips A (2011) *Attitudes to Guilty Plea Sentence Reductions* Sentencing Council Research Series 02/11, London: Sentencing Council

de Keijser J W (2014) 'Penal theory and popular opinion: the deficiencies of direct engagement' in J Ryberg and J V Roberts (eds) *Popular Punishment: On the Normative Significance of Public Opinion in Penal Theory* Oxford: Oxford University Press

Demleitner N V (2013) 'Collateral Sanctions in the United States and Europe: Retroactivity and Proportionality' Paper presented to the Robina Workshop on Collateral Sanctions, University of Minnesota Law School, USA

Denning A Lord (1979) *The Discipline of Law* Oxford: Oxford University Press

Dhami M K (2013) 'A "decision science" perspective on the old and new sentencing guidelines in England and Wales' in A Ashworth and J V Roberts (eds) *Sentencing Guidelines: Exploring the English Model* Oxford: Oxford University Press

Dignan J (2003) 'Towards a systemic model of restorative justice: reflections on the concept, its context and the need for clear constraints in restorative justice and criminal justice' in A von Hirsch, J Roberts, A E Bottoms, K Roach, and M Schiff (eds) *Restorative Justice & Criminal Justice: Competing or Reconcilable Paradigms?* Oxford: Hart Publishing

Doak J (2009) 'Redress, Reconciliation and the Law: In Search of Principle' Unpublished paper

Doak J (2011) 'Honing the Stone: Refining Restorative Justice as a Vehicle for Emotional Redress' *Contemporary Justice Review* 14/4: 439

Doak J, Henham R, and Mitchell B (2009) 'Victims and the sentencing process: developing participatory rights?' *Legal Studies* 29: 651

Donoghue J (2014) *Transforming Criminal Justice? Problem-Solving and Court Specialisation* Abingdon: Routledge

Douzinas C and Gearty C (eds) (2014) *The Meanings of Rights: The Philosophy and Social Theory of Human Rights* Cambridge: Cambridge University Press

Dryzek J S (2013) 'The deliberative democrat's Idea of Justice' *European Journal of Political Theory* 12: 329

du Bois-Pedain A (2017) 'Punishment as an inclusionary practice: sentencing in a liberal constitutional state' in A du Bois-Pedain, M Ulväng, and P Asp (eds) *Criminal Law and the Authority of the State* Oxford: Hart Publishing Publishing

Dubber M (2006) *The Sense of Justice: Empathy in Law and Punishment* New York: New York University Press

Duff R A (1990) *Intention, Agency and Criminal Liability: Philosophy of Action and the Criminal Law* Oxford: Basil Blackwell

Duff R A (2001) *Punishment, Communication and Community* Oxford: Oxford University Press

Duff R A (2007) *Answering for Crime: Responsibility and Liability in the Criminal Law* Oxford: Hart Publishing

Duff R A, Farmer L, Marshall S, and Tadros V (2007a) *The Trial on Trial: Volume 2: Towards a Normative Theory of the Criminal Trial* Oxford: Hart Publishing

Duff R A, Farmer L, and Marshall S E (eds) (2014) *Criminalisation: The Political Morality of the Criminal Law* Oxford: Oxford University Press

Durkheim E (1984) *The Division of Labour in Society* trans. of Durkheim (1893) London: Macmillan

Durkheim E (2008) *The Elementary Forms of Religious Life* trans. of Durkheim (1912) Oxford: Oxford University Press

Dzur A W (2012) *Punishment, Participatory Democracy and the Jury* New York: Oxford University Press

Dzur A W (2014) 'Repellent institutions and the absentee public: grounding opinion in responsibility for punishment' in J Ryberg and J V Roberts (eds) *Popular Punishment: On the Normative Significance of Public Opinion in Penal Theory* Oxford: Oxford University Press

Easton S (2008) 'Dangerous waters: taking account of impact in sentencing' *Criminal Law Review* 105

Easton S and Piper C (2012) *Sentencing and Punishment: The Quest for Justice* Oxford: Oxford University Press, 3rd edn

Edwards I (2004) 'An Ambiguous Participant: The Crime Victim and Criminal Justice Decision-Making' *British Journal of Criminology* 44: 967

Edwards I (2012) 'Sentencing Councils and Victims' *Modern Law Review* 75/3: 324

Emsley C (1996) *Crime and English Society 1750–1900* London: Longman, 2nd edn

Ewald U (2006) 'Large-Scale Victimisation and the Jurisprudence of the ICTY—Victimological Research Issues' in U Ewald and K Turkovic (eds) *Large-Scale Victimisation as a Potential Source of Terrorist Activities—Importance of Regaining Security in Post-Conflict Societies* NATO Security through Science Series, E: Human and Societal Dynamics

Farrall S and Maruna S (2004) 'Desistance from Crime: Implications for Public Policy' *Howard Journal of Criminal Justice* 43/4: 358

Fawcett Society (2010) *Realising Rights: Increasing Ethnic Minority Women's Access to Justice* London: The Fawcett Society 5/34

Feeley M (2014) Review of A W Dzur (2012) 'Punishment, Participatory Democracy and the Jury' *Punishment & Society* 16/5: 602

Feeley M and Simon J (1992) 'The new penology: notes on the emerging strategy of corrections and its implications' *Criminology* 30/4: 449

Feilzer M (2015) 'Exploring public knowledge of sentencing practices' in J V Roberts (ed) *Exploring Sentencing Practice in England and Wales* London: Palgrave Macmillan

Findlay M (2001) 'Juror Comprehension and Complexity: Strategies to Enhance Understanding' *British Journal of Criminology* 41/1: 56

Findlay M (2008) *Governing through Globalised Crime* Cullompton: Willan Publishing

Findlay M and Henham R (2005) *Transforming International Criminal Justice: Retributive and Restorative Justice in the Trial Process* Cullompton: Willan Publishing

Findlay M and Henham R (2007) 'Integrating theory and method in the comparative contextual analysis of trial process' in M McConville and W H Chui (eds) *Research Methods for Law* Edinburgh: Edinburgh University Press

Findlay M and Henham R (2010) *Beyond Punishment: Achieving International Criminal Justice* London: Palgrave Macmillan

Flynn N (2014) 'Advancing Emotionally Intelligent Justice within Public Life and Popular Culture' *Theoretical Criminology* 18/3: 354

Foucault M (1977) *Discipline and Punish: The Birth of the Prison* Harmondsworth: Penguin

Fox F, Albertson K, and Wong K (2013) *Justice Reinvestment: Can the Criminal Justice System Deliver More for Less?* Abingdon: Routledge

Franklin S and Ramamurthy U (2006) 'Motivations, Values and Emotions: Three Sides of the Same Coin' Proceedings of the Sixth International Workshop on Epigenetic Robotics, Paris, France, September 2006, Lund University Cognitive Studies, 128: 4

Frase R S (1998) 'Comparative criminal justice policy' in *Comparative Criminal Justice Systems: From Diversity to Rapprochement* Nouvelles Etudes Penales No 17, International Association of Penal Law, Toulouse: Editions Eres

Frase R (2013) *Just Sentencing: Principles and Procedures for a Workable System* New York: Oxford University Press

Freiberg A and Gelb K (2008) *Penal Populism, Sentencing Councils and Sentencing Policy* Cullompton: Willan Publishing

Frost D and Phillips R (2012) 'The 2011 Summer Riots: Learning from History—Remembering '81' *Sociological Review Online* 17/3: 19

Fuller C (2013) 'Action against unlawful "Phoenix" companies doubles' *Accountancy Age* 23 September

Fuller L L (1969) *The Morality of Law* New Haven: Yale University Press, 2nd edn

Gardner J (2012) *Law as a Leap of Faith* Oxford: Oxford University Press

Garland D (1990) *Punishment and Modern Society* Oxford: Clarendon Press

Garland D (2001) *The Culture of Control: Crime and Social Order in Contemporary Society* Oxford: Oxford University Press

Garside R (2006) 'Right for the wrong reasons: Making sense of criminal justice failure' in R Garside and W McMahon (eds) *Does Criminal Justice Work? The 'Right for the Wrong Reasons' Debate* London: Crime and Society Foundation

Garside R (2014) 'The Coming Probation Privatisation Disaster' London: Centre for Crime and Justice Studies

Gelsthorpe L (2005) 'Back to Basics in Crime Control: Weaving in Women' in M Matravers (ed) *Managing Modernity. Politics and the Culture of Control* Abingdon: Routledge

Gelsthorpe L (2010) 'Working with women offenders in the community: a view from England and Wales' in R Sheehan, C Trotter, and G McIvor (eds) *What Works with Women Offenders* Cullompton: Willan Publishing

Gelsthorpe L (2013) 'Legitimacy, law, and locality: making the case for change' in M Malloch and G McIvor (eds) *Women, Punishment and Social Justice: Human rights and penal practices* Abingdon: Routledge

Gelsthorpe L and Sharpe G (2015) 'Sentencing women: challenges and choices' in J V Roberts (ed) *Exploring Sentencing Practice in England and Wales* London: Palgrave Macmillan

Giddens A (1979) *Central Problems in Social Theory* London: Macmillan

Giddens A (1984) *The Constitution of Society: Outlines of a Theory of Structuration* Cambridge: Polity

Gilbert B (2013) 'Public Protection? The Implications of Grayling's 'Transforming Rehabilitation' Agenda on the Safety of Women and Children' *British Journal of Community Justice* 11/2–3: 123

Gomm R (2013) 'What will "Count" and be Transformed for Women in the Criminal Justice System' *British Journal of Community Justice* 11/2–3: 153

Gordon I, Scanlon K, Travers T and Whitehead C (2009) 'Economic impact on the London and UK economy of an earned regularisation of irregular migrants to the UK' London: Greater London Authority http://www.london.gov.uk/mayor/economic_unit/docs/irregular-migrants-report.pdf

Green E (1961) *Judicial Attitudes in Sentencing* London: Macmillan

Green L (2013) 'Should Law Improve Morality' *Criminal Law and Philosophy* 7: 473

Habermas J (1998) *Between Facts and Norms: Contributions to a Discourse Theory of Law and Democracy* trans. of Habermas (1992) Cambridge, MA: MIT Press reprint

Hales L and Gelsthorpe L (2012) *The Criminalisation of Migrant Women* Cambridge: Institute of Criminology

Hall S, Critcher C, Jefferson T, Clarke J N, and Roberts B (1978) *Policing the Crisis: Mugging, the State and Law and Order* London: Palgrave Macmillan

Hammersley M (2000) *Taking Sides in Social Research: Essays on Partisanship and Bias* Abingdon: Routledge

Harcourt B L, Meares T L, Hagan J, and Morrill C (2005) 'Seeing Crime and Punishment through a Sociological Lens: Contributions, Practices and the Future' *University of Chicago Legal Forum 525*

Harding A and Orucu E (eds) (2002) *Comparative Law in the 21st Century* The Hague: Kluwer

Harris L (2015) 'Aggravation and mitigation: Have we lost our way?' *Current Sentencing Practice News* 1: 7

Harris N (2011) 'Shame, ethical identity and conformity: lessons from research on the psychology of social influence' in S Karstedt, I Loader, and H Strang (eds) *Emotions, Crime and Justice* Oxford: Hart Publishing

Hart H L A (1968) *Punishment and Responsibility: Essays in the Philosophy of Law* Oxford: Oxford University Press

Hawkins K (ed) (1995) *The Uses of Discretion* Oxford: Clarendon Press

Henham R (1990) *Sentencing Principles and Magistrates' Sentencing Behaviour* Aldershot: Avebury

Henham R (1994) 'Attorney-General's References and Sentencing Policy' *Criminal Law Review* 499

Henham R (1998) 'Making Sense of the Crime (Sentences) Act 1997' *Modern Law Review* 223

Henham R (1999) *Sentence Discounts and the Criminal Process* Aldershot: Ashgate

Henham R (2003) 'The Philosophical Foundations of International Sentencing' *Journal of International Criminal Justice* 1: 64

Henham R (2005) *Punishment and Process in International Criminal Trials* Aldershot: Ashgate Publishing

Henham R (2012) *Sentencing and the Legitimacy of Trial Justice* Abingdon: Routledge

Henham R (2014) *Sentencing: Time for a Paradigm Shift* Abingdon: Routledge

Henham R and Mannozzi G (2003) 'Victim Participation and Sentencing in England and Italy: A Legal and Policy Analysis' *European Journal of Crime, Criminal Law and Criminal Justice* 11: 278

Herzog-Evans M (2015) *Offender Release and Supervision: The Role of Courts and the Use of Discretion* Nijmegen: Wolf Legal Publishers

Hindman M D (2013) Review of Dzur, Punishment, Participatory Democracy, and the Jury *Law and Politics Book Review* 23:8

Hohl K, Stanko B and Newburn T (2013) 'The effect of the 2011 London disorder on public opinion of police and attitudes towards crime, disorder, and sentencing' *Policing* 7/1: 12

Hood R (1992) *Race and Sentencing* Oxford: Oxford University Press

Hough M, Roberts J V, Jacobson J, Bredee A, and Moon N (2008) *Attitudes to the Sentencing of Offences Involving Death by Driving* London: SAP Research Report

Hough M, Farrall S and McNeill F (2013) *Intelligent Justice: Balancing the Effects of Community Sentences and Custody* London: The Howard League for Penal Reform

House of Commons (2009), Business and Enterprise Committee, The Insolvency Service: Government Response to the Committee's Sixth Report of Session 2008–09, Fourth Special Report of Session 2008–09, 14 July

Howard J (2013) 'Punishment, Socially Deprived Offenders, and Democratic Community' *Criminal Law and Philosophy* 7/1: 121

Hucklesby A L (2007) *Prisoner Resettlement: Policy and Practice* Cullompton: Willan Publishing

Hudson B (1987) *Justice through Punishment: A Critique of the 'Justice' Model of Corrections* Basingstoke: Macmillan

Hudson B (1993) *Penal Policy and Social Justice* Basingstoke: Macmillan

Hudson B (1996) *Understanding Justice: An Introduction to Ideas, Perspectives and Controversies in Modern Penal Theory* Buckingham: Open University Press, 1st edn

Hudson B (1998) 'Doing justice to difference' in A Ashworth and M Wasik (eds) *Fundamentals of Sentencing Theory* Oxford: Clarendon Press

Hudson B (2003) *Justice in the Risk Society: Challenging and Re-affirming Justice in Late Modernity* London: Sage Publications

Hudson B (2006) 'Balancing the ethical and the political normative: reflections on the institutionalization of restorative justice' in I Aertsen, T Daems, and L Robert (eds) *Institutionalizing Restorative Justice* Cullompton: Willan Publishing

Hutton N (2006) 'Sentencing as a social practice' in S Armstrong and L McAra (eds) *Perspectives on Punishment: The Contours of Control* Oxford: Oxford University Press

Hutton N (2008) 'Institutional mechanisms for incorporating the public' in A Freiberg and K Gelb (eds) *Penal Populism, Sentencing Councils and Sentencing Policy* Cullompton: Willan Publishing

Hutton N (2013) 'The definitive guideline on assault offences: the performance of justice' in A Ashworth and J V Roberts (eds) *Sentencing Guidelines: Exploring the English Model* Oxford: Oxford University Press

Hutton N (2014) 'Invisible Sentencing' Paper presented at the Fourth Symposium of The Sentencing and Penal Decision-Making European Group (ESC), University of Reims, France, 16 May

Indermaur D (2008) 'Dealing the Public In: Challenges for a transparent and accountable sentencing policy' in A Freiberg and K Gelb (eds) *Penal Populism, Sentencing Councils and Sentencing Policy* Cullompton: Willan Publishing

IPPR (2006) 'Irregular migration in the UK' https://www.ippr.org/files/images/media/files/publication/2011/05/irregular_migration_1493.pdf

IPPR North (2014) *Decentralisation Decade: A Plan For Economic Prosperity, Public Service Transformation and Democratic Renewal in England* http://www.ippr.org/publications/decentralisation-decade

Jackson J (2009) 'Finding the best epistemic fit for international criminal tribunals: beyond the adversarial-inquisitorial dichotomy' *Journal of International Criminal Justice* 7: 17

Jackson J, Tyler T R, Hough M, Bradford B, and Mentovich A (2015) 'Compliance and legal authority' in J D Wrights (ed) *International Encyclopedia of the Social and Behavioural Sciences* Oxford: Elsevier, 2nd edn

Jacobson J and Hough M (2011) 'Personal mitigation: an empirical analysis in England and Wales' in J V Roberts (ed) *Mitigation and Aggravation at Sentencing* Cambridge: Cambridge University Press

Jamieson F (2014) 'Judicial Interdependence in the Sentencing Process' Paper presented at the Fourth Symposium of The Sentencing and Penal Decision-Making European Group (ESC), University of Reims, France, 16 May

Jarman N (2006) 'Punishing Disorder: Sentencing of Public Order Offences in Northern Ireland' ICR Working Paper No 2 http://

conflictresearch.org.uk/reports/conflict-violence/Punishing-Disorder.pdf

Jeffries S and Bond C (2010) 'Narratives of Mitigation: Sentencing Indigenous Criminal Defendants in South Australia's Higher Courts' *Journal of Sociology* 46/3: 219

Karstedt S, Loader I, and Strang H (eds) (2011) *Emotions, Crime and Justice* Oxford: Hart Publishing

Kaufman A (ed) (2014) *Distributive Justice and Access to Advantage: G. A. Cohen's Egalitarianism* Cambridge: Cambridge University Press

King N J (2012) 'Procedure at sentencing' in J Petersilia and K R Reitz (eds) *The Oxford Handbook of Sentencing and Corrections* New York: Oxford University Press

Kirby A (2014) 'Inter-Professional Dynamics in the Sentencing and Penal Decision-Making Process' Paper presented at the Fourth Symposium of The Sentencing and Penal-Decision Making European Group (ESC), University of Reims, France, 16 May

Kirby A and Jacobson J (2014) 'Public attitudes to the sentencing of drug offences' *Criminology and Criminal Justice* 14/3: 334

Koch I (2016) 'Moving beyond punitivism: Punishment, state failure and democracy at the margins' *Punishment & Society* 17/5: 598

Lacey N (1988) *State Punishment: Political Principles and Community Values* London: Routledge

Lacey N (2008a) *The Prisoners' Dilemma: Political Economy and Punishment in Contemporary Democracies* The Hamlyn Lectures, Cambridge: Cambridge University Press

Lacey N (2008b) 'Philosophy, Political Morality and History: Explaining the Enduring Resonance of the Hart-Fuller Debate' *New York University Law Review* 83/4: 1059

Lacey N (2012) 'Punishment, (Neo)Liberalism and Social Democracy' Max Weber Lecture No 2012/02, Max Weber Progamme, European University Institute, Florence, Italy

Lacey N and Pickard H (2015a) 'The Chimera of Proportionality: Institutionalising Limits on Punishment in Contemporary Social and Political Systems' *Modern Law Review* 78/2: 216

Lacey N and Pickard H (2015b) 'To Blame or to Forgive? Reconciling Punishment and Forgiveness in Criminal Justice' *Oxford Journal of Legal Studies* 35/4: 665

Larsen A (2012) 'Gendering criminal law: sentencing a mothering person with dependent children to a term of imprisonment' *Australian Journal of Gender and Law* 1/1: 21

Law Commission (2017) Sentencing Code https://www.lawcom.gov.uk/project/sentencing-code/

LCCS (Local Crime Community Sentence) (2010) *A Blueprint for Practical Community Engagement* http://www.lccs.org.uk/handbook.php

Lea J and Young J (1984) *What is to be Done About: Law and Order?* Harmondsworth: Penguin

Lee A (2015) 'Reflective Equilibrium: The Role of Public Opinion in Normative Theoretical Work' http://crim.law.ox.ac.uk/reflective-equilibrium-the-role-of-public-opinion-in-normative-theoretical-work/

Legrand P and Munday R (eds) (2011) *Comparative Legal Studies: Traditions and Transitions* Cambridge: Cambridge University Press

Leveson B (2015) *Review of Efficiency in Criminal Proceedings* https://www.judiciary.gov.uk/wp-content/uploads/2015/01/review-of-efficiency-in-criminal-proceedings-20151.pdf

Lichterman P (2012) 'Religion in Public Action: From Actors to Settings' *Sociological Theory* 30/1: 15

Liebling A and Arnold H (2005) *Prisons and their Moral Performance: A Study of Values, Quality, and Prison Life* Oxford: Clarendon Studies in Criminology

Lightowlers C and Quirk H (2015) 'The 2011 English "Riots": Prosecutorial Zeal and Judicial Abandon' *British Journal of Criminology* 55: 65

Lippke R L (2014) 'Criminal prosecutors: experts or elected officials?' in J Ryberg and J V Roberts (eds) *On the Normative Significance of Public Opinion* Oxford: Oxford University Press

Loader I (2006) 'Fall of the Platonic Guardians: Liberalism, Criminology and Political Responses to Crime in England and Wales' *British Journal of Criminology* 46: 561

Loader I (2011) 'Playing with fire? Democracy and the emotions of crime and punishment' in S Karstedt, I Loader, and H Strang (eds) *Emotions, Crime and Justice* Oxford: Hart Publishing

Loader I and Sparks R (2011) *Public Criminology?* Abingdon: Routledge

LSE/*Guardian* (2011) *Reading the Riots: Investigating England's Summer of Disorder* http://eprints.lse.ac.uk/46297/1/Reading%20the%20riots(published).pdf

Luhmann N (1992) 'Operational Closure and Structural Coupling: The Differentiation of the Legal System' *Cardozo Law Review* 13: 1419

Luhmann N (2013) *A Sociological Theory of Law* Abingdon: Routledge, 2nd edn

Luna E and Wade M (eds) (2012) *The Prosecutor in Transnational Perspective* New York: Oxford University Press

Lundy P and McGovern M (2008) 'The role of community in participatory transitional justice' in K McEvoy and L McGregor (eds) *Transitional Justice from Below: Grassroots Activism and the Struggle for Change* Oxford: Hart Publishing

Macormick N (2007) *Institutions of Law: An Essay in Legal Theory* Oxford: Oxford University Press

Mair G and Millings M (2011) *Doing Justice Locally: The North Liverpool Community Justice Centre* London: Centre for Crime and Justice Studies

Malloch M, McIvor G, and Burgess C (2014) '"Holistic" Punishment and Criminal Justice Interventions for Women' *Howard Journal of Criminal Justice* 53/4: 395

Mannozzi G (2011) 'The allocation of sentencing discretion in the Italian legal experience about security policies' Paper presented at the ESC Working Group on Sentencing and Penal Decision-Making, Vilnius, Lithuania, September

Manson A (2011) 'The search for principles of mitigation: integrating cultural demands' in J V Roberts (ed) *Mitigation and Aggravation at Sentencing* Cambridge: Cambridge University Press

Manuell J (2009) *The Fernando Principles: The Sentencing of Indigenous Offenders in NSW* Sydney: NSW Sentencing Council

Marchetti E (2015) 'An Australian Indigenous-focussed Justice Response to Intimate Partner Violence: Offenders' Perceptions of the Sentencing Process' *British Journal of Criminology* 55/1: 86

Maslen H (2015) 'Penitence and persistence: how should sentencing factors interact?' in J V Roberts (ed) *Exploring Sentencing Practice in England and Wales* London: Palgrave Macmillan

Mason T, de Silva N, Sharma N, Brown D, and Harper G (2007) *Local Variation in Sentencing in England and Wales* London: Ministry of Justice

Mathiesen T (1990) *Prison on Trial* London: Sage Publications

Matrix Evidence (2009) *Make Justice Work: Are Short Term Prison Sentences an Efficient Use of Public Resources?* http://www.ohrn.nhs.uk/resource/policy/MakeJusticeWork2009.pdf

Mazzacuva F (2014) 'Justifications and purposes of negotiated justice for corporate offenders: deferred and non-prosecution agreements in the UK and US systems of criminal justice' *Journal of Criminal Law* 78/3: 249

McBarnet D (2007) 'The new corporate accountability: corporate social responsibility beyond law, through law, for law' in D McBarnet, A Voiculescu, and T Campbell (eds) *The New Corporate Accountability: Corporate Social Responsibility and the Law* Cambridge: Cambridge University Press

McBarnet D (2013) 'Questioning the legitimacy of compliance: a case study of the banking crisis' in A Crawford and A Hucklesby (eds) *Legitimacy and Compliance in Criminal Justice* Abingdon: Routledge

McConville M and Marsh L (2014) *Criminal Judges: Legitimacy, Courts and State-Induced Guilty Pleas in Britain* Cheltenham: Edward Elgar

McEvoy K and McGregor L (2008a) 'Letting go of legalism: developing a "thicker" version of transitional justice' in K McEvoy and L McGregor (eds) *Transitional Justice from Below: Grassroots Activism and the Struggle for Change* Oxford: Hart Publishing

McEvoy K and McGregor L (2008b) 'Transitional justice from below: an agenda for research, policy and praxis' in K McEvoy and L McGregor L (eds) *Transitional Justice from Below: Grassroots Activism and the Struggle for Change* Oxford: Hart Publishing

McIvor G and Burman M (2011) *Understanding the Drivers of Female Imprisonment in Scotland* Glasgow: Scottish Centre for Crime & Justice Research

McNeill F (2009) 'What Works and What's Just?' *European Journal of Probation* 1/1: 21

McNeill F (2013) 'Transforming Rehabilitation: Evidence, Values and Ideology' *British Journal of Community Justice* 11/2–3: 83

McNeill F (2014) 'Punishment as rehabilitation' in G Bruinsma and D Weisburd (eds) *Encyclopedia of Criminology and Criminal Justice* New York: Springer Science and Business Media

McNeill F (2016) 'The Fuel in the Tank or the Hole in the Boat? Can sanctions support desistance?' in J Shapland, S Farrall, and A Bottoms (eds) *Global Perspectives on Desistance: Reviewing What We Know and Looking to the Future* Abingdon: Routledge

McNeill F, Burns N, Halliday S, Hutton N, and Tata C (2009) 'Risk, responsibility and reconfiguration: Penal adaption and misadaptation' *Punishment & Society* 11/4: 419

McNeill F and Robinson G (2013) 'Liquid legitimacy and community sanctions' in A Crawford and A Hucklesby (eds) *Legitimacy and Compliance in Criminal Justice* Abingdon: Routledge

McWilliams W and Pease K (1990) 'Probation practice and an end to punishment' *Howard Journal* 29: 14

Melossi D, Sosso M, and Sparks R (eds) (2011) *Travels of the Criminal Question: Cultural Embeddedness and Diffusion* Onati International Series in Law and Society, Oxford: Hart Publishing

Ministry of Justice (2010) *Breaking the Cycle: Effective Punishment and Sentencing of Offenders* London: TSO

Ministry of Justice (2011) *Increasing Community Access to Local Justice* https://www.gov.uk/government/uploads/system/uploads/attachment_data/file/217257/increasing-access-local-criminal-justice.pdf

Ministry of Justice (2012a) *Swift and Sure Justice: The Government's Plans for Reform of the Criminal Justice System* London: Ministry of Justice, Cm 8388

Ministry of Justice (2012b) 'The effectiveness of different community order requirements for offenders who received an OASys assessment'

Ministry of Justice Research Series 17/12 London: Ministry of Justice https://www.gov.uk/government/uploads/system/uploads/attachment_data/file/217383/niesr-report.pdf

Ministry of Justice (2013a) *Simple Cautions for Adult Offenders* https://www.gov.uk/government/uploads/system/uploads/attachment_data/file/397867/adult-simple-caution-guidance.pdf

Ministry of Justice (2013b) *Impact Assessment on Her Majesty's Courts and Tribunals Service Proposals on the Proposed Closure of North Liverpool Community Justice Centre (NLCJC)* https://consult.justice.gov.uk/digital-communications/north-liverpool-community-justice-centre/results/nlcjc-ia.pdf

Ministry of Justice (2013c) *Transforming the CJS: A Strategy and Action Plan to Reform the Criminal Justice System* London: Ministry of Justice

Ministry of Justice (2013d) *Story of the Prison Population 1993–2012 England and Wales* London: Ministry of Justice

Ministry of Justice (2014) *Transforming Criminal Justice* https://www.gov.uk/government/publications/transforming-the-criminal-justice-system-strategy-and-action-plan

Mitchell B (2011) 'Sentencing riot-related offending: considering Blackshaw and others' *Archbold Review* 4

Mooney G, Croall H, Munro M, and Scott G (2015) 'Scottish Criminal Justice: Devolution, Divergence and Distinctiveness *Criminology and Criminal Justice* 15/2: 205

Morris N and Tonry M (1990) *Between Prison and Probation: Intermediate Punishments in a Rational Sentencing System* New York: Oxford University Press

Munby J Sir (2013) 'Law, Morality and Religion in the Family Courts' Keynote address given by Sir James Munby, President of the Family Division at the Law Society's Family Law Annual Conference 'The Sacred and the Secular: Religion, Culture and the Family Courts' London, 29 October

Murphy J G (2012) *Punishment and the Moral Emotions: Essays in Law, Morality, and Religion* New York: Oxford University Press

National Audit Office (2014) *The Criminal Justice System: Landscape Review* http://www.nao.org.uk/report/the-criminal-justice-system-landscape-review/

Nelken D (ed) (1997) *Comparing Legal Cultures* Aldershot: Dartmouth

Nelken D (1998) 'Blinding Insights? The Limits of a Reflexive Sociology of Law' *Journal of Law and Society* 25: 407

Nelken D (ed) (2000) *Contrasting Criminal Justice: Getting from Here to There* Aldershot: Ashgate

Nelken D and Feest J (eds) (2001) *Adapting Legal Cultures* Oxford: Hart Publishing

New Economics Foundation (NEF) (2008) *Unlocking Value: How we all benefit from investing in alternatives to prison for women offenders* London: New Economics Foundation

New Economics Foundation (NEF) (2013) *Better Courts: Cutting Crime through Court Innovation* London: New Economics Foundation

Newburn T (2015) 'The 2011 England Riots in Recent Historical Perspective' *British Journal of Criminology* 55: 39 2/28

Newburn T, Cooper K, Deacon R, and Diski R (2015) 'Shopping for Free? Looting, Consumerism and the 2011 Riots' *British Journal of Criminology* 55/5: 987

Newlove H (2015) 'A Review of Complaints and Resolution for Victims of Crime' http://victimscommissioner.org.uk/wp-content/uploads/2015/01/A-Review-of-Complaints-and-Resolution-for-Victims-of-Crime_January20151.pdf

Norrie A (2000) *Punishment, Responsibility and Justice* Oxford: Oxford University Press

Nuffield Foundation (2014) *Changing Lifestyles, Keeping Children Safe: An Evaluation of the First Family Drug and Alcohol Court (FDAC) in Care Proceeding* http://www.nuffieldfoundation.org/evaluation-pilot-family-drug-and-alcohol-court

Nussbaum M (2013) *Creating Capabilities: The Human Development Approach* Harvard: Harvard University Press

Nyakudya K (2013) 'Eradicating DVA in faith communities over the long haul' http://kahrmelwellness.com/2013/12/07/eradicating-over-the-long-haul/

O'Mahony D and Doak J (2007) 'The Enigma of Community and the Exigency of Engagement: Restorative Youth Conferencing in Northern Ireland' *British Journal of Community Justice* 4/3: 9

O'Malley P (1999) 'Volatile Punishments: Contemporary Penality and the Neo-Liberal Government' *Theoretical Criminology* 3/2: 175

O'Malley P (2004) *Risk, Uncertainty and Government* London: Cavendish Publishing

O'Malley P (2009) 'Neo-liberalism and Risk in Criminology' Sydney Law School Research Paper No. 09/83 https://ssrn.com/abstract=1472862

O'Malley P (2010) *Crime and Risk* London: Sage Publications

Ostrom E (1990) *Governing the Commons: The Evolution of Institutions for Collective Action* Cambridge: Cambridge University Press

Padfield N (2009) 'Parole and early release: the Criminal Justice and Immigration Act 2008 changes in context' *Criminal Law Review* 166

Padfield N (2013) 'Exploring the success of sentencing guidelines' in A Ashworth and J V Roberts (eds) *Sentencing Guidelines: Exploring the English Model* Oxford: Oxford University Press

Padfield N (2014) 'Shifting the Paradigm from Sentencing to the Sentence: Understanding sentencing as a process not an event' Paper presented at the Centre for Criminal Law and Criminal Justice seminar, Durham Law School, University of Durham, 7 February

Padfield N (2016) 'Editorial: Deferred Prosecution Agreements' *Criminal Law Review* 449

Parry J P (1986) *Democracy and Religion: Gladstone and the Liberal Party 1867–1875* Cambridge: Cambridge University Press

Paternoster R, Brame R, Bachman R, and Sherman L W (1997) 'Do Fair Procedures Matter?' *Law and Society Review* 31: 163

Pavarini M (2001) 'Italy – the politics of punishment: the death of prison reform in Italy' in D van Zyl Smit and E Dunkel (eds) *Imprisonment Today and Tomorrow: International Perspectives on Prisoners' Rights and Prison Conditions* The Hague: Kluwer Law International, 2nd edn

Perez O (2003) 'Normative Creativity and Global Legal Pluralism: Reflections on the Democratic Critique of Transnational Law '*Indiana Journal of Global Legal Studies* 25

Pickering S, Bosworth M, and Aas K F (2014) 'The criminology of mobility' in S Pickering and J Ham (eds) *The Routledge Handbook on Crime and International Migration* Abingdon: Routledge

Pina-Sanchez J and Linacre R (2013) 'Sentencing Consistency in England and Wales: Evidence from the Crown Court Sentencing Survey' *British Journal of Criminology* 53: 1118

Pina-Sanchez J, Lightowlers C, and Roberts J (2017) 'Exploring the punitive surge: Crown Court sentencing practices before and after the 2011 English riots' *Criminology and Criminal Justice* 17/3: 319

Piper C (2007) 'Should Impact Constitute Mitigation?: Structured Discretion versus Mercy' *Criminal Law Review* 141

Piper C (2011) 'The English riots and tough sentencing' http://dspace.brunel.ac.uk/bitstream/2438/5785/2/Fulltext.pdf

Pitt B (2011) 'Daily Mail's bigoted and inaccurate reporting provokes more right-wing anti-Muslim hysteria' *Islamophobia Watch* 12 December

Player E (2012) 'Sentencing women: towards gender equality' in L Zedner and J V Roberts (eds) *Principles and Values in Criminal Law and Criminal Justice: Essays in Honour of Andrew Ashworth* Oxford: Oxford University Press

Player E (2013) 'Women in the criminal justice system: The triumph of inertia' *Criminology and Criminal Justice* 14/3: 276

Policy Exchange (2014) *Future Courts: A New Vision for Summary Justice* http://www.policyexchange.org.uk/images/publications/future%20courts.pdf

Pratt J (2011) 'The Power and the Limits of Populism: An Illustration from Recent Developments in New Zealand' in S Karstedt, I Loader, and H Strang (eds) *Emotions, Crime and Justice* Oxford: Oxford University Press

Prinz J (2006) 'The Emotional Basis of Moral Judgments' *Philosophical Explorations* 9/1: 29

Prison Reform Trust (2011) *Response to the Ministry of Justice Consultation, Punishment and Reform: Effective Community Sentences* London: Prison Reform Trust

Prison Reform Trust (2014) *Submission Theft offences guideline consultation* http://www.prisonreformtrust.org.uk/Portals/0/Documents/Prison%20Reform%20Trust%20submission%20-%20Theft%20Offences%20Guideline%20consultation.pdf

Provost R and Sheppard C (2012) 'Introduction: Human rights through legal pluralism' in R Provost and C Sheppard (eds) *Dialogues on Human Rights and Legal Pluralism* London: Springer

Quinney R (1980) *Class, State and Crime* New York: Longman, 2nd edn

Radzinowicz L (1966) *Ideology and Crime* London: Heinemann

Radzinowicz L and Hood R (1979) 'Judicial Discretion and Sentencing Standards' *University of Pennsylvania Law Review* 127: 1288

Radzinowicz L and Hood R (1990) *The Emergence of Penal Policy in Victorian and Edwardian England* Oxford: Clarendon Press

Ramsey P (2006) 'The Responsible Subject as Citizen: Criminal Law, Democracy and the Authoritarian State' *Modern Law Review* 64: 29

Rawls J (1972) *A Theory of Justice* Oxford: Oxford University Press

Reiner R (2012) 'What's Left?: The prospects for social democratic criminology' *Crime, Media, Culture* 8: 135

Reitz K R (2013) 'Comparing sentencing guidelines: do US systems have anything worthwhile to offer England and Wales?' in A Ashworth and J V Roberts (eds) *Sentencing Guidelines: Exploring the English Model* Oxford: Oxford University Press

Rex S (1998) 'A new form of rehabilitation?' in A von Hirsch and A Ashworth (eds) *Principled Sentencing: Readings on Theory and Policy* Oxford: Hart Publishing, 2nd edn

Riots, Communities and Victims Panel (2012) *After the Riots: The Final Report of the Communities and Victims Panel* London: Riots, Communities and Victims Panel

Roberts J V (2008) *Punishing Persistent Offenders: Exploring Community and Offender Perspectives* Oxford: Oxford University Press

Roberts J V (2011a) 'The future of state punishment: the role of public opinion in sentencing' in M Tonry (ed) *Retributivism Has a Past: Has it a Future?* New York: Oxford University Press

Roberts J V (2011b) 'Punishing, more or less: exploring aggravation and mitigation in sentencing' in J V Roberts (ed) *Mitigation and Aggravation in Sentencing* Cambridge: Cambridge University Press

Roberts J V (2012) 'Points of Departure: Reflections on Sentencing Outside the Definitive Guidelines Ranges' *Criminal Law Review* 439

Roberts J V (2013) 'Complying with sentencing guidelines: latest finding from the crown court sentencing survey' in A Ashworth and J V Roberts (eds) *Sentencing Guidelines: Exploring the English Model* Oxford: Oxford University Press

Roberts J V (2014) 'Clarifying the significance of public opinion in sentencing policy and practice' in J Ryberg and J V Roberts (eds) *Popular Punishment: On the Normative Significance of Public Opinion in Penal Theory* Oxford: Oxford University Press

Roberts J V (ed) (2015a) *Exploring Sentencing Practice in England and Wales* London: Palgrave Macmillan

Roberts J V (2015b) 'Sentencing Council Update' *Current Sentencing Practice News* 1: 9

Roberts J V and de Keijser J (2014) 'Democratizing Punishment: Sentencing, Community Views and Values' *Punishment & Society* 16: 474

Roberts J V and Hough M (2002) *Changing Attitudes to Punishment: Public Opinion, Crime and Justice* Cullompton: Willan Publishing

Roberts J V and Hough M (2005) *Understanding Public Attitudes to Criminal Justice* Maidenhead: Open University Press

Roberts J V and Hough M (2011) 'Exploring public attitudes to sentencing factors in England and Wales' in J V Roberts (ed) *Mitigation and Aggravation at Sentencing* Cambridge: Cambridge University Press

Roberts J V and Hough M (2013) 'Sentencing Riot-related Offending: Where do the Public Stand?' *British Journal of Criminology* 53: 234

Roberts J V and Hough M (2015) 'Empirical sentencing research: options and opportunities' in J V Roberts (ed) *Exploring Sentencing Practice in England and Wales* London: Palgrave Macmillan

Roberts J V and Pina-Sanchez J (2015) 'Paying for the past: the role of previous convictions at sentencing in the crown court' in J V Roberts (ed) *Exploring Sentencing Practice in England and Wales* London: Palgrave Macmillan

Roberts J V and Stenning P (2001) 'Empty Promises: Parliament, the Supreme Court and the Sentencing of Aboriginal Offenders' *Saskatchewan Law Review* 64: 137

Roberts P (2006) 'Theorising procedural traditions: subjects, objects and values in criminal adjudication' in R A Duff, L Farmer, and S Marshall (eds) *The Trial on Trial 2: Judgement and Calling to Account* Oxford: Hart Publishing

Robinson P H (2013) *Intuitions of Justice and the Utility of Desert* New York: Oxford University Press

Robinson P H (2014) 'The proper role of community in determining criminal liability and punishment' in J Ryberg and J V Roberts (eds) *Popular Punishment: On the Normative Significance of Public Opinion in Penal Theory* Oxford: Oxford University Press

Robinson P H, Barton J S, and Lister M J (2014) 'Empirical Desert, Individual Prevention, and Limiting Retributivism: A Reply' *New Criminal Law Review* 17/312 U of Penn Law School, Public Law Research Paper No 13–19 SSRN: http://ssrn.com/abstract=2312655

Rogers J (2006) 'Restructuring the Exercise of Prosecutorial Discretion in England' *Oxford Journal of Legal Studies* 26/4 775

Rogers L J and Erez E (1999) 'The Contextuality of Objectivity in Sentencing among Legal Professionals in South Australia' *International Journal of the Sociology of Law* 27: 267

Rossner M (2013) *Just Emotions: Rituals of Restorative Justice* Oxford: Oxford University Press

Rusche G and Kircheimer O (1939) *Punishment and Social Structure* New York: Columbia University Press

Ryberg J and Roberts J V (2014) 'Introduction: exploring the normative significance of public opinion for state punishment' in J Ryberg and J V Roberts (eds) *Popular Punishment: On the Normative Significance of Public Opinion in Penal Theory* Oxford: Oxford University Press

Sandel M J (2010) *Justice: What's the Right Thing to Do?* London: Penguin

Sandel M (2013) *What Money Can't Buy: The Moral Limits of Markets* London: Penguin

Saward M (2002) 'Rawls and deliberative democracy' in M Passerin D'Entreves (ed) *Democracy as Public Deliberation: New Perspectives (Perspectives on Democratization)* Manchester: Manchester University Press

Schwarzmantel J (2008) *Ideology and Politics* London: Sage Publications

Sen A (2001) *Development as Freedom* Oxford: Oxford University Press

Sen A (2010) *The Idea of Justice* London: Penguin

Sentencing Council (2014a) *Environmental Offences Definitive Guideline* http://www.sentencingcouncil.org.uk/wp-content/uploads/Final_Environmental_Offences_Definitive_Guideline_web1.pdf, effective 1 July 2014

Sentencing Council (2014b) *Fraud, Bribery and Money Laundering Offences Definitive Guideline* http://www.sentencingcouncil.org.uk/wp-content/uploads/Fraud_bribery_and_money_laundering_offences_-_Definitive_guideline.pdf, effective 1 October 2014

Sentencing Council (2014c) *Crown Court Sentencing Survey Annual Publication January to December 2013 England and Wales*, 26 June, rev 3 February 2015 https://www.sentencingcouncil.org.uk/wp-content/uploads/CCSS-Annual-2013.pdf

Sentencing Council (2014d) *Robbery Guideline Consultation* https://www.sentencingcouncil.org.uk/wp-content/uploads/Robbery_offences_guideline_consultation_web1.pdf

Sentencing Council (2015a) *Crown Court Sentencing Survey Annual Publication January to December 2014 England and Wales* https://www.sentencingcouncil.org.uk/wp-content/uploads/CCSS-Annual-2014.pdf

Sentencing Council (2015b) *Theft Offences: Response to Consultation* https://www.sentencingcouncil.org.uk/wp-content/uploads/SC-Theft-Offences-Response-paper_FINAL-web_1.pdf

Sentencing Council (2016) *Theft Offences: Definitive Guideline* https://www.sentencingcouncil.org.uk/wp-content/uploads/SC-Theft-Offences-Definitive-Guideline-content_FINAL-web_.pdf

Sentencing Council (2017) *Reduction in Sentence for a Guilty Plea: Definitive Guideline* http://www.sentencingcouncil.org.uk/wp-content/uploads/Reduction-in-Sentence-for-Guilty-plea-Definitive-Guide_FINAL_WEB.pdf

Sentencing Guidelines Council (2004) *Overarching Principles: Sentencing Guideline* http://www.sentencingcouncil.org.uk/wp-content/uploads/web_seriousness_guideline.pdf

Sentencing Guidelines Council (2008) *Definitive Guideline, Causing Death by Driving* London: Sentencing Guidelines Council http://www.sentencingcouncil.org.uk/wp-content/uploads/web_causing_death_by_driving_definitive_guideline.pdf

Shapland J (2011) 'Personal mitigation and assumptions about offending and desistance' in J V Roberts (ed) *Mitigation and Aggravation at Sentencing* Cambridge: Cambridge University Press

Sheirs V (2014) 'What does [re-]integration mean for the Belgian sentence implementation courts?' Paper presented at the European Society of Criminology Conference, Prague, 10–13 September

Sherman L W and Strang H (2012) 'Restorative justice as evidence-based sentencing' in J Petersilia and K R Reitz (eds) *The Oxford Handbook of Sentencing and Corrections* New York: Oxford University Press

Shute S (1994) 'Prosecution Appeals Against Sentence: The First Five Years' *Modern Law Review* 57: 745

Shute S, Hood R, and Seemungal F (2005) *A Fair Hearing? Ethnic Minorities in the Criminal Courts* Cullompton: Willan Publishing

Siddiqui M (2012) *The Good Muslim: Themes in Classical Islamic Law and Theology* Cambridge: Cambridge University Press

Simon J (2007) *Governing Through Crime: How the War on Crime Transformed American Democracy and Created a Culture of Fear* New York: Oxford University Press

Slapper G (1994) 'Corporate Punishment' *New Law Journal* 29

Slater T (2011) 'From "Criminality" to Marginality: Rioting against a Broken State' *Human Geography* 4/3: 106

Smith G (2007) 'Margaret Thatcher's Christian Faith: A Case Study in Political Theology' *Journal of Religious Ethics* 35:2 233

Sobel-Read K B (2014) 'Global Value Chains: A Framework for Analysis' Transnational Legal Theory 5/3: 364

Sparks R (2011) 'Divided sympathies: David Hume and contemporary criminology' in S Karstedt, I Loader and H Strang (eds) *Emotions, Crime and Justice* Oxford: Hart Publishing

Spencer M E (1970) 'Weber on Legitimate Norms and Authority' *The British Journal of Sociology* 21/2: 123

Starmer K (2014) 'Human Rights, Victims and the Prosecution of Crime in the 21st Century' *Criminal Law Review* 777

Tadros V (2011) *The Ends of Harm: The Moral Foundations of Criminal Law* Oxford: Oxford University Press

Tamanaha B Z (1997) *Realistic Socio-Legal Theory* Oxford: Clarendon Press

Tankebe J and Liebling A (2013) *Legitimacy and Criminal Justice: An International Exploration* Oxford: Oxford University Press

Tata C (2010) 'A Sense of Justice: the Role of Pre-Sentence Reports in the Production and Disruption of Guilt and Guilty Pleas' *Punishment & Society* 12/3: 239

Tata C (2014) 'What Else do the non-Judicial Sentencing Professions Do?' Paper presented at the Fourth Symposium of The Sentencing and Penal-Decision Making European Group (ESC), University of Reims, France, 16 May

Telegraph View (2014) 'Honesty in sentencing policy is long overdue' 8 May http://www.telegraph.co.uk/news/uknews/law-and-order/10813871/Honesty-in-sentencing-policy-is-long-overdue.html

The Broadwater Farm Inquiry (1986) *The Broadwater Farm Inquiry: Report of the Independent Inquiry into Disturbances of October 1985 at the Broadwater Farm Estate, Tottenham*, chaired by Lord Gifford, London: Karia Press

The Guardian (2014a) 'Rolf Harris's prison sentence will not be increased despite complaints' 30 July https://www.theguardian.com/uk-news/2014/jul/30/rolf-harris-prison-sentence-not-increased

The Guardian (2014b) 'Dave Lee Travis sentence not "unduly lenient"' 21 October https://www.theguardian.com/uk-news/2014/oct/21/dave-lee-travis-sentence-attorney-general

The Guardian (2014c) 'Police cautions replaced with punitive sanctions for three English Forces', 1 November https://www.theguardian.com/law/2014/nov/01/police-cautions-abolished-staffordshire-west-yorkshire-leicestershire-forces-chris-grayling

The Migration Observatory (2011) 'Irregular Migration in the UK: definitions, pathways and scale' http://www.migrationobservatory.ox.ac.uk/resources/briefings/irregular-migration-in-the-uk-definitions-pathways-and-scale/

Thomas D A (1979) *Principles of Sentencing* London: Heinemann, 2nd edn

Thomas D A (2012) Case Comment 'Sentencing: public disorder—offences committed in context of public disorder' *Criminal Law Review* 57

Thorburn M (2012) 'Proportionate sentencing and the rule of law' in L Zedner and J V Roberts (eds) *Principles and Values in Criminal Law and Criminal Justice: Essays in Honour of Andrew Ashworth* Oxford: Oxford University Press

Tomaino J (1997) 'Guess who's coming to dinner? A preliminary model for the satisfaction of public opinion as a legitimate aim in sentencing' *Criminal Law & Social Change* 27: 109

Tombs J and Jagger E (2006) 'Denying responsibility: Sentencers' accounts of their decisions to imprison' *British Journal of Criminology* 46/5: 803

Tonry M (2011) *Punishing Race: A Continuing American Dilemma* New York: Oxford University Press

Tonry M (2012) 'Can twenty-first century punishment policies be justified in principle' in M Tonry (ed) *Retributivism Has a Past: Has it a Future?* Oxford: Oxford University Press

Tonry M and Rex S (2002) 'Reconsidering sentencing in England and Wales' in S Rex and M Tonry (eds) *Reform and Punishment: The Future of Sentencing* Cullompton: Willan Publishing

Travis A (2014) 'MPs warn of Risks in Probation Service Privatisation' *The Guardian*, 20 May

Travis J (2007) 'Back-End Sentencing: A Practice in Search of a Rationale' *Social Research* Punishment: *The US Record* (SUMMER) 74/2: 631

Treacy C T (2016) Letter to the Editor *Criminal Law Review* 489

Turley T, Kerr J, Kenny T, Simpson I, and Keeble J (2014) *Process Evaluation of the Neighbourhood Justice Panels* Ministry of Justice Analytical Series, London: Ministry of Justice

Tyler T R (2006) *Why People Obey the Law* Princeton: Princeton University Press

Tyler T R (ed) (2008) *Legitimacy and Criminal Justice* New York: Russell Sage Foundation

Underdown A (2001) 'Making "what works" work, challenges in the delivery of community penalties' in A Bottoms, L Gelsthorpe, and S Rex (eds) *Community Penalties: Change and Challenges* Cullompton: Willan Publishing

Van Dijk T (1989) 'Race, riots and the press: An analysis of editorials in the British press about the 1985 disorders' *Gazette* 43: 229

van Zyl Smit D and Snacken S (2009) *Principles of European Prison Law and Policy: Penology and Human Rights* Oxford: Oxford University Press

Vogel D (2005) *The Market for Virtue: The Potential and Limits of Corporate Social Responsibility* Washington, USA: The Brookings Institution

Vogel M E (1999) 'The Social Origins of Plea Bargaining: Conflict and the Law in the Process of State Formation, 1830–1860' *Law and Society Review* 33: 161

von Hirsch A (1993) *Censure and Sanctions* Oxford: Clarendon Press

von Hirsch A and Ashworth A (2005) *Proportionate Sentencing: Exploring the Principles* Oxford: Oxford University Press

Wacquant L (2009) *Punishing the Poor: The Neoliberal Government of Social Insecurity* Durham NC, USA: Duke University Press

Walker N (1972) *Sentencing in a Rational Society* Harmondsworth: Penguin, rev edn

Wandall R H (2008) *Decisions to Imprison: Court Decision-Making Inside and Outside the Law* Aldershot: Ashgate

Ward J (2014) 'Are problem-solving courts the way forward for justice?' Howard League What is Justice? Working Papers https://d19ylpo4aovc7m.cloudfront.net/fileadmin/howard_league/user/pdf/Research/What_is_Justice/HLWP_2_2014.pdf

Ward J (2015) 'Transforming "Summary Justice" Through Police-Led Prosecution and "Virtual Courts"' *British Journal of Criminology* 55: 341

Warner K (2011) 'Equality before the law: racial and social background factors as a source of mitigation at sentencing' in J V Roberts (ed) *Mitigation and Aggravation at Sentencing* Cambridge: Cambridge University Press

Wasik M (2004) 'What guides sentencing decisions?' in A Bottoms, S Rex, and G Robinson (eds) *Alternatives to Prison: Options for an Insecure Society* Cullompton: Willan Publishing

Wasik M (2012a) 'Editorial: The Crown Court Sentencing Survey' *Criminal Law Review* 569

Wasik M (2012b) 'The test for dangerousness' in G R Sullivan and I Dennis (eds) *Seeking Security: Pre-empting the Commission of Criminal Harms* Oxford: Hart Publishing

Wasik M (2014) 'Sentencing—the last ten years' *Criminal Law Review* 477

Weale A (2011) 'The Deliberative Social Contract' Lecture delivered at the Centre for Ethics and Global Politics, LUISS Guido Carli University, Rome, 14 April

Weber M (1954) *On Law in Economy and Society* trans. by E Shils and M Rheinstein Cambridge, MA: Harvard University Press

Weber M (1958) 'The Three Types of Legitimate Rule' trans. by Hans Gerth *Berkeley Publications in Society and Institutions* 4/1: 1

Weber M (1971) *The Sociology of Religion* trans. by E Fischoff London: Methuen & Co Ltd

Wemmers J (1996) *Victims in the Criminal Justice System* Amsterdam: Kugler

Wernick A (2001) *Auguste Comte and the Religion of Humanity: The Post-theistic Program of French Social Theory* Cambridge: Cambridge University Press

Wilkins L T (1964) *Social Deviance: Social Policy, Action, and Research* London: Tavistock

Williams R (2002) *The Richard Dimbleby Lecture* http://www.theguardian.com/world/2002/dec/19/religion.uk

Williams R (2012a) *Faith in the Public Square* London: Bloomsbury

Williams R (2012b) *Archbishop's Address to the Welsh Assembly* 26th March 2012 http://rowanwilliams.archbishopofcanterbury.org/articles.php/2424/#Lecture

Wolff J (2002) 'Addressing Disadvantage and the Human Good' *Journal of Applied Philosophy* 19/3: 20

Wolff J and de-Shalit A (2007) *Disadvantage* Oxford: Oxford University Press

Worrall A (2015) 'Grace Under Pressure: The Role of Courage in the Future of Probation Work' *Howard Journal of Criminal Justice* 54/5: 508

Worsdorfer M (2014) '"Free, Prior and Informed Consent" and Inclusion: Nussbaum, Ostrom, Sen and the Equator Principles Framework' *Transnational Legal Theory* 5/3: 464

Young J (1974) 'Drugs and deviance' in P Rock and M Macintosh (eds) *Deviance and Social Control* London: Tavistock

Young W and King A (2011) 'Addressing problematic sentencing factors in the development of guidelines' in J V Roberts (ed) *Mitigation and Aggravation at Sentencing* Cambridge: Cambridge University Press

YouGov-Cambridge (2013) *Public Trust in Banking* https://yougov.co.uk/news/2013/04/17/special-report-public-trust-banking/

Zedner L (2010) 'Security, the State, and the Citizen: The Changing Architecture of Crime Control' *New Criminal Law Review* 13: 379

Index

The manufacturer's authorised representative in the EU for product safety is Oxford University Press España S.A. of el Parque Empresarial San Fernando de Henares, Avenida de Castilla, 2 – 28830 Madrid (www.oup.es/en or product.safety@oup.com). OUP España S.A. also acts as importer into Spain of products made by the manufacturer.

www.ingramcontent.com/pod-product-compliance
Lightning Source LLC
LaVergne TN
LVHW011511200926
848484LV00001B/12
9780198718895